D0771289

Perspectives on the South: Agenda for research

Perspectives on the South: Agenda for research

Edited by Edgar T. Thompson

Contributors:

Avery Leiserson
Marshall R. Colberg
B. U. Ratchford
Robert J. Harris
John T. Caldwell
Rupert B. Vance
Gordon W. Blackwell
David M. Potter
George Tindall
Willard Thorp
Louis D. Rubin, Jr.
Raven I. McDavid, Jr.
J. Kenneth Morland
Edwin C. Kirkland
C. Arnold Anderson
Samuel S. Hill, Jr.

Sponsored by The Center for Southern Studies in the Social Sciences and the Humanities, Duke University
Published by Duke University Press / Durham, N. C. 1967

Library of Congress Catalogue card no. 67-20397

Printed in the United States of America by the
Seeman Printery, Inc., Durham, N. C.

Prefatory Note

The series of papers presented in this volume originated in a decision made by the governing body of the Duke University Center for Southern Studies in the Social Sciences and the Humanities. It was felt that in beginning its program, the Center would be greatly benefited by the visit of outstanding authorities from other institutions in the disciplines associated with the Center at Duke. Each visitor was asked to present a paper giving his views on the proper place and function of a Center for Southern Studies and to offer suggestions for a fruitful program of study and research. Accordingly, an oral symposium was held at Duke University on February 10 and 11, 1966, with Professor Avery Leiserson of Vanderbilt University delivering the keynote address. Along with the commentaries, the papers presented on that occasion follow in this volume in the order in which they were then given. The remaining papers, equally important and useful in other disciplines in which the Center is interested, were invited for publication here. The extensive range of suggestions and advice offered by the contributors deals with matters of organization, library resources, orientation, points of view, frames of reference, and particular problems regarded as urgently in need of research.

The editor is under obligation to Dr. W. J. Jokinen, Louisiana State University, Dr. Charles McGlamery, University of Alabama, and Mrs. Elizabeth Tornquist, Durham, North Carolina, who read all or parts of the manuscript and offered critical suggestions. Various members of the Center Committee assisted in many ways. Mrs. Katherine Pearson prepared the index.

Edgar T. Thompson

Duke University

Contents

Introduction

Fetch me a better answer.
King Lear

Better answers to the insistent social and scientific problems of a society will not be forthcoming until better questions are asked, and better questions require more imaginative and persistent questioners. The South has not had a strong tradition of questioning and answering except in the field of public politics, and here the questioner has been more interested in vote-getting answers than in the kind of real answers that accumulate knowledge. Real questions are compelling and moving inquiries into the nature of things which invite new and unorthodox comparisons leading to new insights and better understanding. The student who raises and pursues real questions systematically and methodically is an engine of change in every field of discovery. He is the chief determiner of the nature and direction of new knowledge.

Social discovery is the business of the scholars who have contributed to this interdisciplinary symposium volume on the research tasks now facing the South. They are men of learning who are, however, acutely sensitive to the vast areas of ignorance lying beyond the frontiers of knowledge in their particular intellectual divisions of labor. To sense an area of ignorance is itself an advance. The contributors to this symposium are probing for new dimensions in the study of this region of the United States, and some of them do not hesitate to repudiate conventional ways of looking at sectional relationships, past and present, in the life of the nation of which the South is a part.

The contributors arrive from many fields of scholarship, fields differentiated from each other by the kind of questions they ask of the data. The common ground they share is the South, but they do not waste much time over the question of what and where the South is. Perhaps they should have. It is enough for them that the South is constituted by people rather than by territory; it is that part of the nation where people who regard themselves as Southerners live in numbers exceeding those who do not regard themselves as Southerners. No Gallup poll has yet determined the boundary lines.

It has been said that "every country has a South"—a social South if not a geographical South.[1] The parts or regions of probably every country, particularly the larger ones, change at uneven rates of advance marking

1. Seymour Martin Lipset, *Political Man* (Garden City, N. Y.: Doubleday and Company, Inc., 1963), pp. 273-274.

some as relatively progressive and prosperous and others as relatively poor and backward. The search for status differences between our South and other regions of the United States, including economic, political, social, and cultural factors entering into these differences, has long engaged much of the attention of Southern scholars and will continue to do so; but at some point we must follow the lead of Professor Potter and others who are encouraging us to utilize wider frames of comparison. For only on the assumption that all human societies are comparable, that beneath the differences are institutional similarities and regularities, is a social science possible. If we are better to utilize the facts of Southern life to advance our general knowledge of society we must curb our traditional preoccupation with North-South contrasts and at least supplement it by comparative analysis with other societies. We shall not discover the irreducible core of Southern society, if there is an irreducible core, until we have done so.

Actually, we shall have to make a greater effort to free ourselves from the peculiarities of our time and place, not only because modern scholarship and science demand it, but also because modern transportation and communication have placed this region and every other region on earth in a comparative universe to stay. Every region has now become a social laboratory. But there are still some romantic Southerners who would like to remain in, or escape into, the relative isolation of the past despite the fact that no longer is it possible to withdraw like Candide and cultivate our own private garden, especially when the produce of that garden is encountering more and more difficult marketing and labor problems.

The relative isolation of the past gave the South a more or less distinctive culture. Culture, in one of its aspects, is a way of life, a body of beliefs, and an organization of conventional understandings in which all or nearly all questions are automatically and convincingly answered. Propositions inconsistent with it do not have to be rejected because they are not even entertained; what debate there is occurs well within the area of unquestioned cultural assumptions. But as the world shrinks unevenly and turns at different speeds creating stresses and strains among its parts, ambiguous social situations develop here and there which force new questions and make old answers obsolete. Ideas about geography, the community, the state, and society are differentiated, and speculations about each of these and their relations to each other launch new fields of scientific investigation and research. Every people will want to know who they are, how they came to be, how and why they differ from neighboring peoples, and in what direction they are moving. Thus society, science, and the humanities develop and change together as aspects of a single historical process brought to public consciousness. In the more advanced societies the process at last comes to provide institutional means for self-examination. Confident that there is always more to learn, peoples organize themselves for deliberate discovery. Southern society has reached this stage, as the chapters in this book and many earlier books testify.

Before and since Henry W. Grady used the expression in 1886, every generation of Americans has been told that the South of its day was a "New South." After the Civil War it was one way of telling the North that the South accepted defeat and looked forward to a new day for all its people, white and black alike. From a term of repentance it came to stand for industrial progress and employment. The cliché has appeared again and again with each change or advance, real or supposed, particularly in the fields of education and race relations. Each "New South" has raised new problems and new questions, but not always new answers.

We are hearing the expression again today. What is "new" about the present South? Identifying the present South, or anything else for that matter, as genuinely new, is a very uncertain business, for every society has a natural tendency to repeat ancient doctrines and old experiences. But recently there have been shifts in the South's orientation to the rest of the nation and to the world. One shift involves a change in race relations. Throughout most of its history the place of the Negro has been the South's chief problem and, as Louis Rubin and Robert Jacobs point out, its chief symbol of change.[2] He is still very much in the picture, but there has been a shift of focus from the Negro as the South's chief problem to a recognition of a complex of problems in which he figures along with poverty, education, industrialization, urbanization, and many other economic, political, and social problems. It is a new focus which presents him as a phase, albeit a highly charged one, in the South's broad complex of problems in regional, national, and international contexts.

Closely related to this shift in focus, and also a part of whatever is new about the present South, is the advent of a more widespread disposition to interrogate ourselves. The new mood is perhaps the latest phase of the long dialogue between the American South and the other regions of the country concerning the concept of national unity. In this vast country we no longer are haunted, as we were through the period of the Civil War, by the fear that the country might one day fall apart; but the problem of incomplete regional integration into the mainstream of American life is still under debate. As this debate has proceeded, we have been conscious of regional differences in public opinion. Masked behind the regional trends in public

2. *South: Modern Southern Literature in its Cultural Setting* (Garden City, N. Y.: Doubleday and Company, Inc., 1961), p. 15.

opinion, however, changes even more fundamental and revolutionary seem now to be occurring. These are changes in orientation and in points of view—that is, ideological changes. One indication of this is that Americans, North and South, presently are engaged in more self-study and analysis than ever before.

Few people have administered to themselves and digested so much praise, at least on the popular level, as have Southerners since the Civil War. This is the familiar phenomenon of ethnocentrism which has been accentuated in the South by the reception of a considerable amount of abuse from outside the region. It is a reaction to be expected and written off, or itself made an object of study. But it has to be admitted that many of the scholars and writers whom we have allowed to praise the region have been working without comparative knowledge. There has been an increasing number of splendid exceptions, but until recent years Southerners have discovered relatively little about either themselves or the South, perhaps because they assumed they knew enough already. If they are increasingly being stimulated into a reassessment of the region, its relations with other regions of the United States and the nation as a whole, it is because it is clear that the South can no longer survive and prosper in the maintenance of an older order which everywhere is crumbling with the dissolution of the physical and social distances upon which it has rested. Such is the inevitable consequence of secularization. But, goaded by the ignorance and even hostility of a host of commentators on the Southern scene, North and South, students are now in a mood to probe into the conditions of Southern life perhaps more intelligently than has been the case in the past. The discussion is being brought to bear on fundamental issues and on the vast potential of unrealized development. There is a growing realization that the future holds infinitely more promise than the past. It might be suggested that we are now in a period of clarification, when almost everything traditional is being questioned. It is almost as if students in the South are saying that the unexamined society is not worth living in. We now have, or are getting, the institutional machinery in the form of great universities in which the examination can proceed systematically, scientifically, and fruitfully. If this is true, then we indeed have a "New South."

The Center for Southern Studies in the Social Sciences and the Humanities was formally established at Duke University on July 1, 1965, as another step in the institutionalization of study and research in this region. It is a natural outgrowth of scholarly interest in the region which goes back to the early history of this institution when it was Trinity College. A similar interest is stirring in many another Southern institution. American civilization, in both its Northern and Southern aspects, is increasingly one in which liberal values predominate; and it is understandable that scholars in these institutions, as well as politicians and laymen outside them, should be caught up in the drive toward the goals of the Great Society. As we experience the upheaval of the hard, dry ground on which has rested our whole social fabric, it is inevitable that there should be a felt need for more "applied" research to help us face and deal with our more immediate social and practical problems. The result is a growing contempt for the impractical theorist and impatience with basic research. It seems evident that basic research in both the physical and social sciences is in trouble in spite of the fact that long experience has demonstrated that without it, "applied" research grinds to a halt for lack of fundamentally new ideas and knowledge. Real progress in science has its own laws and tempos and it would be most unwise for Southern scholars to ignore them.

Edgar T. Thompson

Duke University
April, 1967

Perspectives on the South: Agenda for research

The changing South: Some social science applications / Avery Leiserson

I

It is a privilege for an up-country Tennessean to be invited to a Piedmont symposium on research needs and opportunities in our Southern region. Some forty years ago two approaches to the South were emanating from my home territory which today we would do well to avoid. I refer to the liberal optimism of Edwin Mims's *The Advancing South* (1925) and the embattled traditionalism of the Agrarians' manifesto, *I'll Take My Stand* (1930). I do not say that clarification of conceptual issues through disputes like that between Mims and the Agrarians has no utility or importance. To attribute ultimate reality to intellectual categories and currents, however, and to present these as factual description can have and has had unfortunate, even tragic, results. It is possible that our true-believers in the South may force us back into old-style trench warfare between prepared philosophical positions, but this is becoming increasingly unlikely in view of the more sophisticated forms of regional analysis developing today. The establishment by Duke University of a "center of excellence," dedicated to the identification and analysis of basic facts and trends in our society, is evidence of a prevailing tendency. We are coming to realize that discussion of inevitable human differences over the purposes, the rate, the methods, and the consequences of change must be organized in contexts that transcend the merely preferential, literary argument. Humanists and scientists together,[1] we seek knowledge in contexts of meaning that are relevant to what is actually going on in the world outside and within ourselves. The enemy is not the mistaken idea, but the destructive fanaticism and cynicism of ignorance, including our own. There is a barb in the old folktale epigram attributed to Artemus Ward: "Ignorance ain't so much not knowin', as knowin' so derned well what ain't so!"

1. "There is not, in particular, any formal difference between the humanities and the sciences in the appropriate method of theory formation, conceptualization, classification, verification and evaluation—although substantive differences will modify research strategies and the availability of proof will vary considerably." R. E. Lane, *The Liberties of Wit, Humanism, Criticism and the Civic Mind* (New Haven: Yale University Press, 1961), p. 122. See also K. Polanyi, *Personal Knowledge* (Chicago: University of Chicago Press, 1958); J. Bronowski, *Science and Human Values* (New York: Harper and Row Torchbooks, 1959); T. W. Wann, ed., *Behaviorism and Phenomenology* (Chicago: University of Chicago Phoenix Books, 1964), particularly S. Koch, "Psychology and Emerging Conceptions of Knowledge," pp. 1-38.

What are some of the meaningful contexts which strike common chords of human feeling as we enter the final third of our century? With no claim whatever to originality, I venture to suggest three features of twentieth-century civilization which offer significant criteria of choice to a research institution seeking support from a society that desires to understand the crucial processes of its own transformation. The first is *interdependence*, the sense of worldwide human involvement which led Adlai Stevenson to say:

> . . . we travel together on a little space ship, dependent on its vulnerable reserves of air and soil; all committed for our safety to its security and peace; preserved from annihilation only by the care and work and love we give our fragile craft. We cannot maintain it half fortunate, half miserable, half confident, half despairing, half slave to the ancient enemies of man, half free in a liberation of resources undreamed of until this day.[2]

The idea of interdependence and world order of course generates its opposite, the desirability of independence and pluralistic autonomy for intermediate foci of human loyalty and effort—local, regional, and national, as well as international. Given the disparity of demographic and technological resources between autonomous units of political mobilization, we arrive at the second significant focus of contemporary interest, the notion of *comparative competitive development*, or progress, through improved technology and efficient resource utilization, toward wider, mass sharing of the gains in economic growth, and broader participation in the political decisions affecting the distribution of social goods upon which the achievement of human dignity and fulfilment depend. In Harold Lasswell's words:

> What emerges . . . is the importance of recognizing and living with controversial models of political development. I join with all who recommend a conception that gives expression to the overriding goal of human dignity and defines this phrase to include effective general participation in the decision process. . . .[3]

The third universal I would specify as giving significance to research in our time is the demand that John Gardner has done so much to articulate: the need of the individual to acquire a sense of *competence and ca-*

2. Address to the 39th Session of the U. N. Economic and Social Council, Geneva, July 9, 1965. Also, K. Boulding, *The Meaning of the Twentieth Century* (New York: Harper & Row, 1964).
3. "The Policy Sciences of Development," *World Politics*, XVII (Jan., 1965), 290-291.

pacity to meet the requirements of effective living in a changing culture. In part this involves a conception of society as a "system or framework within which continuous innovation, renewal and rebirth can occur," but it also implies an educational system that produces men and women skilled in the "processes of bringing the results of change in line with our purposes."[4] The old-fashioned words for this were "calling" or "craftsmanship," and it is important to remember that the old emphasis upon personal competence, no less than the new stress on capacity for self-renewal, includes not only the acquisition of technical skill, but the attainment of the moral responsibility of belonging and contributing to that more inclusive society which sustains and rewards the exercise of initiative and ability.

What does all this have to do with the agenda for the Center for Southern Studies in the Social Sciences and the Humanities? Here I can do no better than quote a distinguished Southern scientist-administrator, the Director of the Oak Ridge National Laboratories:

> Society does not "a priori" owe the scientist, even the good scientist, support any more than it owes the artist or the musician or the writer support. Science must seek its support from society on grounds other than that it is carried out competently and is ready for exploitation . . . curiosity for its own sake [*sic*] . . . or because scientists find it an enchanting diversion . . . . We are led inevitably to consider external criteria for the validity of science—criteria external to science or a given field of science.[5]

Dr. Weinberg goes on to specify three such external criteria: (1) technological or applied end-use, (2) contribution to and illumination of neighboring scientific disciplines, and (3) relevance to human welfare and the values of man. Recognizing that the criteria of scientific merit do not move in the same direction, he applies them to five fields of rapidly-growing scientific knowledge. What he has to say about the behavioral sciences deserves careful scrutiny.

> The workers are of high quality; the sciences are significantly related to each other; they are deeply germane to every aspect of human existence. . . . On the other hand, it is not clear to me that the behavioral scientists on the whole see clearly how to attack the important problems of their sciences. Fortunately, the total sum in-

4. *Self-Renewal: The Individual and the Innovative Society* (New York: Harper & Row Colophon Books, 1965), pp. 5-6.

5. Alvin M. Weinberg, "Criteria for Scientific Choice," reprinted in *Congressional Record*, 88th Cong., Oct. 22, 1963, pp. 18996-18999, from *Minerva* (Winter, 1963).

volved in behavioral science research is now relatively tiny, as it well must be when what are lacking are deeply fruitful, and generally accepted, points of departure.

We may be able to agree, objectively, with our physical and biological science brothers that the social and behavioral sciences are "little science" rather than "big science" in terms of the dollar volume of government support they receive. However, I take it we are here precisely in order to specify the contribution that the humanities and social sciences can make toward understanding the South in transition, and, so far as may be, toward bringing the results of change in line with our shared national purposes.

II

Duke University has already established its position as a focal point of resource information, and of faculty and institutional commitment to the study of cultural, social, economic, and political change in the South. The symposia volumes edited by Sindler (1963) and McKinney and Thompson (1965), and the organic document of February, 1965, which culminated in the official establishment of the Center, testify to a determination and ability to pursue this commitment through the time-honored activities of research, teaching, and advisory, consulting services. Both the proposal to establish the Center and the program of the present symposium contemplate a number of research projects which would undeniably add to our knowledge about the South. Recognizing this, a visitor will be forgiven, I hope, the impertinence of raising the question as to whether the Center should limit itself in practice to acting as (*a*) an impresario, organizing external conferences and fostering interdisciplinary communication within the university, and (*b*) a functional point of administrative co-ordination, formulating research programs and distributing financial and personnel support to established departments. These are undoubtedly determinate and valuable objectives which should be carried forward, but they are also quite compatible with a broader programmatic conception, which would place the Center more explicitly in a context of basic regional research and contribution to public policy.

What I have in mind parallels, I believe, Professor Spengler's suggestion of separate institutes for (*a*) "regional science," and (*b*) metropolitan and community planning. While I understand his reasons for separating the collection and analysis of basic data about the region from the formulation of programs and participation in policy development with representatives of private and public groups, it seems to me that both in public attitudes and in government and philanthropic financing, we have reached the point where a university may engage in both basic research and policy discussion on a technical basis, without calling into question the validity of basic categories and indices that technically competent people use in analyzing the underlying problems. I would therefore propose that the Center, either under its own name or through the University administration, consider the establishment of its own staff, composed of a director, demographers, lawyers, economists, social anthropologists, and political scientists, whose salaries would be paid by the Center and whose primary responsibilities would be research, but who would also be acceptable as members of their respective departments and available for part-time, advanced seminar teaching. As a beginning, the director and his associate might assemble a small group of research associates to develop on a continuing basis the systematic, quantitative information upon which high-level scientific and policy analysis depends. If a separate name and identity were desirable, something like the Duke Institute for Regional and Community Planning would describe the twofold function I would associate with the projected program for the Center. Difficult organizational questions would have to be faced, but I believe it is by this path that the social sciences will acquire a public image and status of usefulness justifying larger-scale financial support.

The issue at stake here involves the idea of the university, but also the meaning of basic and applied research in relation to the social sciences. No one questions that the university should be organized on a disciplinary or cross-disciplinary basis so far as basic research and teaching are concerned. Both private and public sources of support are already agreed that their objective is to encourage competent individuals and groups of scholars in the universities to pursue lines of inquiry that panels of their peers consider important and promising.[6] The statistical categories are none too clear, but there is general understanding that on the order of ten to fifteen per cent of national research and development funds is a proper allocation for basic research in the physical and biological sciences. The major portion goes for "hardware"—the instrumentation and deployment of research toward such public goals as national defense, space exploration, atomic energy development, public health, and so on. The question

6. National Academy of Sciences, Committee on Science and Public Policy, *Basic Science and National Goals* (1964); 89th Congress, 1st Session, Hearings Before the (Daddario) Subcommittee on Science, Research and Development of the Committee on Science and Astronautics, U. S. House of Representatives, *Government and Science: Review of the National Science Foundation* (1965).

is not whether the social sciences need more money, which is debatable, nor whether more or less than ten per cent should be allotted for basic research; rather, the point is that the line between basic and applied research is probably clearer in the case of the physical than the behavioral and social sciences, which have been defined in the most fundamental sense by the President of the Social Science Research Council as those "institutions who have a way of getting into the problems of people and working with them." Even if we know and wish to maintain a distinction between basic and applied research in history, literature, economics, sociology, and politics, it is just as futile and self-defeating for us to separate them too rigidly as it was for the so-called "hard" sciences in the eighteenth and nineteenth centuries. The lesson of public and private support for research, therefore, is that society is willing to pay for end-uses it recognizes as publicly beneficial and that it is legitimate for some portion of end-use funds to be devoted to the production of basic knowledge essential to the achievement of such "social engineering" goals or "applied" missions.

If regional and community planning in the South is such a goal, a major portion of the activities of the Center might be oriented toward the people of the region engaged in and affected by such planning. Research projects undertaken or supported by the Center, including those proposed by members of the basic disciplinary departments, would be defined in terms essential to the "mission" of the Center, though of course this should be interpreted to have a specifically constructive, and not a broadly restrictive, meaning. On such terms, the Center would not convey the impression that it was thinking primarily about the university, and, by omission, dissociate itself from "working with people directly involved in shaping and guiding the course of regional development." It would of course make itself useful to all persons seriously interested in studying the data on the continuing basis that is required to understand the basic social trends and potentialities of the South. Its staff should also be in constant communication with leaders of government and non-governmental opinion concerning contemporary issues and *effects* of alternative policies of Southern growth and development. The great opportunity for the Center goes beyond the "storehouse" function of making scientific knowledge available to other scholarly workers: it lies in the imagination with which it selects its problems and *finds its appropriate emphases in the process of working with other groups*, and in the ingenuity with which it presents its findings for public attention and discussion.

III

Our modern age is often characterized as the era of science and technology, or some facet thereof, like "nuclear," "atomic," or "space." Thorstein Veblen once suggested that "the scientific age" is a historical time period in which events are evaluated by reference to *matters of fact,* as opposed to previous epochs in which the controlling criteria were the presumed will of God, the Fates, or some popular myth upholding a prevailing system of social relations based upon military, class, or racial domination, honor, privilege, money, or some form of economic organization. Whether or not our present society has wholly transcended such values, there seems to be no question today that "modernization" is measured very largely by changes in such mundane statistical indices as we have of population characteristics, mobility, natural resources, urbanization, industrialization, employment, income, educational and occupational distribution of the labor force, bureaucratization, communication, and political and other forms of group participation and allegiance. The collection and assessment of data indicating trends and possibilities in such basic facts about our region is therefore a logical and appropriate function of a modern Center for Southern Studies. The question is whether this should be its primary function, as a sort of regional Census Bureau, or whether it should focus upon particular areas of Southern concern, like race relations, employment and manpower, urban and industrial growth, political and governmental transformations, artistic and cultural activity.

This is no idle question. Bertram Gross and others have drawn our attention to the desirability of a national Report on the Social State of the Union,[7] corresponding to the President's Annual *Economic Report.* No social scientist who has paid any attention to the legislative antecedents and subsequent developments under the Employment Act of 1946 has any doubt about the unforeseen influence upon national economic policy exercised by the systematic, continuously published economic indicators furnished to the President, and from him to Congress and the nation, by a skilful, trained staff of economic advisers. The question now raised is whether this type of information should not be systematically developed for a whole series of non-economic, social, cultural, and political activities that a democratic society carries on. This is separate from, but not unrelated to, the problem of finding an appropriate vehicle for formulating issues raised by the indicators, and focusing public discussion over alternative means of achieving desired objectives.

7. *Transaction* (published by Washington University Community Leadership Project), I, 3 (Nov.-Dec., 1965), 14-17.

Fascinating as such a vision is, a private university center is probably not an appropriate vehicle for an attempt to specify the whole broad range of public interests and objectives. It could perform an important advisory and stimulating role in such an enterprise, particularly in collaboration with state and city governments and regional agencies. But on the whole, the dynamic role of private intellectual enterprise is played to best advantage in particular functional areas rather than in attempts to cover the whole spectrum, which raise the difficult question of establishing priorities among quite legitimate and urgent, but competing, public goals. What areas then, what aspects, of Southern life and culture, economy and polity, should by virtue of their timeliness or ripeness for exploitation be selected by the Center as deserving of special emphasis, thrust, and scientific energy? Here it must be candidly confessed one speaks from intuition and hunch rather than from sure and complete information on what already is being done and who is doing it at the several institutions presently engaged in the collection and analysis of basic social intelligence about our region.

The number-one area in which there seems to be no comprehensive, systematic, continuing effort anywhere in the South outside of national government agencies is scientific manpower—the identification, education, flow, and utilization of trained, specialized talent. Within the broad field of education and the basic demographic census information, there is almost an open field for a regional center constantly concerned with the availability and flow of manpower to urban, agricultural, and industrial development, the factors affecting the supply and demand for different types of labor, and the resources and objectives for training and utilization of workers in industry, government, and universities. With all due respect to the initiative of the Oak Ridge Institute of Nuclear Studies,[8] the South needs more analytical research and fewer overall surveys of needs and opportunities. For a number of years Columbia University has had a national program of manpower research whose studies and publications provide an outstanding model of the level of analysis to which a Southern institution should reasonably aspire. The 1954 Wolfle Report is being replicated under the same sponsorship of four national learned societies and two private foundations, and it would be a tremendous step forward if a Southern institution could undertake studies, using similar benchmarks and categories, associated with such projects of national scope.

8. *Resources for Southern Manpower Development: A Report to the U. S. Department of Labor, Office of Manpower, Automation and Training,* Oct., 1965, by the Oak Ridge Institute of Nuclear Studies (since January 1, 1966, incorporated as Oak Ridge Associated Universities).

The second area in which I am unaware of a major concentration of research energy and talent in the South is that of mass communications and popular culture. This is a field in which we take legitimate pride in our distinctive regional identity, and it of course provides a focus to which students of history and literature, as well as the dramatic arts and journalism, have much to contribute. Regardless of the point of view one takes with respect to the vulgarization and standardization of taste evidenced in the mass media, it is really surprising that no Southern institution has inaugurated a modern communications research program to provide a regional counterpart and flavor to those around New York and Boston, Illinois, Michigan, Missouri, and the California bay area. Indices of communication have become part of the standard stock-in-trade for the analysis of transitional societies in the Near East, Africa, and Asia, yet we in the South still lack a center for systematically exposing our future journalists and creative writers to the analytic tools and insights of sociology, anthropology, and psychology and to the processes of interpersonal and intergroup communication.

A third focus of interdisciplinary attention that has characterized the study of changing societies is the analysis of bureaucratic and organizational behavior. This is a field in which students of public and business administration, sociologists and economists, not to mention social psychologists, have pressed forward the frontiers of our understanding with respect to both the internal dynamics and the external conditions of democracy. The populist model of mass majorities composed of abstract human individuals as the typical structure of democratic action, has long since been recognized as an inadequate analytical tool for investigating human behavior in the context of the multitude of groups, institutions, and associations with which most individuals are affiliated in modern societies. Over the last century in social science research, the populist model has gradually been replaced by something like John C. Calhoun's conception of "the concurrent majority," transformed, however, from the static Calhounian notion of minority groups and elites leading or vetoing the non-rational and tyrannical sentiments of mass majorities, into a generic, dynamic *process of intergroup conflict and adjustment.* The factor that has been added to the theory of democracy is bureaucracy, or organization, as a universal component of both public and private interests, which has somehow to be brought into line with the demands and aspirations of the more inclusive membership which it both serves and represents. Nowadays we hear that the ambiguous concept of group process, under the influence of general theorists, mathematicians, and the technology of communications, is being supplanted by the concept of self-sustaining *systems of human action,* in which groups become *subsystems* and individuals occupy varying *roles.* However that may be, the field of administration, analytically conceived as the factor of human planning, skilled direction, and intelligent co-ordination in the interplay between the bureaucratic organization of technical skills and the equally necessary political adjustment of internal demands and external pressures in order to establish practicable goals of collective human effort, constitutes a focus of empirical attention that should be applied to the phenomena of change on the contemporary Southern scene. The connections with conceptual and interdisciplinary interests in the study and training of leadership, a topic of perennial social-scientific and foundation concern, scarcely need elaboration.

Two fields of salient Southern concern, race relations and natural resources, in my fallible judgment are either already being handled or are likely to be handled by a number of other regional institutions. I cannot refrain from mentioning one aspect of our regional culture which should be the special object of one or more private universities whose dedication to, and indigenous knowledge of, the South cannot be questioned. I refer to the role of anarchic violence or individualistic non-violent resistance to externally imposed change that seems to have been endemic to our politics at least since the 1830's, if not before. I do not mean to say that this is the main or typical feature of Southern politics; but one of the basic indices of societal cohesion and disorganization in any society undergoing transition is the frequency and incidence of extremist movements which challenge the fundamental structure of authority upon which the maintenance of law and order depends. The South should be a natural place for trained social scientists to measure and study systematically the leadership, organization, ideology, membership, and tactics of "resistance groups" to the objective processes of internal and external societal change.[9] Although such a project need not be given explicit organizational recognition, the Center's research program would provide a felicitous meeting-ground for the variety of analytical skills required.

IV

To this point, we have been considering a number of contexts in which the program of the Center for Southern Studies might be connected with some of the main currents in contemporary social science. Let me suggest,

9. R. B. Highsaw, ed., *The Deep South in Transformation* (University, Ala.: University of Alabama Press, 1964), pp. 71-77, 85-86.

briefly, a somewhat outmoded approach to research that may point to certain lines of inquiry that were not mentioned, although not necessarily excluded, by the able report of the Founding Committee. You will recall the notorious controversy in biology several generations ago of hereditary vs. environmental influences on behavior, and the "great man" vs. "social forces" dispute in sociology. Long before them, Tocqueville ranked the determinative factors affecting societal evolution in ascending order of influence as follows: (1) historical and geographic situation (we should now say demographic, natural, and technological resources); (2) "the laws," including formal, constitutional, and legal arrangements, as well as the informal political practices that acquire the status of constitutional principle; and (3) the customs, manners, and religion of the people. Such broad categories sound much too philosophical to many present-day social scientists, and it must be admitted that broad concepts are usually logically ambiguous and empirically overlapping. To mention just one famous example, Karl Marx's contribution as a sociologist could be ascribed to the way he broke down the old category of "customs, manners, and beliefs" and formulated the relationships between the modern terms "social structure" and "ideology." Without debating the character of that contribution to social science, I should like to argue that it would greatly benefit social science if only every once in a while we desisted from our preoccupation with quantitative indices of micro-individual and macro-analyses of mass aggregate behavior, and focused upon developing more satisfactory points of departure for research.

There is no escaping the fact that such efforts involve the analyst in personal conflicts which generate highly charged emotional feelings. A case in point is William Nicholls' *Southern Tradition and Regional Progress*, which literally throbs with the conviction that the historic Southern values, social structure, and political institutions are unalterably opposed to the economic development he sees as feasible and necessary for the universal achievement of democratic values made possible by modern technology. But this very case highlights the difference between a social scientist who decides he must "take a stand" on the big issues, and the ones who, while feeling just as deeply, devote their professional energies to demonstrating, for example, that congeniality of ideas (good or bad) is a stronger determinant of individual social choice than race,[10] or that the single-member electoral system based on equitable apportionment produces a socio-political type of representative which differs from that produced by mathematical schemes of proportional group representa-

10. Milton Rokeach, ed., *The Open and Closed Mind* (New York: Basic Books, 1960).

tion.[11] The immediate motivation of research is not so much my point, however, as the desirability of orienting analytical inquiries to the *dynamic interaction of conditioning or determining variables in behavior*, to the end that objective evidence may be produced for our fellow citizens and policymakers willing to use their senses and intelligence. In colloquial terms, our function may be described as that of society's *non-secret* CIA, showing to all who will listen that: (*a*) "things that were thought to be necessary and inevitable aren't necessarily so," and (*b*) things that were thought to be impossible may, under certain conditions, be brought about. The job of the social scientist is less to predict how things will happen, than to reveal how things do happen, to delineate trends, to specify probable effects, and to indicate the conditions under which alternative goals may be achieved.

It is not necessary to repeat that demographic resources and economic institutions are a necessary, but not a sufficient, condition for democracy; nor need we go back to Tocqueville for inspiration on the relative influence of laws and political institutions as against belief and value systems and social structure. But neither do we need to be reminded that Supreme Court decisions and national education acts affect Southern regional progress along with urbanization, industrialization, and Negro out-migration. As a professional political scientist, I hope those who guide the destinies of the Center for Southern Studies will find appropriate ways to "crank the political variable" into their models of development and change. Altogether too many social scientists have made the mistake of forgetting that since government is the formal organization of controversy in society, politics is society's vehicle for mobilizing opposition and consent, and not a mere institutional derivative or non-rational obstacle to preferred schemes of economic organization, cultural values, and status systems. Empirical political science has in the past concentrated too much on historic-descriptive analysis of institutions, but in the past twenty years great progress has been made in analyzing the attitudes, motivation, participation, and affiliation of individual voters and citizens, and the complex processes of intergroup policy and decision-making, in settings ranging from the local community to the strategy of international conflict. From the standpoint of the Center, the requisite analytical quality, in addition to the recognized cultural, psychological, economic, and historical skills, is that of the specialist in collective decision-making, whose training and experience in the various modes of structuring group and governmental decisions—in public and private, formal and informal, organized and un-

11. M. Duverger, *Political Parties*, trans. Barbara and Robert North (New York: John Wiley, 1954).

organized, settings—equip him to inject the political variable into the interdisciplinary construction of analytic, hypothetical models of societal change.[12]

How would this be done? The path I would indicate, all too briefly and schematically, is to differentiate between (*a*) external conditions, (*b*) policy outcomes, and (*c*) political structures and processes, and to try to identify those independent and intervening variables with which varying types of political structure and decision-making are properly related.[13] Here again, political scientists may be criticized for paying too much attention to the relation between formal structures and informal processes within political systems, and not enough to the external conditions and policy effects that economists and sociologists emphasize; but this is simply to say that all analytical specialties have something to learn from the sister disciplines in which they are imbedded, and political science is not immune to such learning.

V

In conclusion, permit me to note the sense of comradeship and collaboration with which all Southerners who identify with the goals of democratic progress welcome the inauguration of the Center for Southern Studies. True toilers in the vineyard will see it not so much as a symbol of the triumph of personal values as the timely assertion of leadership in applying the instruments of scientific intelligence to measuring and analyzing steps toward or away from modernization and development of our region. In such an enterprise the Center cannot hope to avoid controversy, but it can look forward to the support of persons who cherish deeply conflicting value positions, provided that it relates its research objectively and competently to the goals of those who perceive constructive creative innovation as the paramount task facing an interdependent world undergoing development at differential rates of change. The history and the traditions of the South contain many strands, and the Duke Center is a portent perhaps that we are breaking out of the old vicious circle, which we share with the Great Plains and mountain sections of the Midwest and North, of low educational standards combined with out-migration

12. C. E. Lindblom, *The Intelligence of Democracy* (New York: Macmillan, The Free Press, 1965).

13. R. A. Dahl, *Modern Political Analysis* (New York: Prentice-Hall, 1963); G. A. Almond and J. A. Coleman, eds., *The Politics of the Developing Areas* (Princeton: Princeton University Press, 1960); J. A. Robinson, "The Major Problems of Political Science," in L. K. Caldwell, ed., *Politics and Public Affairs* (Bloomington: Indiana University, Department of Government, 1962).

of youthful vigor, talent, and ability. At all events, the cumulative building of a great center of research intelligence here in the Carolina Triangle parallels similar movements in Houston and Dallas, Kansas City and St. Louis, and we look forward to the day when it will rival the great concentrations around Boston, Chicago, Los Angeles, and San Francisco. Whether or not the South turns out to be a self-sustaining social system combining structural continuity and the capacity for adjusting to change, we may heartily agree that the Center will help to provide our decision-makers with a more inclusive frame of reference from which, if they wish, they may choose progress and growth.

Southern economic development: Some research accomplishments and gaps* / Marshall R. Colberg

The South is generally considered an underdeveloped region, but the same is not true of research on the South. Benjamin Ratchford, in a recent publication, aptly states, "For many years the South has been studied, surveyed, praised, condemned, evaluated, analyzed, psychoanalyzed, reviewed, and discussed by writers and speakers of all lines and persuasions."[1]

This is not to say that all of the needed research on the South has already been completed. We do not want to make John Stuart Mill's mistake when he wrote, "There is nothing in the laws of value which remains for the present or any future writer to clear up; the theory of the subject is complete."[2] Actually, more than a century later, we are not even able to state fully the nature of a demand curve along which real income remains constant or of a supply curve which can be cut at any point by a demand curve. For similar reasons the theory of price discrimination as it now stands is incorrect.

Much research still needs to be done on the South; and the passage of time inevitably brings new research problems. However, many of the more obvious matters have been rather well taken care of—at least in so far as is possible using easily accessible statistical information on the recent past. Consequently, future economic research has a good launching pad from which to take off, but it has the obligation of approaching its task with more sophistication and of using more detailed, less accessible data.

My intention is to suggest some promising directions for future economic research on the South. I believe that the most useful research on the region should be policy-oriented; that is, it should be directed at problems which can conceivably be solved by private, local, state, or federal action—or in some cases opposition to action. My suggestions may be more meaningful if they are related to work already accomplished. I will not, however, attempt a comprehensive survey of economic research on the South. A good recent survey is available in Clarence Danhof's

* The author is indebted to Professors Zarko Bilbija, William P. Dillingham, George Macesich, and Ernst Swanson for useful suggestions.

1. B. U. Ratchford, "Economic Development in the South," *South Atlantic Quarterly*, LXIV (Autumn, 1965), 496.

2. J. S. Mill, *Principles of Political Economy,* Book III, Chapter i, par. 1.

essay entitled "Four Decades of Thought on the South's Economic Problems."[3]

The federal minimum wage

Perhaps a good place to begin is with that perennial favorite, the federal minimum wage. John Van Sickle, in his surprisingly entitled book, *Planning for the South*, published in 1943,[4] argued that economic development of the South is hampered by this type of legislation. I agree with him. The lower level of wages in the South, especially for the least skilled workers, serves as an attraction to capital—particularly that used in manufacturing for a national or international market. A legislated minimum wage reduces the pull of this magnet, especially since expectations of future legislative action, as well as the prevailing minimum, can affect private investment decisions. It is interesting to note that the AFL-CIO is now pushing for a $2.00 per hour minimum, although a $1.75 per hour bill was defeated in the first session of the 89th Congress.

I believe it is not unfair to call the federal minimum wage a "Yankee trick" on the South. In an important sense it is also a city trick on the small town and country folks, because money wage rates tend to be lower in the rural areas.[5] To some extent minimum-wage legislation promotes urban agglomeration of manufacturing because rural labor surpluses are not permitted to exert their full pull on industry. Professor Spengler has pointed out that the South may need an increase in the number of urban growth points about which to locate new manufacturing and other activities.[6] Agglomeration has natural advantages for many types of economic activity, but I do not believe that the rural areas should be subjected to legislated disadvantages.

A higher minimum wage also has important effects on the distribution of income. These are difficult to measure. Even if measured they are difficult to evaluate. When some persons gain and others lose we cannot with confidence say that society has gained. From the point of view of economic development alone, there is little doubt that the South is adversely affected.

3. M. L. Greenhut and W. T. Whitman, eds., *Essays in Southern Economic Development* (Chapel Hill: University of North Carolina Press, 1964), pp. 7-68.

4. Nashville: Vanderbilt University Press.

5. M. R. Colberg, "Minimum Wage Effects on Florida's Economic Development," *Journal of Law and Economics*, III (Oct., 1960).

6. Joseph J. Spengler, "Southern Economic Trends and Prospects," *The South in Continuity and Change*, J. C. McKinney and E. T. Thompson, eds. (Durham: Duke University Press, 1965), p. 127.

The same sort of wage differential found between urban and rural areas tends to exist between wage rates of whites and non-whites within a given area, especially in the South. Gary Becker has considered an employer's "taste for discrimination" to be reflected in his willingness to forfeit income in order to avoid certain transactions.[7] Following this line of analysis, we can say that an increase in the legal minimum wage lowers the price of discrimination to employers, and hence promotes discrimination. More simply, it reduces the attractiveness to employers of relatively abundant non-white labor by reducing the wage differential between whites and non-whites.

Unfortunately, racial breakdowns of labor data are scarce. It is common for one federal agency deliberately to neglect to secure and publish data in the detail needed by other agencies. Racial employment and unemployment data would be very useful to the Area Development, Appalachia, Manpower Retraining, and Poverty programs, for example. To the extent that racial breakdowns are available in the census and in special tabulations, I believe that investigation of minimum-wage effects on employment by race provides a useful field of research and one of special interest to the South. Most of the available studies attempt to show effects by industry only.

Somewhat similarly, studies of the effects of minimum-wage changes on employment in small areas such as counties should provide useful insights. A great deal of under-utilized data on employment may be found in the "shuttle reports" which go back and forth monthly between state agencies such as the Florida Industrial Commission (in co-operation with the Department of Labor) and a large sample of non-agricultural firms in the state. One advantage is that man-hours, as well as number of employees, are reported. When employment information is tabulated on a county basis it can be reinforced with data on unemployment compensation payments, retail sales, and other variables for the same county. This provides a useful picture of conditions just before and after a change in the legal minimum wage. I have used Florida data before and after the $1.00 minimum was established. A greater reduction in employment in Florida's underdeveloped rural counties showed up quite strikingly. Similar data should be available in all states, providing a wealth of information for studying effects of the $1.00 and $1.25 minima, for example. There will probably soon be a $1.50 minimum wage to study. It is inappropriate that the Department of Labor, which administers the Fair Labor Stan-

7. *The Economics of Discrimination* (Chicago: University of Chicago Press, 1957), p. 8.

dards Act, is also the principal appraiser of its economic effects. One difficulty is that methods of analyzing the impacts tend to become stereotyped. Also, evasion of the law may be a problem but it is unlikely to be publicized by the administration.[8]

The usefulness of a county approach to research was well illustrated by Anthony Tang in his study of twenty-one contiguous counties in the Georgia-South Carolina Piedmont area.[9] From such sources as the Censuses of Population, Manufactures, and Agriculture, Tang compiled a great many measures of economic conditions in these counties and of their changes over time. This enabled him to test various hypotheses such as the tendency of urbanization to follow industrialization.

Research using counties instead of states as the geographic unit seems to me to hold much promise. Carefully grouped counties can provide study areas that are reasonably homogeneous economically. A sufficient number of variables are then fairly constant between counties to permit the effects of changes in other variables to show up. For some purposes a broad division of counties within a state into "urban" and "rural," or "developed" and "underdeveloped" is useful for analysis. An advantage of intensive research on a county basis is that economic information thus gathered is close to that needed by businessmen for locational decisions. The small size of most Southern counties is helpful in this respect. In some cases, of course, cities or groups of cities provide the desired geographic unit for analysis.

Equal Pay Act of 1963

So far as I know, there has been little investigation by economists of a federal law that bears some resemblance to the minimum wage law, namely, the Equal Pay Act of 1963. This law provides that employers engaged in interstate commerce may not discriminate in rate of pay between employees on the basis of sex for work of comparable character requiring comparable skills, except on grounds of seniority or an established merit system. The law sounds entirely fair and logical, but like minimum wage laws, it is based on the idea that employers do not respond to the forces of supply and demand but rather, are able to set wage and salary rates arbitrarily for any given quality of worker. It is based on the idea that men

8. See G. Macesich and C. T. Stewart, Jr., "Recent Department of Labor Studies of Minimum Wage Effects," *Southern Economic Journal*, XXVI (April, 1960).

9. *Economic Development in the Southern Piedmont 1860-1950* (Chapel Hill: University of North Carolina Press, 1958).

will use this power to discriminate against women—though it is hard to see why they would not, in fact, pay a premium for the presence of the more pulchritudinous.

Where wage and salary rates for women are lower than for men, the basic supply-demand situation is usually less favorable for women. In part this is due to employers' lesser willingness to invest in their specialized training because of shorter average tenure on the job. As a consequence, a law requiring equal pay for women may deprive them of an essential price advantage in securing employment. That is, when the broader picture of what is needed to provide jobs for all who want them is kept in mind, much of the apparent logic of equal pay for equal work disappears.

Salary schedules in most school systems call for the same rate of pay for men and women. However, differentials above the schedule are frequently given for athletic or debate coaching, publications advising, or other extra work.[10] Usually these differentials go to men and are required to induce them to fill teaching positions, in view of alternative opportunities. Actual earnings of male teachers consequently average more in spite of a deliberate attempt at equalization. Men are more often high school teachers, which also aids their average salary level. Market forces are usually too powerful to contravene fully by law.

Some implications for regional economic development are inherent in the Equal Pay Act, although they are less striking than those of minimum wage legislation. The incomes of white women in the South with only an elementary school education and of Negro women with an elementary or high school education compare especially poorly with the non-South. High school diplomas have little economic value to Negro girls in the South unless used as a stepping-stone to college degrees. Men, both white and non-white, have lower incomes in the South than elsewhere, but their incomes do not compare as unfavorably with those of other regions as do those of women.[11] Consequently, the legislated need to pay equal wage rates for similar work and skill to men and women will tend to raise the costs of Southern firms more than those outside the region. This will occur for firms that use both men and women in similar jobs. If only a few men are employed in jobs held mainly by women, the tendency will be to lay off the men in order to prevent comparison of pay rates. In other cases there will be a tendency to lay off female workers instead of equalizing their pay rates with those of men.

Research on the effects of the Equal Pay Act on Southern economic

10. S. J. Knezevich and J. G. Fowlkes, *Business Management of Local School Systems* (New York: Harper and Row, 1960), p. 77.
11. Colberg, "Minimum Wage Effects," p. 99.

development appears to be worthwhile. The "shuttle reports" already mentioned should be a source of "before" and "after" data, since employment and earnings are shown separately for men and women. Logically, this research is closely related to that of measuring the effects of minimum-wage fixing. Looked at as a single project, the research would seek to uncover what, if any, structural unemployment or unwanted intrastate employment has been induced among persons of low productivity. Such persons are especially prevalent in Southern towns and rural areas. A likely hypothesis is that the effects on interstate jobs for non-white women are the greatest.

Regional effects of federal lending

Another research project connected with federal legislation that appears to be worthwhile is a study of loans and grants under the Area Redevelopment Act. In general the South seems to have an appropriate share of redevelopment counties.[12] The actual effect on Southern economic development depends, however, on the way in which the law is administered. Many plants serving local markets in other parts of the country are not prospects for the South under any mode of financing. Other new plants which serve broader markets may have great latitude in location, and federal subsidies may be decisive. Consequently, analysis of redevelopment loans made to relatively "footloose" types of industry might indicate whether this law is aiding or retarding Southern economic development.

A further survey, by questionnaire if necessary, might reveal the nature of employment within these federally assisted plants. For example, in the typical Deep South states, the proportion of non-whites in the population is normally much larger in the redevelopment counties than in other counties. It would be interesting to learn whether the impecunious Negroes who caused the counties to be classified as "distressed" were also the beneficiaries of newly created jobs. The general ability of this sort of program to cope with severe unemployment by area also needs to be appraised objectively.

A similar research project would involve tabulation and analysis of loans made by the Small Business Administration in order to determine their regional dispersion. An especially interesting aspect of this study would be relative use of the preferential 4 per cent interest rate

12. M. R. Colberg, "Area Redevelopment and Related Programs: Effects on the South," *Essays in Southern Economic Development*, p. 371.

in the South and elsewhere. The Small Business Administration is permitted to make loans at this low rate in "areas of substantial unemployment" designated by the Department of Labor. While this designation may be only a temporary one, the preferentially low interest charges to borrowers may go on long after the area's employment classification improves. This is a sort of distressed-area program under which criteria for eligibility are easier than under the Area Redevelopment Act. The SBA criteria appear to be somewhat unfavorable to the South since rural poverty does not provide eligibility for the preferential rate. Instead, the lower rate may favor other regions, since "areas of substantial unemployment" are usually the larger industrial cities. The South is rather short of these.

Research on the developmental effects of the Small Business Administration loan program is facilitated by the regular listing by that agency of all loans, including those in which it participates with banks. The researcher has to be prepared to work with many thousands of loans, but the project appears to be both important and feasible because of the good data that are available.

I believe on the basis of limited investigation that comprehensive study of SBA interest rates would show that preference has generally been given to borrowers in the urban centers. On the other hand, this does not appear to be the case with commercial banks which are members of the Federal Reserve System. My colleague George Macesich has found no significant difference in interest rates between centers and peripheries of economic development within the Sixth Federal Reserve District, which covers much of the South.[13] His study excluded non-member banks. If similar data can be obtained, it would be useful to determine whether the same situation exists for non-member banks or whether their interest rates are higher in the less developed places. This investigation could best be made on a county basis. A related investigation would seek to determine whether unit or branch banking is more likely to provide banks for small Southern towns. Availability of banking facilities seems to be especially important to the establishment of small industrial, commercial, and service organizations. Large firms are usually able to tap other sources of funds.

13. G. Macesich, *Commercial Banking and Regional Development in the United States, 1950-1960* (Tallahassee: Florida State University Studies, No. 45, 1965), p. 95.

Industrial plant inventory and subsidization of firms

Some states, including Florida, regularly publish lists of new industrial plants and major expansions of such plants. While it is useful, the Florida Development Commission's list exaggerates the amount of new employment being created, especially since the closing down or out-migration of plants is not publicized. In addition, relocations of plants from one part of the state to another are likely to be counted as new plants.[14]

Along this line, I believe a worthwhile project would be compilation and maintenance of an up-to-date inventory of manufacturing plants established anywhere in the South since a specified date, say 1950. Eventually this could be expanded to constitute a complete enumeration of plants above a certain size in existence in the region. Special care would have to be exercised with respect to those which had shut down or relocated. A possible objection to this project is that it overemphasizes the importance of manufacturing. Unfortunately, small-scale activities in most other fields would make a similar project too difficult.

State and local subsidies to industry

Even before completed, an inventory of manufacturing plants would provide the basis for investigation of a great many hypotheses pertaining to the development of industry in the South. Some of these hypotheses relate to state and local subsidization of industry. John Moes has defended such subsidies as a means of improving the allocation of resources, since federal intervention and other forces have caused initial disequilibrium in the labor markets.[15] Local subsidies are viewed by Moes as an appropriate countervailing power. James Rinehart has calculated that the rates of return to communities from the subsidization of twenty-two plants were extremely high.[16] The effectiveness of local subsidies to industry, however, is in need of further study. For example, unsuccessful efforts such as investment in industrial parks which so far have attracted no industrial customers need to be entered as negative items in calculating the net rates of return to local efforts. The sample is biased when only successes are analyzed.

14. M. L. Greenhut and M. R. Colberg, *Factors in the Location of Florida Industry* (Tallahassee: Florida State University Studies, No. 36, 1962), p. 106.

15. John E. Moes, *Local Subsidies for Industry* (Chapel Hill: University of North Carolina Press, 1962).

16. James R. Rinehart, "Rates of Return on Municipal Subsidies to Industry," *Essays in Southern Economic Development.*

The relative effectiveness of different types of local, state, and federal lures to industry needs to be measured. Several researchers have already observed that most of the plants attracted by subsidies are stable, rather than "fly-by-night" operations. More complete appraisal of this situation might well be attempted, since critics of local subsidies continue to level the charge that gains from subsidized plants are ephemeral. Also, an appraisal needs to be made as to whether the South as a whole has gained from the extensive use of local subsidies, or whether the effect has been mainly on the distribution of new facilities among Southern communities. Even in the latter case, however, the region might gain if the more needy communities have also been the more successful. It should be recognized that strong developmental efforts in such states as Pennsylvania and New York also affect the South, especially by altering the profitability of establishing branch plants in Dixie. Frequently it is a close decision whether to serve growing Southern markets from Northern plants or to establish branch plants in the South in order to reduce delivery costs.

Migration

A number of excellent studies of interstate migration, some pertaining especially to the South, have already been made from the 1960 Census of Population. The special census volume on migration, which covers population movements between 1955 and 1960, is a particularly useful source of data.

James M. Henderson and John L. Fulmer are among those who have recently analyzed migration into and out of the South. Henderson has emphasized the extent of out-migration from rural areas and in-migration to urban areas. Among Southern states he found that only Florida had net rural in-migration during the 1950-1960 decade.[17] This state also had net urban in-migration, as did all of the Southern states except West Virginia. Fulmer has emphasized the importance of the growth of urban centers in the South in contributing to the leadership, technical know-how, and financial power needed to generate economic growth.[18]

Good use has been made by Rashi Fein of the special census volume on migration.[19] He concentrated on the qualitative aspect of migration into

17. James M. Henderson, "Some General Aspects of Recent Regional Development," *Essays in Southern Economic Development*, p. 175.
18. John L. Fulmer, "Trends in Population and Employment in the South from 1930 to 1960 and Their Economic Significance," *ibid.*, p. 228.
19. Rashi Fein, "Educational Patterns in Southern Migration," *Southern Economic Journal*, Supplement (July, 1965), pp. 106-124.

and out of the South, as measured by educational level. While substantial out-migration of well-educated non-white males from the South occurred, Fein found only a very minor loss of white human capital by the region. The largest division, the South Atlantic, had net in-migration of well-educated white males.

A similar migration study for 1955-1960 has been made by Charles Hamilton. He found that better educated youth were more likely to leave the South than were the poorly educated. Above the age of thirty, net migration into the South was found to be frequent among the better educated whites.[20]

In my own recently published study,[21] which covers females as well as males for the period 1939 to 1959, I estimated that the Census South had 23 per cent of the nation's stock of human capital in 1939, 28 per cent in 1949, and 30 per cent in 1959. The rate of gain appears definitely to have diminished, in view of the Fein and Hamilton findings. The South's share of non-white human capital declined from 53 to 37 per cent during the twenty-year period, according to my estimates.

The relative gain to the South in human capital over the two decades probably reflects net in-migration of well-educated persons rather than an outstanding performance by the South in educating its own population. Nevertheless, the results raise the question of whether the commonly heard complaint that Southern college graduates have to go North to secure adequate employment is correct. Probably it is true for some Southern states. It could still be true of all of them, if Southern universities do not provide the types of advanced education needed by expanding Southern activities, including those related to space exploration. Perhaps Southern college graduates are having to go North and West at the same time that the South is importing graduates from other regions to fill the best jobs. If so, Southern programs of higher education are in need of sharp reappraisal.

This suggests that a useful research project would be determination for each Southern state of changes in the inventory of college graduates and the import, export, production, and mortality components of the changes. Numbers of persons, by sex and race, with at least a bachelor's degree can be determined decennially for each state, if one is willing to accept the Census of Population as accurate in this respect. (There is a tendency to exaggerate educational attainment, especially in talking to the relatively well-educated census taker.) The problem of determining domestic "pro-

20. C. H. Hamilton, "Continuity and Change in Southern Migration," *The South in Continuity and Change*, p. 74.

21. Marshall R. Colberg, *Human Capital in Southern Development, 1939-1963* (Chapel Hill: University of North Carolina Press, 1965).

duction" of such persons is more difficult. The U. S. Office of Education combines bachelor's and first professional degrees in its reports. However, universities and colleges publicize their granting of degrees, so that a separation could be made by an alert statistician. A method would have to be devised to avoid counting the same individual two or more times when he receives advanced degrees. Despite the difficulties, the project appears to be worthwhile. It is unfortunate that we know so much more about the production, inventories, and interstate flows of commodities than we know about college graduates.

According to Herman Miller, lifetime earnings of males with sixteen or more years of formal education are about a quarter million dollars higher than for those who left school after only eight years.[22] Even after these earnings are discounted for futurity, college graduates are indeed valuable items!

Successful measurement of the output, export, import, and inventory of college graduates would permit states better to judge the value of investment in higher education of residents. Also, there could be better appraisal of the value of investment in activities which tend to attract educated persons from other states or to retain those already in the state. Expenditures to improve the quality of primary and secondary education, for example, are highly important in attracting industry of the types that use many professional workers. The reason, of course, is that such workers are aware of the importance of quality education for their children.

Educated persons in industry

In this connection and others we need to have better measures of "labor intensive" and "capital intensive" production. There is still a tendency to treat the contribution of professional persons as that of labor, whereas actually it is more akin to the contribution of capital. That is, the productive contribution is possible only because of a great deal of previous investment in individuals. One consequence is that we hear too many politicians and even economists claim that what a state needs is high-wage industry rather than "sweat shops." Often the former gives employment mainly to professional and other highly skilled workers and to machines. Indirectly, some employment may be gained by other persons through local multipler effects, as Ernst Swanson has pointed out.[23] In addition,

22. Herman P. Miller, "Annual and Lifetime Income in Relation to Education: 1939-1959," *American Economic Review*, L (Dec., 1960), Table 11.

23. Ernst W. Swanson, "Appraising Economic Development Potentials: The General Case," a paper presented at a Conference on Area Redevelopment at Athens, Georgia, Jan. 8-10, 1962.

the South needs a great deal of relatively low-wage industry to give employment primarily to large numbers of persons of low productivity. Often these people are residents of small towns and rural areas, and often they are non-whites.

I believe a useful research project would involve the separation of value added by Southern manufacture into the contribution of "human capital," material capital, and ordinary labor. Special interest would attach to changes in their proportionate contribution over a period of time. This would relate interestingly to analysis of migration by educational status and occupation. Even zero net migration may involve considerable out-movement of some types of persons and in-migration of other types. In general, the simpler and more homogeneous commodities such as tobacco products, textiles, and apparel seem to use relatively little human capital, while complex, heterogeneous items such as machinery and aircraft use a great deal. Since regional differences in the remuneration of highly skilled persons are not great when degree of urbanization is held constant, it follows that non-pecuniary perquisites such as educational facilities, cultural advantages, recreational opportunities, and good climate can become decisive factors in attracting new "human-capital intensive" enterprise. The South is strong in the last two attributes but relatively weak in the first two.

Problems of desegregation

Another field of research that is clearly important to the South at the present time might be called "the economics of desegregation." Segregated facilities—whatever their impact on quality may have been—have provided sheltered employment for Negro teachers, professors, nurses, clergymen, and the like. Segregation in these cases has been like a protective tariff in keeping out competition from white persons. Where private resources alone are relied upon, as for clergymen, the protection has had little economic value. The situation is different, however, for teachers, professors, and nurses, who are usually on public payrolls. Here the historic desire of Southern legislators and administrators to maintain separate societies has frequently led to respectable salaries for non-white professionals.

An outstanding example is found in the earnings of school teachers. According to data in the 1960 Census of Population, median earnings of female school teachers were higher for non-whites than for whites, even in the South. Ten Southern states paid more to non-white and six paid more to white women in teaching. Eleven Northern states paid more to non-white women while five paid more to white women. Taken by themselves, these figures suggest substantial discrimination in pay against white teachers! Actually this is seldom the case, the difference in median earnings being attributable to the greater urban concentration of non-whites. The adjustment for urban residence is more important in the North, but even in the South there is a greater tendency toward city-dwelling for Negroes than for whites.

Carefully analyzed, the 1960 census data suggest little, if any, discrimination in pay against non-white female school teachers in either the North or South. The situation is quite different, however, for the number of teaching jobs in relation to the non-white school-age population. Here the non-South discriminates much more than the South does. That is, openly segregated Southern education has brought a close relationship between the number of Negro pupils and the number of Negro teachers. In the Northern states only about half as many non-white teachers were employed in 1959 in relation to the corresponding population.[24]

This raises the specter of unemployment among Negro school teachers and professors if Southern states adopt Northern hiring practices as school desegregation proceeds. Recent reports indicate that only 6 to 7½ per cent of the Negro students in the South are attending desegregated schools. Only about 7 per cent of the 104,000 Negro teachers in the South are now assigned to integrated schools.[25] Approximately 40,000 of these teaching positions can be traced to the higher propensity of Southern schools to employ non-white teachers in order to maintain fully segregated schools, according to estimates I have made from 1960 census data.

There have already been a substantial number of reports of lay-offs of Negro teachers in the Southern states and even a CBS news broadcast on the subject. Rather typically, the poor record of the Northern states with respect to hiring Negro teachers has not been emphasized. One interesting and important topic for research is whether non-white teachers who lose their jobs in the South are able to secure other professional jobs within or outside the region. There is much cause for concern, since almost 60 per cent of all non-white "professional, technical, and kindred" workers in the South in 1959 were teachers. It is unlikely that Negro nurses will be affected adversely by desegregation because of the more physical nature of their work and because of the imminence of Medicare.

Fuller desegregation of employment in Southern factories should help

24. Colberg, *Human Capital in Southern Development, 1939-1963.*

25. "New Moves to Speed School Desegregation Readied in Government," *Wall Street Journal,* Jan. 24, 1966, p. 1.

the South attract labor-oriented industry. Frequently, prospective employers have surveyed Southern towns in order to determine the number of available white female workers, for example. Less frequently the surveys have sought to determine only the number of available Negro workers. As further integration of working forces in factories occurs, many localities will be able to show prospective employers a more adequate working force. Research to determine which communities are more likely to be favorably affected in this way may be a useful guide to new industry seeking a home.

Vocational training needs

Somewhat related and much-needed research is the development of an improved methodology for forecasting the number of persons with various skills that will be required within various geographic areas. With the expansion of federal, state, local, and private funds available for vocational training, this has become an important problem. The usual practice is to survey existing firms regarding their probable future requirements for various types of labor. This technique fails to register the needs of new plants that will be established. Serious errors in planning vocational training programs can be made in the absence of good forecasts.

While we tend to think primarily of the importance of vocational training for jobs in manufacturing and in numerous service activities, there is also a need to forecast requirements for skilled agricultural labor. The increasing mechanization of agriculture requires workers who can handle and maintain expensive farm equipment. The stake of the South in efficient vocational training is especially high because of its relative labor surplus.

Transportation

In the field of transportation there is a need to study the actual and potential effect of construction of the federal interstate highway system on the location of economic activity. In general, transportation costs appear to be diminishing in importance as a factor in locational decisions. Still, so important a development as this new superhighway network will clearly aid some communities at the expense of others. In general it should bring populous and opulent Northern and Far Western markets closer in an economic sense to Southern manufacturers and distributors. As was pointed out by Hoover and Ratchford in their classic study of the region, the

South has an inherent advantage in attracting industry by means of good highways because of the ease with which they may be used during the winter months.[26] At the same time, the interstate highway system brings the rapidly growing Florida and Texas markets closer to the North, reducing the need for branch plants in the South. The regional advantages, like the traffic, appear to be two-way.

Uniformity vs. ad hoc *approach*

Edgar Dunn has written that there is need for a new approach to research on Southern economic development.[27] As I understand it, his recommendation calls for studies that will be co-ordinated in regard to such matters as regional definition, time span, and industrial classification. They should fit together so that each study will aid the others and so that the relations to other regions and the national economy may be measured. In part the research he recommends would, I believe, be aggregative in approach, employing such techniques as input-output analysis and regional income accounting with definitions comparable to those used in the national income accounts.

I am sure this sketch does not do justice to Dunn's proposal. Undoubtedly more should be done to tie in the results of Southern research with those pertaining to other regions and to the nation as a whole. Frank Hanna's well-known work on income has helped us to gain perspective on the changing position of the Southern states.[28] Much has already been accomplished in the uniform treatment of regions and industries by Perloff, Dunn, Lampard, and Muth in their ambitious study published in 1960.[29] This approach is also used in part by Victor Fuchs in his 1962 volume dealing with changes in the location of manufacturing.[30] His book has the advantage of special access to census data which permits four-digit industry detail. One's conception of "slow growth" and "fast growth" industries depends heavily on the narrowness or broadness of classifications. For example, some parts of the textile industry are growing rapidly.

26. C. B. Hoover and B. U. Ratchford, *Economic Resources and Policies of the South* (New York: Macmillan, 1951), p. 388.

27. E. S. Dunn, Jr., "The Need for a Research Design in Southern Regional Economic Studies," *Southern Economic Journal*, XXIX (July, 1962).

28. F. A. Hanna, *State Income Differentials 1919-1954* (Durham, N. C.: Duke University Press, 1959). Also see "Income in the South since 1929," *Essays in Southern Economic Development*, pp. 239-292.

29. H. S. Perloff, E. S. Dunn, E. E. Lampard, and R. F. Muth, *Regions, Resources, and Economic Growth* (Baltimore, Md.: Johns Hopkins Press, 1960).

30. W. R. Fuchs, *Changes in the Location of Manufacturing in the United States Since 1929* (New Haven: Yale University Press, 1962).

Aggregation at the four-digit level seems to me to provide more interesting and more useful information than two-digit classification. In the same way, however, even greater detail is likely to be more pertinent to the actual problems faced by the South. For this reason, I believe there is much to be said for the *ad hoc* approach to research, utilizing whatever classifications of data and methods of analysis seem best for the variety of problems at hand. A danger in this approach is that we may not be able to see the forest because of the trees. However, it may help us locate and remove some of the trees that are blocking the path to development.

Commentary / B. U. Ratchford

It has been a pleasure to study Marshall Colberg's thoughtful survey of economic research in the South and his suggestions for future undertakings. While some of the suggestions appeal to me more than others, I do not believe that I disagree with any of them. Certainly much work needs to be done, and perhaps the greatest need is for some scale of priority to indicate which should be done first. Since I will not take issue with Professor Colberg's ideas, I shall confine my efforts to suggesting some regrouping of those recommendations and adding a few of my own. Perhaps this approach may make some small contribution toward the uniformity which he mentions near the end of his paper as a desirable but probably not a feasible goal.

Perhaps the principal theme of my remarks is the need for a wide focus and a broad perspective in studying the economic problems of the South. We need breadth with respect both to geography and to the economic and political structures. The South is a large region—larger both in population and geography than most nations of the world. Our economy is becoming more complex, more highly specialized, and more like the national economy of which it is a growing component. Professor Potter has said that students of a region should concern themselves with the aspects of the region which are peculiar to that region and different from the aspects of the nation as a whole. Regional economists in the South have devoted much of their efforts to discovering ways in which the

Southern economy may produce per capita incomes equal to or higher than those in the rest of the nation. This goal, if realized, would inevitably mean that the distinctive characteristics of the Southern economy would be reduced or eliminated. Thus economists, unlike historians, may find that if they are successful they will have worked themselves out of their jobs. But if that should happen, the reward would be worth the cost.

As a secondary theme I should like to suggest the desirability of taking a close look at those areas in the South which have made the greatest economic progress recently, to see how they accomplished it. Against a broad context of the economic, social, and political environment, an examination should be made of the resources available, the policies adopted, and the results obtained. This is a highly empirical field, and we should not overlook experiments which are going on all the time. This reminds us, also, that we are here engaged in *applied* research and that it should be as *realistic* as possible. While it can and should be intelligent and imaginative, we are not permitted the flights of fancy permissible to those who engage in research in pure theory. If perchance we should in the process discover some new basic principles, that would be welcome, but we should not expect it.

With these preliminary remarks, let me now turn to Professor Colberg's suggestions. Early in his paper he discusses minimum wage laws, the Equal Pay Act, and subsidies to industry. I would group these under a broad heading which might be called programs of subsidy and special advantages, and I would add the federal farm program, the union shop provision of the Taft-Hartley Act, and others of a like character. I would suggest that these programs should be analyzed carefully and critically, not with the purpose of collecting evidence to discredit them, but to see whether they are economically sound and whether they have, in fact, contributed to economic development.

Attention should be given also to the institutional and political characteristics of these programs. They tend to perpetuate themselves indefinitely, even though the conditions which give rise to them may have vanished. Like all special favors, they tend to breed demand for similar ones in other fields. Perhaps most important, they may be barriers to progress. Beneficiaries naturally want to continue their eligibility for benefits. If their incomes rise too rapidly or if they change the nature of their activities in accordance with the needs of a rapidly changing economy, they may find themselves disqualified. So they may content themselves with mediocre incomes and rigid, antiquated economic practices rather than face the risk of change. Finally, in order to keep the programs growing and expanding, the beneficiaries may find themselves more and more enmeshed with and dominated by political considerations. The result may be an economy influenced more and more by political ideas rather than by the free play of economic forces.

In this connection, regional economists have a special responsibility to avoid encouraging the growth of legislation which confers subsidies or special advantages. Often, in concentrating on a special regional problem, they may conclude that the problem can be solved most directly and most quickly by legislation which would aid some special group or area, without considering fully whether it would do so by imposing burdens or limitations on others. This is a special danger in an era when it is often assumed that a new law is the proper solution for any and all problems.

Four of Professor Colberg's suggestions, it seems to me, fall naturally into a broad program of research on the human resources of the South. They are the ones dealing with migration, educated personnel in industry, desegregation, and vocational training. These are interrelated to some extent and might be undertaken jointly or co-operatively. In view of the contributions he has already made in this field, Professor Colberg would seem to be a fitting leader or director of such a group of studies.

Another broad area that should be studied is that of the political and governmental environment. One of Professor Colberg's suggestions—that dealing with transportation—falls in this area, but several other facets might be investigated. They include the level and costs of community services, the economy and efficiency with which state and local governments are conducted, and the level of political integrity. More broadly, there is the question of the general attitude of government toward organized business. Many of these factors are not susceptible to precise measurement, and some ingenuity would have to be exercised in weighing their influence on economic development. Also, some of them would have to be handled with extreme caution, because it would hardly be wise to state baldly that state X is handicapped in its economic development by a weak and dishonest governor. But there can be no doubt that these factors are of considerable importance in the development of local enterprise, and perhaps even more in attracting business from the outside. This area, incidentally, is one in which it may be feasible and desirable to conduct some interdisciplinary research with students from the field of political science.

In the past few years we have not heard as much about the problem of financing economic development as we did formerly. Since development has been proceeding, it may be that better methods of financing have been found. In his brief study Joe Floyd found very substantial increases in savings and liquid funds within the region, an increase in the inflow of insurance investments from outside the region, and a decline in interest rates relative to the rest of the country.[1] But much more is needed. We need to know how much progress we have made in developing local investment-banking facilities for underwriting security issues, and commercial-banking resources to meet the current needs of business. We need to know the extent to which national companies with headquarters outside the region are financing new plants and equipment. In this connection, if Professor Colberg's suggestion for an inventory of new plants should be implemented, I should hope that it would cover methods of financing and the sources of funds.

Finally, there is a large area of potential research which has long interested me and in which, to my knowledge, very little has been done. It is that area which might be called the infrastructure, or the area of supporting services for industry and commerce. It includes specialized services for industry and commerce in such fields as law, engineering, accounting, insurance, marketing, finance, and many others. In the nature of the case, these services cannot be developed profitably until industrial and commercial development has attained a certain critical stage. But once that stage is reached, they become of considerable importance, both in supporting business and in enabling it to be locally self-sufficient in these areas, as well as in providing employment for a substantial number of well-educated, high-income people. It would be most useful to know where, when, and how these services develop. Among other things, it would give our colleges and universities some indication of the future demands for training in the relevant fields.

1. Joe S. Floyd, Jr., "Trends in Southern Money, Income, Savings, and Investment," *The South in Continuity and Change*, J. C. McKinney and E. T. Thompson, eds. (Durham: Duke University Press, 1965), p. 127.

The South: Research for what? / Robert J. Harris

The profusion of books, articles, and private and official reports published on the South has resulted in a condition reminiscent of Edward Gibbon's description of the state of Roman law at the time Justinian ascended the throne. Then, according to Gibbon,

> the reformation of the Roman jurisprudence was an arduous but indispensable task. In the space of ten centuries, the infinite variety of laws and legal opinions had filled many thousand volumes, which no fortune could purchase and no capacity could digest. Books could not easily be found; and the judges, poor in the midst of riches, were reduced to the exercise of their illiterate discretion.[1]

A cursory examination of publishers' notices of new books or of the catalogue of any university library or the Library of Congress Catalogue reveals ample testimony of the interest and diligence with which scholars and publicists have pursued the Southern theme. The literature of Southern history alone is staggering in its immensity, and to this is added a plethora of materials on race relations, economic development, population movements and changes, urbanization, natural resources, social conditions, literature, and a congeries of other categories, a listing of which would attain the prolixity of an index. The books and other materials can be easily found, but even in an affluent society few fortunes can purchase all the materials dealing with the South, and in an age of the specialization of knowledge no mind can digest them. Hence, publicists, statesmen, and leaders of thought and opinion, like the judges in Justinian's Rome, are poor in the midst of riches and are frequently reduced to the exercise of their illiterate discretion.

This state of affairs raises to some degree the question of why more research on the South is needed, and it suggests even more significantly the necessity for introducing order and system into the materials we already have and bringing them into the fullest utilization.[2] Unlike the law, knowledge is hardly subject to codification, and, even if it were, codifiers of the quality of Justinian's able coadjutors are not in sight. Nevertheless, knowledge can be systematized, concepts introduced, and generalizations made.

1. J. B. Bury, ed., *The History of the Decline and Fall of the Roman Empire* (7 vols.; London: Methuen, 1901), IV, 461.

2. An argument can be made that the South, having already received disproportionate attention from scholars and publicists, should be ignored in the interest of more pressing issues; but the South is a live political, economic, and social phenomenon that is not going to vanish if ignored, or be further inflated by attention.

A major task confronting universities and other research organizations embarking upon a study of the South is that of bringing unity out of the dispersed and sometimes vagrant fragments of knowledge already in our possession—for knowledge and yet more knowledge is in itself hardly enough in a South which is under heavy stress in an effort to reconcile continuity with dramatic political, economic, and social change. "Knowledge comes, but wisdom lingers," lamented Tennyson, and in the South of the twentieth century it is not amiss to say that the accumulation of knowledge has outrun the acquisition of wisdom. The time has come, therefore, when greater emphasis must be placed upon wisdom, understanding, and reason in the study of Southern life; when necessary, we must take paths to truth other than empirical knowledge, whether these paths be myths, new or old, or even poetry and art.

To avoid possible confusion let it be made clear that these suggestions in no wise disparage the accumulation of knowledge for its own sake or encourage the suspicion that more knowledge is unnecessary. Far from it. All they indicate is that we need to bring existing knowledge into a degree of order in which it can be put to use in the solution of the problems confronting the South and the nation and in the building of a better society. After all, to paraphrase Jefferson, scholars "are here to enrich the world," and they impoverish themselves if they "forget the errand." If these observations are correct, they lead to the conclusion that any program of meaningful study of the South must contain an element of applied research which can be directed to the attainment of identifiable and specified goals. If research is to be more than a species of intellectual coma, as the late Harold Laski used to call it, it behooves governments, foundations, and universities not only to work together in applying knowledge to existing needs, but in some instances, to take active steps in influencing and even molding public opinion through a popular diffusion of knowledge.

What is now being proposed is a large and vigorous program of research designed for social action. Research for social action is no novel concept, and it has its share of advocates and critics and its potential dangers and benefits. Even so, it is possible for Southern universities and other research units to engage in applied research without becoming regional Fabian societies. A few examples taken from the field of race relations will suffice to illustrate what is meant.

Any casual student of Supreme Court cases dealing with race relations during the nineteen years preceding the 1954 decision could have predicted an early revolution in the law of race relations and the ultimate demise of segregation by law. The jury and grand jury cases of the 1930's,[3] the suffrage cases of the 1940's and 1950's,[4] and the judicial injuries inflicted upon the equal-but-separate fiction in 1938 and 1950[5] were more than ample warnings of the greater developments yet to come through the decision in the public school segregation cases and the decisions which followed it. The warnings were heard, to be sure, but state and local governments in the South misinterpreted them. Instead of preparing for an orderly transition to meet what should have been known as the inevitable outcome of future litigation, Southern officialdom sought to prolong a dying order by making frenzied expenditures to improve Negro schools and by improvising schemes for regional professional education of Negroes. When the desegregation decision did come, Southern white leadership displayed an even more inexcusable lack of awareness of the facts of legal and political life by resorting to a bizarre combination of sophisticated and simple-minded subterfuges to circumvent the law as declared by the Supreme Court and to defy federal authority at great financial expense and at greater social costs. It would, of course, be expecting too much of research and education to think that they could have made politicians and other leaders react wholly rationally in a situation in which immediate political profits were to be made by the exploitation of irrational fears and appeals to primitive ignorance, but they might have helped mitigate the difficulties of the years after 1954 had there been a wider diffusion of existing knowledge among the public generally and leaders in particular.

Just as the course of Supreme Court decisions in race relations was predictable, so were many aspects of the Civil Rights Movement. The improved educational and economic status of Negroes, the growth of political awareness among them, the rise of militant leaders, a growing impatience with the slowness of litigation, and the growth of a sense of injustice were all evident to serious students of race relations long before the advent of demonstrations and other forms of political action. However, Southern leaders in and out of office persisted in the delusion that Negroes were happy with their lot and that all the difficulties in race relations were instigated by outside agitators, Communists, and other evil genii. They had learned nothing since John Taylor of Caroline thought that when "well

3. *Norris* v. *Alabama*, 294 U.S. 587 (1935); *Pierce* v. *Louisiana*, 306 U.S. 354 (1939).

4. *Smith* v. *Allwright*, 321 U.S. 649 (1944); *Terry* v. *Adams*, 345 U.S. 461 (1953).

5. *Missouri* ex rel. *Gaines* v. *Canada*, 305 U.S. 337 (1938); *Sweatt* v. *Painter*, 339 U.S. 629 (1950); *McLaurin* v. *Oklahoma State Board of Regents*, 339 U.S. 637 (1950). Very important, too, in this context are the restrictive covenant cases. *Shelley* v. *Kraemer*, 334 U.S. 1 (1948); *Barrows* v. *Jackson*, 346 U.S. 249 (1953).

managed by cheap comforts and judicious grants of cider, they [Negro slaves] are happy, useful, docile, and can be made to like their lot indefinitely."[6]

This delusion and others in turn led Southern leaders in some states to adopt a plan of resistance based on a scheme of strategy and tactics designed to produce the very result which they professed to be so anxious to prevent, namely, federal intervention in the form of the use of troops to enforce national authority, voting-rights legislation, anti-discrimination laws, and again more voting-rights legislation. Indeed, it would not be inaccurate to call the Act of 1965 the Wallace-Clark Act, or if one prefers to be impersonal about it, the Alabama Act, because some of the leaders of Alabama did more to promote its enactment than the whole of the Civil Rights Movement. Here again, it would have been expecting too much to hope that knowledge could have resulted in a wholly rational approach to the difficult subject of race relations, but it could have deterred the white resistance in pursuing a course of indefatigable futility, and it might at least have taught this resistance the lesson of the simple rustic who after being chided for running from a bear retorted that it is always better to make a good run than to take a bad stand.

The isolation of the white resistance from the basic facts of Negro opinions and attitudes resulted in a failure in leadership compounded by malice and ignorance; perhaps more seriously, it resulted in a failure of the informed to educate the political leadership of the South in a critical period of history. Whether anything has been learned from partaking of the bitter fruits of resistance to changes in race relations remains to be demonstrated. Some leaders have learned, but in 1966 no one could say with confidence that resistance would not continue to the point that the Civil Rights Movement would abandon its non-violent strategy and answer violence with violence. Certainly in 1966 indications of danger were sufficiently present to disturb the thoughtful. In any case, the whole area of race relations is a subject eminently worthy of study in both its pure and applied aspects. Again it must be emphasized that man cannot live by knowledge alone. Even so he cannot survive without it. There must be a change in the minds and hearts of men, as a prominent American who led the nation's armies in war and lulled its people in peace was wont to remind us. However, it is not too much to expect that knowledge fortified by wisdom can be instrumental in changing the minds and hearts of men.

These unpleasant matters are mentioned not in order to begin a parade of horribles, but rather to demonstrate how public policy and issues of

6. E. T. Mudge, *The Social and Political Philosophy of John Taylor of Caroline* (New York: Columbia University Press, 1939), p. 205.

great moment should not be approached. Although it is obvious that the more pressing issues confronting the South in the sixth decade of the twentieth century yield to no magic solution and that many of them will endure for ages to come, efforts to resolve them must be made. Such efforts involve first an identification and analysis of the major social and political issues concerning the South. Goals must be established and defined. Careful attention must be given to the formulation of public policy; recommendations must be made, and action taken. All of these involve a considerable program of research for social action. For better or worse, universities are not the best place for laying the foundations of public policy, but they can help; and it has been the misfortune of the South that little communion has existed between the universities and state governments comparable to that which was once the glory of Wisconsin. In applied research it may well be that the universities, through special bureaus or institutes, should confine themselves to the collection and distribution of information to government agencies and private organizations, leaving the controversial task of policy-making to official and unofficial groups. Some of this work is already being done through specialized research organs, and it should be expanded. The task of defining goals is also one which is best performed outside the universities—lest they run the risk of becoming special pleaders or, even worse, of assuming pretensions to an academic elitism.

Any program of research is bound to encounter obvious difficulties, especially in its applied aspects. The development of new knowledge and the diffusion of existing information are always unsettling influences upon established modes of thinking and acting, long engrafted traditions, myths, and customs. This difficulty is particularly intense in the South, where tradition, myth, and custom are generally allied in opposition to the kind and degree of change which must occur if racial animosities are to be mitigated, economic development expanded, and human and physical resources conserved. Parochialism in politics, fundamentalism in religion, reaction in economics, a certain anti-intellectualism, and the persistence of stereotypes regarding the Negro, the federal government, and non-conformists are potent deterrents to change and serious handicaps to a program of research which would promote it.

Tradition, at least, is not all on one side. There are Southern traditions of nationalism with a respectable ancestry. John Marshall was a great Southerner, but a greater American. So was Washington before him. Calhoun in his early career, and Henry Clay, hardly an outsider, espoused political and economic nationalism in the form of a central bank, tariffs, and internal improvements. The South also has a tradition of liberal reform and individual freedom. Foremost among their proponents was Thomas Jefferson, who was not afraid of alien and noxious ideas, who advocated change to the point of a new constitution or a revolution in every generation, and who in his time emphasized to the utmost individual freedom and equality. Jacksonian Democracy in many of its aspects was a movement of liberal reform and social change, with elements of political equality, equality of economic opportunity, and the removal of artificial legal shackles from a developing economy. Even before the Civil War, publicists like Hugh Swinton Legaré saw industrialism as a necessary and desirable prerequisite to Southern economic development, though it would be an exaggeration to say that he and other Southern Whigs established an industrial tradition. After the Civil War, however, Henry W. Grady and his cohorts did. On the academic side, Francis Lieber saw clearly the need for relevant and useful information in the development of public policy.

The voices of Washington, Jefferson, Marshall, and Jackson were muted by secession and Civil War; and Calhoun as a nullificationist attained an influence in death that he never possessed in life. Defeated in war, the South retreated to a romantic past that never was, but in this retreat it regrouped its forces and waged assaults with substantial victories. First it conquered constitutional law in a succession of Supreme Court decisions which circumscribed the effect of the Civil War Amendments and returned the control of race relations and political and civil rights to the states. Then it conquered American history. The Civil War, once labeled "the late wicked rebellion"[7] by Justice David Davis, became the War for Southern Independence. Reconstruction was denuded of all its favorable and idealistic features and depicted as a vindictive humiliation of a prostrate people by profligate and corrupt carpetbaggers and illiterate and swaggering Negroes. In these assaults the South found some allies among biologists and social scientists, who provided what passed for scientific proof of the superiority of the white race. It also found support in the teachings of the social Darwinians and jurists like James Coolidge Carter, who in different contexts averred that laws, legislation, and government are powerless to change social customs, and that efforts at social change are at best doomed to failure, and at worst productive of a long chain of social evils.

Confident and complacent in the security of this mythology fortified by respectable scholarship, the South chose to follow the path of John C. Calhoun's dogmas of states' rights and natural inequality rather than the road of nationalism and liberal reform. Accordingly, it did little with the victories it had won in law, politics, and historiography and was intellectually ill-

7. *Ex parte Milligan*, 4 Wallace 2, 109 (1866).

prepared in the twentieth century to meet the great social changes wrought by depression, war, and the revolution of rising expectations by submerged people everywhere. Its leaders accepted the New Deal with an enthusiasm which was not infectious and thereafter engaged in a series of rear-guard actions, some of which have been noticed.

Although succeeding generations of historians, scientists, social scientists, and jurists have produced studies which seriously undermine the mythology of the South as briefly outlined here, the fruits of their labor have not become common property. Public policy must either be made within the framework of popular ideology, or the ideology must be changed. Perhaps the two approaches have to be combined, but the choice of means is the task of applied research. Certainly, it would not be inappropriate for popular historians and other publicists to introduce to the South and some of its leaders those lost or ignored traditions which could act as counterpoises to the views which are so frequently expressed in newspaper editorials, speeches by public officials and other leaders, and pamphlets of special organizations, and which depict the federal government as an alien enemy, change as Communist-inspired, and expansion of government services as steps in the march to a concentration camp.

It thus becomes the role of applied research, working within tradition where possible, to expose ancient errors and provide a kind of domestic technical-assistance program comparable in many respects to programs now being conducted in the developing countries of Africa and Asia. The South is large, rich in natural resources, and favored by nature with a benign climate, yet it is relatively undeveloped as compared with other sections of the country. Its workers are less skilled and more poorly paid; its educational system at all levels is less than the best; its people are less literate; and its per capita income is lower. Yet its great resources, combined with the changes and improvements that have occurred at an accelerated tempo, point to future development if only the will to excellence can be generated and the knowledge mobilized to bring about the fullest development of the capacities of the Southern people—physical, moral, intellectual, and spiritual.

Any program of utilitarian studies must have the firm support of basic research, which is primarily a task for the universities and private foundations. In the field of basic research the South provides a remarkable laboratory for the conduct of clinical case studies in history, law, and the social sciences, and it furnishes an abundance of materials for empirically testing hypotheses and laying the foundations for the advancement of theoretical knowledge. Although there is no such discipline as Southern historiography, law, or political science, the South as a distinctive region does present some unique phenomena which ought not to be ignored by scholars in law and the social sciences. To be of the greatest significance a program of basic research centered upon the South should be conceived within the broadest possible context of law and the social sciences and should employ the newer methods of historical and social research to the end that studies of the South will advance the knowledge of human behavior generally. Purely sectional studies may serve a useful purpose, but research which ignores the broader claims of scientific knowledge can easily degenerate into sterile narratives by antiquarians and deadly analyses by pedantic drones, whereas research directed both to the South and to the expansion of scientific knowledge can fulfil a dual purpose.

Accordingly, one of the first tasks of social scientists who would study the South is to ascertain and isolate those features of Southern society which are distinctively Southern and at the same time relevant to scientific knowledge and social theory. Without attempting to exhaust all of these features, I might suggest a number of them which are immediately apparent. These include the whole fabric of Southern politics in terms of factional and party alignments, race relations, economic development, urbanization, leadership both official and unofficial, the uses and limits of law, and sectionalism versus nationalism. Many of these matters are interrelated to the point of being inseparable. With the obsessive racial preoccupation of politics and politicians, party politics, race relations, law, federalism, and leadership all tend to become fused into one mass.

Since the epochal study *Southern Politics in State and Nation* by V. O. Key, Jr., appeared in 1948, much has happened to change the pattern of Southern politics, and the introduction of more refined methods of political inquiry has altered the study of politics. The time is now at hand for political scientists to prepare a study of comparable magnitude and originality in the light of these developments. Among the more important political changes which are occurring at an accelerated tempo are those arising from the impact of increased Negro voting as a result of federal court decisions, congressional legislation, an active Negro leadership, and an aroused political consciousness. In a number of states of the old Confederacy, Negro voters now hold the balance of power in primaries and in some instances in general elections, particularly presidential contests. In these states Negro voting has added a new dimension to politics, and candidates for party nominations in Democratic primaries compete openly for the Negro vote or ignore it at their peril. In a few states, too, the Negro vote may be decisive in a statewide general election in non-presidential years, as was demonstrated in the election of a governor of Virginia in 1965.

The Negro vote is worthy of interest in other ways. Will Negroes vote in indiscriminate blocs, as many opponents of Negro suffrage have argued? Will they automatically vote for candidates of their own race when they constitute a majority in a governmental unit, or will they follow the recent pattern of selectivity along the lines of Tuskegee and elect a majority of white officials? It is now far too early to reach definite conclusions respecting Negro voting behavior in the South and its impact upon political institutions and public policy. The immediate task for the scholar in this rapidly changing area is to compile the data as they accumulate and await conclusions until the evidence supports them. In the meantime, the evidence points to some interesting conjectures. The growth of the political influence of Negroes will bring about the election of officials, white and Negro, who are more responsive to the needs of Negroes and other submerged groups; there will be substantial changes in party and factional structure, and the emergence of Southern legislators, judges, and executives more attuned to national trends. These developments in turn will affect party and factional alignments, and party or factional organizations will either have to adjust to the new developments (as was done in a number of Southern states in the presidential election of 1964 and in the Virginia state election of 1965) or shorten their political life expectancy. What could emerge would be a coalition of Negroes and so-called moderate and liberal whites in a mass-oriented party, in opposition to a party directed toward a traditionalist folk society and composed of more conservative groups.

Should such a pattern evolve, the South would have for the first time since the Civil War a viable two-party system at both state and national levels, instead of a confused situation in which many voters are Democrats in state and local elections and Republicans in presidential elections. There were some indications in the presidential election of 1964 of an increased awareness by state and local officials of at least a partial unity in state and national parties. So long as local party fortunes were not affected by the outcome of presidential elections, it mattered not to many state and local Democratic officeholders that their constituents were presidential Republicans. However, when the Republicans, buoyed by national victories in a number of states for three successive presidential elections and by heavy increases in Republican strength in other states, had the temerity and indecency to run in state and local elections and sometimes win, the official indifference of local Democratic leaders to national party success vanished. In 1964, indeed, state and local leaders in a number of Southern states which had been safely Republican for the elections of 1952, 1956, and 1960 bestirred themselves with a vigor hardly characteristic of Southern hedonism, and with the aid of the Negro vote they carried their states for President Johnson.

Another factor making for accelerated change in Southern politics is industrialization and the accompanying movement of the population from the farms to the cities. Industrialization in itself brings changes in its wake, including the rise of labor as a political force. Despite the active resistance by employers to unionization, and the apathy and sometimes hostility of many laborers to labor unions, the organization of labor is ultimately a consequence of industrialization. Unionization in turn produces more political cohesiveness among workers. Although labor unions in the South have not attained an economic strength or political influence comparable to those unions in the heavily industrialized sections of the United States, they have in some of the more industrialized Southern states become a force which candidates for statewide office cannot ignore and upon which successful candidates in large urban centers are dependent.

Industrialization has also brought to the South scientific, technical, and skilled personnel, many of whom have strange names and speak with unfamiliar accents. Their impact upon Southern communities and the South's impact upon them are insufficiently known, but we can be sure of substantial changes in political and social attitudes on a mutual basis. Urbanization itself produces changes in the habits and thoughts of men, despite the tendency of migrants from the farms to the factory to take their rustic attitudes with them, but we know altogether too little of these matters.

Another major development which has emerged since Key and his able collaborators wrote *Southern Politics* is legislative reapportionment. This subject provides special opportunities for inquiry by political scientists throughout the whole of the United States, but the greatest opportunities are in the South, where malapportionment in state legislatures and congressional districts, reinforced by a limited suffrage, safe legislative seats for incumbents, the one-party system, and the rule of seniority have contributed to a specious kind of elite in city halls, county court houses, state capitals, and the Congress of the United States. What all the consequences of legislative reapportionment on the principle of "one man, one vote" will be in the South is something that no prudent scholar will forecast, and the most that political science can now do is to record developments as they come and endeavor to classify them and fit them into some pattern of legislative behavior. There are observers who believe that the whole issue of malapportionment has been over-dramatized and who point to big city delegations with an influence in legislatures beyond their numbers, and to the dominance of the governor over legislation. Others equally competent and confident regard legislative malapportionment as a curse upon the cities and their suburbs and as a deterrent to official responsiveness to demands for the satisfaction of long-felt needs. As newly apportioned legislatures begin to convene in 1966, they will provide a partial laboratory for the testing of these assumptions and for the study of the whole subject of representation.

Any attempt to assess completely the effects of reapportionment in the South is complicated by the simultaneous fact of an enlarged suffrage and by the difficulty of isolating these two factors. We can be sure on the basis of some experience prior to 1966 that an enlarged suffrage and an increase in Negro votes combined with reapportionment have produced some notable results. Judicial abrogation of Georgia's county-unit vote system and a more equitable apportionment of congressional districts have produced some novel developments in Georgia which transcend its boundaries. In the Atlanta area a Dixiecrat congressman has been replaced by two more progressive representatives, one of whom, before the arrival of his colleague from Atlanta under a new districting plan, voted for the Civil Rights Act of 1964. At the same time, candidates for statewide office who know that the first duty of every public servant is to see to it that he continues to be a public servant have displayed a capacity for natural adaptation and an instinct for survival that would have interested Charles Darwin. It may be that, in the words of the late Senator Henry Ashurst, if they have not seen the light, they have felt the heat. All of these changes so deserving of political inquiry were epitomized in a colloquy between Senator Herman Talmadge and a Negro before the Hungry Club in Atlanta in the winter of 1965. In the period for questions and answers a spokesman in the audience chided the Senator by saying, "You would not have come to talk to us five years ago." The resourceful Mr. Talmadge quickly replied, "You did not invite me five years ago." Both were right.

Other examples could be adduced to illustrate the changes and the incentives to even greater change wrought by an expanded electorate and legislative reapportionment, but here it will be sufficient merely to note that well before 1966 the old Confederacy no longer presented a united front in Congress; the power of the Southern congressional oligarchs, previously secure, sometimes serene, and always effective in their committee chairmanships, had been broken. That this result is due in part to a strong President who treated the oligarchs as no more than equals and in part to the surly advance of old age in no way disparages the influence of an extended suffrage and reapportionment, and it surely points to a new breed of Southerner in Congress once the old captains and kings have departed.

For many years to come race relations will have a large share in the study of the South as two conscious minorities. It is unfortunate but true that the Negro has in a peculiar way occupied the thought and political life of the South since the Nat Turner slave revolt in 1831. With few and often no votes, without money, and without access to the common means of communication, he has dominated political campaigns, deliberations in legislative assemblies and constitutional conventions, private conversations, and unspoken thoughts. Gunnar Myrdal was not exaggerating when he wrote, "The intellectual energy agent on the Negro problem in America should, if concentrated in a single direction, have moved mountains."[8] It would be comforting, to be sure, to be rid of the preoccupation and obsession with race, but so long as the racial issue remains as the most important domestic issue of the South and the nation in the twentieth century, it must be faced. Accordingly, intellectual effort directed in a different way and sufficient to move mountains must be devoted to the study of race relations. Even after it ceases to be a major domestic problem, this issue will continue to be a matter of historical interest.

Few political issues have involved the interest of so many fields of the social sciences as those arising from the Supreme Court's decision in the public school segregation cases of 1954. The constitutional and legal aspects of desegregation have been amply treated in books and articles in professional journals. The role of the federal district and circuit judges has been described in one book.[9] Southern patterns of resistance have been portrayed,[10] and the general subject of civil rights for Negroes has been documented in agency reports and congressional committee hearings. Nevertheless, the full story with interpretative analysis remains to be written.

Such a story should begin with what may appropriately be called a judicial revolution in the law of race relations culminating in *Brown* v. *Board of Education of Topeka*[11] and a host of succeeding cases applying the Brown rule. Having fostered a legal revolution, the Supreme Court soon found it difficult to enforce it in the face of active resistance, official lawlessness, and passive disobedience. The federal district courts were given the major responsibility for implementing the Supreme Court's judgment, and the volume of litigation grew. For almost nine years (until 1962) the enforcement of the constitutional guarantee of equal protection of the laws was almost exclusively the responsibility of the judiciary.

President Eisenhower assumed no direct responsibility for the enforce-

8. *An American Dilemma* (New York: Harper, 1944), p. 27.
9. Jack W. Peltason, *Fifty-eight Lonely Men: Southern Federal Judges and School Desegregation* (New York: Harcourt, Brace, & World, 1961).
10. Benjamin Muse, *Virginia's Massive Resistance* (Bloomington: Indiana University Press, 1961); and *Ten Years of Prelude: The Story of Integration since the Supreme Court's 1954 Decision* (New York: Viking, 1964).
11. 347 U.S. 483 (1954).

ment of the 1954 decision (except for permitting the Attorney General to intervene in some desegregation suits) until he was forced by the defiance of Governor Faubus and others to send troops to enforce a court order in Little Rock. In press conferences he refused to say whether he was for or against the decision, lest it complicate his duty to see that the laws were faithfully executed. At times he criticized extremists on both sides and thereby cursed with equal impartiality those who were working within the law and those acting in defiance of it; and only a short time before Little Rock, he declared in a press conference that he could not envisage a situation in which he would use troops to enforce court orders arising out of the racial issue. In contrast to General Eisenhower's silence, President Kennedy was articulate in his endorsement of the decision of 1954 and eloquent in his condemnation of racial discrimination, but like General Eisenhower he was cautiously inactive in the implementation of it until the crises in Oxford, Mississippi, in 1962 and Birmingham, Alabama, in 1963 forced him not only to put down defiance with a massive show of federal force, but also to revise his whole approach to the issue and propose what later became the Civil Rights Act of 1964. Upon the death of President Kennedy, President Johnson pushed the passage of the Civil Rights Act of 1964 and the Voting Act of 1965, but his general plan of operation has not substantially differed from that of Mr. Kennedy.

Congress was the last of the great branches of government to enter the civil rights picture, with the enactment of mild voting laws in 1957 and 1960 and the more comprehensive and effective legislation of 1964 and 1965. Indeed, it can now be argued that legislation has outrun administration in that the full impact of the new laws will not be known until they are enforced, and the administrative mechanism for their execution is incomplete.

These familiar events have been reviewed here in order to provide a context for the gradual evolution of federal policy in civil rights and race relations which has culminated in what some call the Second Reconstruction. For those interested in policy and its formulation, in the role of courts as policy makers, in presidential knowledge of power and its uses, and in the legislative struggle, few episodes in American history provide such rich materials or abundant opportunities. The historian will readily find parallels between the First Reconstruction and the Second—lawlessness, violence, killings, floggings, arson, and other forms of intimidation. Those who read the report of Karl Schurz on conditions in the South and the proceedings of the original congressional committee charged with investigating the Ku Klux Klan, and compare these with the reports of the Civil Rights Commission will find not only that history sometimes repeats itself but also that developments in the South since 1954 add a pertinence and a credibility to the documentation of conditions in the South in 1866 which were denied by conventional historians a generation ago.

Race relations in general and the legal developments pertaining to them since 1954 should attract the attention of lawyers and social scientists for the indefinite future and should constitute an important item in any planned agenda of research for many years to come. Legal scholars have both a large storehouse of laws as formulated in legislation, court decisions, and executive orders, and a great treasure of data on the strategy and tactics of litigation, the use of the courts as policy-making organs, and the whole subject of the uses of law and its limits as a means of social control. The efficacy of legal rules when they run counter to long-established customs and habits has often been a subject of interest to social theorists and speculative jurists, and the South of the twentieth century provides interesting and useful data bearing on this subject. Is law, as Justice Brown believed in *Plessy* v. *Ferguson*,[12] really powerless to change custom? Whether it is or is not, what are the consequences of a conflict between law and custom? We know the answer in part, because recent experiences in the South with respect to Negro voting, the desegregation of public facilities, and employment practices demonstrate that long-established patterns of human behavior, however encrusted by the hard cake of custom, yield sometimes slowly and sometimes quickly to law and its sanctions, and in turn this process results in changed attitudes and opinions, in changes, in short, in the minds and hearts of men. The interaction of law and public opinion is therefore illuminated by racial developments between 1954 and 1966, which provide important data for the lawyer and the social psychologist.

Moving from the law of race relations with its wars of injunctions and other writs, we enter an area of perhaps even greater significance to social scientists, namely, the political, economic, and social aspects of what may loosely be called the Civil Rights Movement. When the struggle for equality took a partial departure from the courtroom and went into the streets, it became an object of direct interest to political scientists and sociologists. The organization and leadership of the Civil Rights Movement and its various components are important individual and social phenomena. The leadership of the movement has required a high order of executive ability, administrative talent, and personal appeal of a charismatic nature. The manner in which leaders emerged, organization evolved, and a militant but orderly following mobilized has few parallels in the his-

12. 163 U.S. 537 (1896).

tory of social action. Abundant materials exist, therefore, not merely for the study of the Civil Rights Movement, but for the general study of leadership, social conflict, and direct political action when laws alone fail to satisfy the felt needs of the times.

Equally important to such a study of social conflict and leadership is an examination of the reactions of the white community to change and to demands for more change. The lawyer and legal historian can find here abundant materials on patterns of resistance through the forms of law—if not always through its substance—to federal court decisions, congressional legislation, and presidential action. Such materials have implications which transcend Southern boundaries and racial conflict and reach the very heart of the American constitutional system, involving as they do individual rights and state power in opposition to national supremacy. Here, too, court records abound with pleadings, briefs, and so-called non-legal materials which are directly relevant to the knowledge of the law and its uses.

The problems faced by the leadership of the white community are equally worthy of attention, and they raise interesting questions because of variations in the kind and quality of leadership. The conditions and factors which produced one type of leadership for states like Georgia, North Carolina, South Carolina, and Tennessee, something of an opposite type in Alabama, Arkansas, Louisiana, and Mississippi, and still a different type in Virginia provide the materials for significant case studies in individual leaders and comparative leadership. In contrast to the rigidity of some leaders, the resilience shown by others and the emergence of new leaders born in this century, inured to change and crisis, indifferent to ancestor worship, and skeptical of old traditions are a dramatic testimonial to the great changes in the South and the heralds of greater changes yet to come.

Regardless of the subject under discussion in the South or about it, the issue of federalism and its concomitants, the nature of the Union, national power, and states' rights have ultimately occupied a place disproportionate to their importance and frequently irrelevant to the matter under consideration. Like the opinions and attitudes on race relations, the Southern theology of federalism and its central dogma of states' rights have been unencumbered by any factual apparatus. Accordingly, Southern resistance to the expansion of national power and federal activity has been irrational to the point of folly and ineffective to the point of futility, so that opposition to alleged federal encroachment has been confined largely to hollow histrionics. The use of hundreds of national guardsmen to keep nine children out of school in Little Rock, the symbolic stand of a governor in a schoolhouse door in Alabama as a final gesture of state defiance, the emergence of a governor of Mississippi as the Director of Admissions of the state university at Oxford, the lurid manifestos, interposition resolutions by state legislatures, school-closing laws, the purging of Negroes from registration rolls, and a host of other actions are all melancholy examples of an ungainly progeny sired by ambition out of ignorance so as to corroborate the recent parody of Lord Acton's dictum that power corrupts but seeking power corrupts absolutely.

The growth of federal activity at a relatively more rapid rate than state functions has two sides and has been an object of concern to serious scholars, to take the late Leonard D. White as only one example, but for the most part Southern opposition to alleged federal encroachment has not made a plausible case for its position. At a time when the cities were groaning under onerous burdens made heavier by an acceleration of urbanization, when education was making more demands because of a burgeoning population and a growing faith in education as a means of secular salvation, and when Negroes were striving to burst the bonds of servility, persons in positions of power and influence with few exceptions took no heed of the warnings. Malapportioned state legislatures—no exclusively Southern phenomenon—did not respond and the issues were taken to Washington. For the most part, indeed, the problems were met by chanting incantations on states' rights and hurling imprecations against federal encroachment. Few studies were made of the serious issues that had to be resolved somewhere, and little attention was paid to the great storehouses of information already available. Indeed, some state legislatures heavily dependent upon federal grants-in-aid were so obsequious to states' rights and so oblivious to the dictates of solvency and self-interest that they enacted resolutions calling for a national constitutional convention to propose an amendment either to repeal or drastically limit the federal income tax.

Aside from a few Southern leaders who have followed the traditions of John Marshall, George Washington, and some other nationalists of the region, many have followed the leadership of John C. Calhoun and, at least publicly, taken seriously the dogma of state sovereignty and regarded nullification as a viable principle of federalism and a prerequisite to constitutional government. The shibboleth of states' rights has been invoked to protect a variety of vested economic interests against federal regulatory, welfare, and civil rights policies. Not once has the dogma of states' rights been invoked in the South to protect basic personal rights, with the possible exceptions of the Virginia and Kentucky Resolutions of 1798. It has been invoked to protect a corporate collectivism against effective national regulation, and to defend entrenched political interests and the legal power of a white minority to enslave a black minority, against judicial decisions and federal statutes aimed at the correction of ancient wrongs and abuses. Except for the Jacksonian Democracy, the more ardent advocates of states' rights have not directed their efforts at effective state action but, on the contrary, have used what Justice Holmes once called the invisible radiations from the Tenth Amendment to foster laissez-faire in economics and stagnation in politics. So persistent has been the virus of states' rights and nullification that it still pervaded portions of the South one hundred years after it had supposedly been eradicated at Appomattox.

The South's concern with states' rights and its unreasoning fear of national power have led it to take a distorted and unrealistic view of the national government detrimental to the substantial interests of the region. Considering the vast sums of federal money spent in the South for highways, welfare, and such direct federal programs as agricultural subsidies, military installations, missile sites, space projects, and a host of others, the South is in the least favorable position of all sections to look upon the national government as an alien intruder. In more than one Southern state the national government is either directly or indirectly the single biggest industry. This is the way the states desire it, and some of the most ardent states' righters have been the most avid seekers of federal projects and money. However, federalism is not a one-way street, nor is the federal government in its relations with the states exclusively a philanthropy which dispenses benefits but abdicates the governance of men. Throughout our history a number of theories of federalism have emerged. All too often the South has followed Chief Justice Taney's conception of federalism as a continuous struggle between angry and truculent sovereigns. Political scientists and lawyers can do much for learning by making studies of Southern regionalism and its relation to federalism, and at the same time they can correct errors sanctioned by longevity and repetition. Until the South discards outmoded and stagnant theories of dual federalism in favor of a vibrant federalism, until it accepts the federal government as a senior partner in the solution of its many problems, it is hardly likely to assume its equal station among the other regions of the country.

Since the end of World War II social scientists in increasing numbers have directed their attention to the developing nations of Asia and Africa. Without in any way disparaging these efforts, it may be suggested that the United States in general and the South especially provide in different ways equally great opportunities for observing economic development. Unlike the new nations of Africa and Asia, the North American colonials were heirs to mature political and legal systems. Even so, they and their descendants were largely responsible for the development of an industrial economy, though they were aided by European capital and technical inventions. The relatively slower industrial development in the Southern region compared with that in the United States as a whole has been accompanied by disadvantages in the form of surplus population, lower wages, less skilled workers, lower standards of living, and the like. On the other hand, it is possible through informed planning to convert the slowness of economic development into a positive benefit. The South has the whole of the experience of the industrialized sectors of the United States upon which to draw; and if it can muster the will and acquire the information to plan an orderly industrialization, it can avoid some of the more obvious errors and more serious consequences of economic development in other regions. In 1966 evidence was largely lacking to indicate that Southern state governments and industrialists had either the will or the information to plan wisely and well. Polluted streams, foul air, the good earth scarred by strip mining, unplanned satellite cities, the decay of the central city, and intensified problems of transportation all testify to the indifference and inertia of the public and private sectors of the political and economic order to the experience of others, and to their failure to see in the fate of others their own. At its best, industrialization is a solvent of old ways of living and a threat to pre-existing institutions. At its worst, it is destructive of human and physical resources. In 1966 the South could still choose between orderly development with the least erosive effects, and haphazard unplanned development productive of a chain of evils which could render industrial development a curse.

Lest it be assumed from most of what has been said that the great changes through which the South has passed and will continue to pass are accompanied exclusively by unmitigated benefits, a warning is in order. Profound changes in any existing order usually result in painful dislocations, serious maladjustments, and even violence. Industrialization and urbanization in particular contribute to the loss of old values and the dissolution of old traditions and institutions without simultaneously providing new substitutes. This condition, too, is an appropriate study for scholars both for the purpose of expanding existing knowledge and for utilitarian ends. In this regard the South has two great advantages. The strength of its traditions may provide a degree of continuity that will obviate the worst personal and social dislocations. Second, it has the experience of other regions and societies from which to learn; but to succeed, the South must know itself. The study of the South in a difficult period of transition for either abstract theory or practical ends is like the reformation of the law in Justinian's empire, "an arduous and indispensable task," and worthy of the ablest intellects of the universities, the philanthropy of foundations, and the support of governments.

Commentary / John T. Caldwell

We have been treated to a brilliant essay by one of the nation's most astute political scientists. Professor (now Dean) Harris has long been a masterful teacher, scholar, and commentator from the faculties of leading Southern universities.

His paper, as an agenda for research, reflects two major facts: (1) that he is primarily a student of the political-legalistic-institutional forces which shape the unfolding future of the region; and (2) that the race question has heavily conditioned and *does* continue, though in fresh patterns, to condition political behavior in the South. We would, therefore, expect his perceptive suggestions for research into the many political phenomena (e.g., Negro voting, reapportionment, states' rights, national power, party alignment, and Civil Rights Movement) in all of which the race question has and continues to play a decisive role. Professor Harris' research agenda also includes the changing labor pattern, industrialization, urbanization, and economic development.

Everyone could, of course, add to his list. And he would expect this to occur. I could suggest an enormous need for research, pure and applied, into the problem of Negro higher education—for example, analysis of the predominantly Negro colleges, public and private. A study of intellectual freedom, especially in the classrooms of elementary and secondary schools, but also in the colleges and universities, of the South might reveal a principal source of retardation in regional development. More study of state and local tax structure and the federal relationship is needed.

But the answer to the question "Research for what?," even in Professor Harris' discourse, is elusive. A hint of the possible answer, though, is found in his early statement, after Tennyson, that "The time has come, therefore, when greater emphasis must be placed upon wisdom, understanding, and reason in the study of Southern life; when necessary, we must take paths to truth other than empirical knowledge, whether these paths be myths, new or old, or even poetry and art." Then, taking pains not to disparage the accumulation of knowledge, he urges that what we need is "to bring existing knowledge into a degree of order in which it can be put to use in the solution of the problems confronting the South and the nation and in the building of a better society." Thus he concludes that meaningful study "must contain an element of applied research" if it is to influence and mold opinion. These observations, to me, are the most important points of Professor Harris' paper. Let me elaborate.

"Research" is a popular word these days. It covers, as one would expect, an infinite variety of activities, some of them remote from the standards of university scholarship. Even university research covers a very broad spectrum of purposes. At one end is the problem-oriented type of research aimed at providing answers for a particular interested user. Examples are disease control in the poultry industry or in human beings, or an analysis of economies of scale in a particular industry. At the other end are the pure researches of the historian and man of letters, or investigation by the physicist of behavior of a particular atom under certain conditions of heat and pressure.

These two extremes can be defined in part in terms of the clientele they purport to serve. The problem-oriented research of the poultry pathologist is designed to serve an anxious poultry farmer who wants to protect his profits. He, as did Mr. Doolittle, stands there "willin' to hear, waitin' to hear, and wantin' to hear" the answer to a problem and to use the answer. But who is waiting and wanting to hear about the hitherto undisclosed facts of what went on in General Grant's mind about the South the day of his inauguration? And to what end? And how many bankers and entrepreneurs are waiting breathlessly to read the physicist's narrow abstract on atoms?

A large portion even of economic research on the South as an economic region has a poorly defined clientele. How many of the changes taking place in the South today (or any other region) can be attributed to scholarly social and economic research? We do not know. "Some," I would feel sure, but "how much" would be hard to identify. For example, is Charlotte's or Atlanta's great growth a result of "economic research"? Are we not compelled to concede that the greatest structural changes in society (e.g., industrialization, urbanization, etc.) stem from the application of research in the natural sciences and technology? But these changes are so impersonal and mechanistic as to present an enormous challenge to the social scientist and humanist. If change is to be progress, it surely must be more than a mechanistic consequence. Will it be sufficient someday to study "what happened" that made our growing Southern cities as ugly and disorganized as those of old vintage to the east and north? Neither Professor Harris nor I wish to underestimate the value of research for the sake of knowledge. The historian, the literary scholar, and the scholarly social scientist all make contributions to a civilization's self-understanding. Indeed, no civilization could claim to be such without such scholarship. Their ultimate contribution depends heavily upon the educational system. Designed in part to insure that each generation is *wiser* than its predecessor, and hopefully more *humane*, the educational system must transmit the product of learned research. But research on what has already occurred or is occurring may make a contribution to a better society only over the long run.

Meanwhile, immediate problems cry out for the wisdom research belatedly produces. Perhaps two needs are suggested: one, for more creative scholars and researchers who dare to suggest solutions; two, for a closer communion of scholars and decision makers.

Political scientists have written and spoken for half a century on county consolidation. Why have there been so few consolidations? On the other hand, educational researchers have been quite successful in demonstrating and effecting school consolidation. Is it indicated that needs have to be felt, recognized, and simplified, and *then* become overwhelming before research is looked to for an answer? Has the research of the social scientist and humanist served exclusively the community of scholars, the educational world? Who is it that needs to know what the scholar learns from his researches? Only other scholars? Is that enough?

Anyway, knowing facts is never enough. The choosing of goals, correctly states Professor Harris, is a task for the man outside the university. The scholar can only supply him with facts to help him in his analysis, his choice among alternatives, his weighing of possible consequences.

Professor Joseph Spengler chose a quotation from Aristotle as one of the epigraphs for his essay in *The South in Continuity and Change:* "The end of the state is the good life." Is this not also the proper end of research, all research, but especially that of the social scientist and humanist? As Professor Harris, paraphrasing Jefferson, reminds us: "Scholars are here to enrich the world."

Most of the social choices that really count are heavily loaded with moral content. Research does not make a moral judgment. Indeed, research is not necessarily inspiring or motivating. Research *can* help motivated people make intelligent decisions. The motivation must come from some other source.

The good society in our region or elsewhere will come through the efforts of right-thinking people acting intelligently on well-researched opportunities.

The South considered as an achieving society / Rupert B. Vance

At a meeting of the Southern Historical Association in Atlanta in 1959, attention was given to the state of Southern regionalism. Among the considerations advanced at the meeting we may note the following: (1) The section had gathered to praise regionalism, not to bury it. (2) But as the South advanced in economic status, the rationale of Southern regionalism was receding. Along with King Pyrrhus regionalists might say: "More such victories and we are undone!" (3) Regionalism was never taken up as a movement by the people; it remained the preoccupation of certain university scholars. (4) The deal is dealt, we were told. Shall we proceed to the next deal?[1]

Now that we are greeting the establishment of a new Center for Southern Studies at Duke University, let us show no hesitation to follow Mark Twain and say that the report of the death of regional studies has been greatly exaggerated. In Atlanta some contradictions seemed in evidence: the movement had never caught on; and it was to be abandoned because it was succeeding.

We are under the obligation to make what use we can of historical perspective in terms of our national and regional trends. The American Civil War has had its centennial; the first hundred years since emancipation has had its commemoration; and now for a hundred years since Appomattox Court House the South has been pursuing the trend line of a developing economy. Only since 1920 has the pursuit seemed real. The value of economic development, "putting first things first," slowly gained acceptance in the South, but two world wars, high postwar productivity, and Keynesian economics were required to make these values operative. With the analysis of the gross national product, measurement of the phenomenon of economic development for regions has become possible. Empirical analyses of components have been plentiful, and I do not propose to read them into this record. Rather we shall seek to discuss interrelationships; to ask whither we are trending; and mayhap to apply what we can of theory and speculation to research in probable developments in the South. And if it seems impossible to keep values out of the account, we may adopt the virtue of frankness and admit a preference for progress. In considering the complementary interaction between quantity and quality in periods of development, one can hardly escape the assessment of values.

1. "The Status and Future of Regionalism," *Journal of Southern History*, XXVI (Feb., 1960), 22-56.

It is the assumption of this paper, then, that the South can be viewed as following along certain lines of development which may or may not reach culmination; that such movements are fairly general phenomena in historical times; and that they have suggested strategy and tactics for research in the transition of an ongoing society. To follow through on such leads bespeaks the efforts of several varieties of social scientists and of humanists, an undertaking congenial, I would assume, to the purposes of the university's new institute. May I in speculative fashion draw on certain assumptions to suggest contiguous areas of ignorance which the research of the future should be able to explore? (1) Here the course of economic development sets the model; (2) the trend line of social process opens up neighboring problems; and (3) the unfolding of new culture in literature and the arts will be related.

I

We lack the trained imagination to realize the great gulf which separates the mentality of underdeveloped societies from that of today's complex economy. Let me cite a parable which I hope will suggest the distance our region has traversed in a century. On certain islands of the Pacific the natives, contemporary primitives comparable to those of the Old Stone Age, were caught up as observers on the fringe of World War II. As transport ships and freight airliners landed with shipments of materials, the natives uttered the cry "Cargo!" and rushed to the harbor to earn porters' wages in unloading inexplicable riches. For this the natives developed their own set of explanations, which anthropologists came to call the "Cult of Cargo." Observing the mass of paper work involved—bills of exchange, bills of lading, invoices, receipts checked and counter-checked, signed and countersigned—they reached an explanation. Desirable cargo was summoned out of the sky and out of the ocean's vastness by marks which white men made on pieces of paper, marks which could not be resisted and which only white men had mastered and understood.[2]

Democracy having been introduced in the islands, one candidate, we are told, mounted his campaign with the promise to teach his people the magic of cargo, to show them how to make the marks that summoned goods from across the ocean and from out of the sky. I like this parable.

2. Peter Worsley, *The Trumpet Shall Sound* (London: MacGibbon and Kee, 1957); J. Van Boal, "Erring Acculturation (Case of the Cargo Cult)," *American Anthropologist*, LXII (Feb., 1960), 108-121, esp. 108-111; "Explaining Cargo Cults," *Hibbert Journal*, LXII (April, 1964), 151-153.

The one thing wrong is that the natives' procedure would start at the top and work its way downward; so far we haven't learned how this is done. One might well ask how the common man was to understand the poverty which gripped the South in the years following Appomattox or understand the wealth-producing qualities of the new industrialism arising in the Northern United States. There is a textbook test of an underdeveloped economy which is often cited—if over one-half of the occupied males work in agriculture the country may be put down as underdeveloped.[3] As late as 1920 slightly over 50 per cent of the Southern total labor force worked in agriculture; by 1960 it was 10.4 per cent; today, it is less.[4]

Industrialization represents a commitment to the improvement of material well-being and the conditions of life as a goal of public policy and private endeavor. In poorer countries outside the West, economic development appears to certain groups well-nigh unobtainable. It calls for drastic changes that include both intended and unanticipated consequences. The acquisition of the skills required in the performance of modern types of economic activity and the deep-seated acceptance of the attitudes and beliefs appropriate to industrialization are to be seen as the problem of the commitment of a society's labor force to a new social discipline.[5] In England's Industrial Revolution no social change, it seemed, could be more drastic than the acquisition of the new industrial discipline. Russia repeated the process with variations that only a totalitarian state could introduce. In the South we are in the midst of the strains, the tensions, and the achievements that accompany the industrialization which is a pervasive feature of modern life. Leon Trotsky called this "the permanent revolution." Great as the tensions are, greater are the rewards; survival lies in no other direction. As the South shifts from an agrarian to an industrial economy, it mechanizes, reorganizes, in fact, "industrializes" its agriculture. Other economies have threatened the agricultural basis of their existence in the transition. The South, along with other regions, has gained efficiency and stored up surpluses of its staples at the same time that it has liquidated small-time agriculture. This should not blind us to the plight of the Negro and poor-white working forces, many of whom have faced liquidation of the only skills they have learned since Appomattox.

3. William Peterson, *Population* (New York: Macmillan, 1961), p. 466.

4. William H. Nicholls, "The South as a Developing Area," in Avery Leiserson, ed., *The American South in the 1960's* (New York: Frederick A. Praeger, 1964), p. 28.

5. See A. F. Feldman and W. E. Moore, "Moot Points in the Theory of Labor Commitment in Developing Areas," S.S.R.C. *Items*, XIV (Dec., 1960), 1 ff.; also the Committee's *Labor Commitment and Social Change in Developing Areas* (New York: S.S.R.C., 1961); and "The Meaning of Discipline," in H. H. Gerth and C. W. Mills, eds., *From Max Weber: Essays in Sociology* (New York: Oxford Press, 1946), pp. 253 ff.

The commitment of the working force is exceeded by that of certain Southern leaders. Floyd Hunter, fresh from studying community power structure in Southern cities, wrote:

> Southern leaders, particularly those in the institutions of business and politics, are convinced that organized efforts on a large scale are necessary to (1) improve agriculture, and (2) to expand and build up new commercial and industrial enterprises. This is seen as "putting first things first." The general agreement from the top down is that nothing must stand in the way of these laudable aims.[6]

Add the pursuit of (3) expansion and excellence in education, however visualized by the educational and political forces, in a movement that extends all the way from public schools to the universities. Finally, the political leaders have united in (4) the support of social security goals. "All major Southern institutions are busily engaged in defining their value systems in terms of progress and development," Hunter wrote in 1954. "They all have the forward look and optimism is abroad in the land."[7]

Many analyses have been made of regional per capita income and deservedly so, for it constitutes the one index of economic achievement and reward. Per capita income in the South was about 46 per cent of that in the rest of the nation in 1929; in 1960 the South's share approached 70 per cent. Professor Howard G. Schaller had developed projections of the South's per capita income which indicate that in fifty years the region will attain equality with the United States per capita income, if the present rates continue. This calculation includes the proviso that migration out of the South also continues at present rates.[8]

Industrialization ran a full course in England, in Japan, and in communist Russia without much importation of capitalization. Japan, we

6. Floyd Hunter, "Community Organization: Lever for Institutional Change?" in R. B. Vance and N. J. Demerath, eds., *The Urban South* (Chapel Hill: University of North Carolina Press, 1954), p. 252.

7. *Idem.*

8. Howard G. Schaller, "Changes in the Southern Economy," in *Manpower Requirements and Human Resource Adjustment* (Raleigh, N. C.: The Agricultural Policy Institute, Series 15 [May, 1965]), pp. 1-14, esp. p. 5. On Southern development in general, see J. J. Spengler, "Southern Economic Trends and Prospects," in J. C. McKinney and E. T. Thompson, eds., *The South in Continuity and Change* (Durham, N. C.: Duke University Press, 1965), pp. 101-131; also chaps. vi-x. See also Clarence Danhof, "Four Decades of Thought on the South's Economic Problems," and Part II in M. L. Greenhut and W. T. Whitman, eds., *Essays in Southern Economic Development* (Chapel Hill: University of North Carolina Press, 1964), pp. 7-68, 169-358. A good reference on regional growth is H. S. Perloff *et al.*, *Regions, Resources and Economic Growth* (Baltimore: Johns Hopkins Press, 1960).

might recall, developed its industry under state socialism and then turned it back to private owners. W. W. Rostow, studying international economic development, holds that underdeveloped countries subject to the thrust of initial capitalization and industrialization reach a take-off stage after which economic growth is self-sustaining.[9] The South's access to capital and the extent to which it has benefited as a component region of the world's richest nation are now very clear.[10] The South's development, however, does not automatically follow from this trend. In Italy's economic growth, the industrial area of Northern Italy has pulled further away from the problem-ridden South, progressively widening the differential.[11]

I have no intention of presenting economic growth as an impersonal, spontaneous evolutionary force. It represents, in fact, a resolution of forces, a merging of the energies of individuals and groups, pushing, striving, wanting, claiming, deciding, struggling, and achieving. To the desire for cargo is added a certain know-how. It is notable that when social psychologists like David McClelland and J. W. Atkinson came to study the achieving society, they took economic development as the prototype and motivation (defined as realized, conscious need to achieve) as the rational component.[12] Undoubtedly the riddle of achievement remains to be riddled; but if the equation were to be written, it would look something like this: IQ (talent) + motivation + opportunity = achievement. We leave to our research people in social science the consideration of how one gets back and forth from individuals to collectivities, from corporate groups to growing cities and achieving regions. Nor does one have to attribute sainthood, superhuman energies, or extraordinary intelligence to businessmen to place a value on the achieving society thus defined.

Given the assumption that economic progress will push through to a plateau of achievement, can the change carry other aspects of regional society and culture along with it? Under one assumption, our region has wanted all things needful and required only the resources to meet the required budgets. Under another assumption, the Southern public has wanted economic development so badly that it was willing to give up certain regional traits and attitudes which stood athwart the line of advance.

9. W. W. Rostow, "The Take-Off into Self-Sustained Growth," *The Economic Journal,* LXVI (March, 1956), 25-48. Also his *The Process of Economic Growth* (New York: Norton, 1956).

10. Joe S. Floyd, "Trends in Southern Money, Income, Savings, and Investment," *The South in Continuity and Change,* pp. 132-144.

11. Lloyd Saville, "Sectional Development in Italy and the United States," *Southern Economic Journal,* XXIII (July, 1956), 39-53.

12. David McClelland, *The Achieving Society* (Princeton: Van Nostrand, 1961), esp. chaps. i-iii, v-viii, and x. Also J. W. Atkinson, "Determinants of Risk-Taking Behavior," *Psychological Review,* LXIV (Nov, 1957), 359-372.

In 1959 a student of the South's economy attempted to come to grips with the question of the impact of non-economic factors on development. W. H. Nicholls of Vanderbilt University devoted his presidential address before the Southern Economic Association to the impact of the Southern tradition on economic progress. In 1960 he published *Southern Tradition and Regional Progress*, stating his firm conviction that the South must choose "between its traditions and progress."[13] Nicholls filed a bill of particulars and the list was a formidable one. Urban and industrial development, he said, run counter to: (1) the persistence of agrarian values, (2) the rigidity of inherited social structure, (3) an undemocratic political structure, (4) the weakness of social responsibility, especially in regard to public education, (5) a forced conformity of thought and behavior, behind which lurked the threats of violence and anti-intellectualism. Nicholls' evidence was familiar to students: the agrarians were taken more seriously than they deserved; racism, while not given the center of the stage, was everywhere in evidence. In Howard W. Odum's terms, the South had turned from regionalism to sectionalism.[14]

One reaction to Professor Nicholls' thesis pointed to the disastrous effect on the life and livelihood of the common man, if tradition should block development. The conflict of values involved was evident in another view: how tragic for the nation and the region if the South carried through to become new-rich and purse-proud only to use its wealth to underwrite its peculiar doctrines. Apparently it was Nicholls' hope that the issue would force a choice and that Southern leaders would be forced to choose development over the implementation of tradition in closed schools and massive resistance. Political compliance, where subsidies and benefits were concerned, was also seen as tied to Southern development. If the region held out its hand for the benefits of equalization funds and railed against the new regulations, it was seen to take the position of saying to the federal powers: "Give us our money and don't ask us what we intend to do with it."

II

Different institutions and different organized ways of doing things have different impacts on the trend of events. We have followed the economic trend closely; others may point to the trend line of compliance and the new federalism in our political structure, to the generating of new

13. The volume was published by the University of North Carolina Press.

14. Howard W. Odum, *Folk, Region and Society: Selected Papers* (Chapel Hill: University of North Carolina Press, 1964), pp. 173-191.

social traditions, or to the talent-releasing power of education. These are the variables of social change and it behooves us not to announce conclusions, but to seek tactics and strategy for the long pull. To my mind this means that in research we must turn to the legitimate use of theory. Certain bodies of older theory do not attempt to explain all phenomena before analysis; rather, they suggest where to look and what questions to ask.

Let us begin by asking if there exist general propositions applying to such social elites as: (1) business leaders, (2) engineers and technicians, (3) political groups and leaders, (4) scholars and research scientists who face change and the demand for change. We do not propose technical answers; we seek rather the general characteristics of social situations. We begin with the assumption that social change involves a learning process —individual, collective, and interactive. A society, a group, an individual is confronted by *X*: an emergency, a crisis, a research problem demanding solution, or at minimum a choice of alternatives, one which may involve public opinion. Such a stimulus arouses a circular reaction, a focus of group attention. A change of direction may follow if the crisis brings forth an invention, an innovation, a research solution, or a new choice of policy. No response or an inadequate response defers the process, which then becomes cumulative. How the crisis is met depends on certain complex conditions which we may state simply.

1. The general level of group culture furnishes the basis for response. Machine retrieval of the stored information in "knowledge banks" has shown how much we expect from the culture basis. Thus in the classic case wartime radar could not have been developed had we lacked any one of a score of previous inventions.
2. The achievement of mastery is dependent on what can quite simply be called the character of ideas in circulation. Thus, the attitudes of the Catholic church and the economics of Lord Keynes greatly affect the chances of innovation to meet economic or population crises.
3. Much depends on the presence of extraordinary individuals in the group. No one should be called on to define genius, but one might say that even Einstein became what he was because of the training he had before he took charge of his own education. It may be entirely possible that many technicians and professional men operate up to the limit of their best training and no further. If so, they are still men of talent.

The elite, the inventors, and innovators of our society thus create new patterns of action, new mechanisms for their achievement, and new ideologies for their justification. If they are problem-solving, such patterns are spread abroad by diffusion and communication, a process as it were of social learning, meeting opposition even as Gabriel Tarde showed in his account of social imitation.

Innovations and inventions come to be incorporated in the social traditions of the group, and the powerful norms of society move in as sanctions. Fortunately, bad laws are occasionally subject to repeal and new science itself is subject to re-evaluation. The final step is taken when elements of the cumulative culture are incorporated in the corpus of knowledge, and are then transferred to the formal curricula of the schools. By the inculcation of new elements in the minds of the young, society establishes a process of intergenerational diffusion, thus molding a new social heritage. Here in simplified form—from the works of Gabriel Tarde, W. I. Thomas, Charles A. Ellwood, Florian Znaniecki, W. F. Ogburn, and Arnold Toynbee[15] is what every young native of Borneo should know about cargo. This represents, of course, a process in which the South is now far advanced.

The interrelations of (1) economic development, (2) changing social conditions, and (3) achievements in the fine arts and the humanities will offer materials for analysis for generations of scholars to come. Certainly the humanities are not to be neglected. Stewart Udall writes: "It is the artists and men of ideas who have done and will do the most to determine our national purpose, to fix our national character, and to shape the American legacy." Nor can the developing South avoid the verdict stated by August Herkcher in his "Quality of American Culture," written for President Eisenhower's Commission on National Goals: "In the eyes of posterity the success of the United States as a civilized society will be largely judged by the creative activities of its citizens in art, architecture, literature, music, and the sciences." One does not have to contend that the arts will remain in total dependence on the marketplace to visualize the impact of Southern development on the humanists.

Problems of interrelations between these areas will call forth suggestions whereby theory may guide further efforts. Alfred Weber gave state-

15. Gabriel Tarde, *Social Laws,* trans. H. C. Warren, Jr. (New York: Macmillan, 1899); William I. Thomas, ed., *Source Book for Social Origins* (Chicago: University of Chicago Press, 1909); Charles A. Ellwood, *Cultural Evolution* (New York: Century, 1927); William F. Ogburn, *Social Change* (New York: Viking, 1956 ed.); Florian Znaniecki, *The Social Role of the Man of Knowledge* (New York: Columbia University Press, 1940); Arnold J. Toynbee, *A Study of History* (abridged by D. C. Somervell) (New York: Oxford University Press), Vol. I (1947) covers Vols. I-VI; Vol. II (1957) covers Vols. VII-X of the original.

ment to one such formulation as early as 1935 in his *Cultural History as Cultural Sociology,* and he returned to the theme in 1951 in *Principles of Historical and Cultural Sociology.*[16] Again we are concerned with hypotheses which have not yet been processed into conclusions. Life to Weber was fundamentally historical in process and the student should face up to this question: What is our place in the stream of history? Here explanations are to be sought in cultural science, not in natural science. Certain it is that if we are to have social dynamics, they must come from the energies and propensities of individuals interacting in groups, however structured.

In the historical process Weber points out a social process, a culture process, and the process whereby civilization accumulates and is integrated. The last may be treated first. The products of civilization are transferable across cultural boundaries and they are cumulative, adding to the stockpile of technology. More than anything else the process represents the idea of development as progressive, unilateral, and irreversible. The civilizational process used to exploit nature's resources reaches culmination in the development of technology and the natural sciences. It is this process, dominated by considerations of utility, rationality, and purpose, which pushes toward a unified civilization—not culture the world over. Culture is superstructural and ideational. In the culture process as Weber defines it, the main uniformity is not accumulation, but unique creativity. Products of high culture represent a synthesis of the world and the mind of individual personalities, uniquely talented. Expressed in art, religion, and philosophy, they furnish no predetermined patterns that we can deduce, no universally valid and necessary criteria except those of taste, no generally applicable laws to relate this creative process to other processes. Such creations, being unique, do not easily transfer from one period or one culture to another. In a work like Dante's *Divine Comedy* we have the epitome of an age and the creative expression of a unique talent, phenomena that cannot be understood without understanding an age.

Both are associated with the social process, which Weber sees as creating a network of interpersonal relation and a *social* heritage. The events of the social process are found in the struggles, the conflicts, and the competitions of the folk: the formation and organization of families, tribes, classes, groups, and nations. The social process then consists of specific events, giving rise to general patterns of social structure and tradition. We see society as a group of groups, all in complex interrelation and

16. Alfred Weber, *Kulturgeschicht als Kultur-Soziologie* (Munich: R. Piper & Co., 1950). *Fundamentals of Culture-Sociology: Social Process, Civilization, Process, and Culture-Movement,* trans. G. H. Weltner and C. F. Hirshman (New York: WPA and Columbia University, 1939).

interaction. It can be viewed as a hierarchy of groups ranging from the national society downward. Regions, as we see it, merit inclusion here, since a region represents a group organized around an interest—in this instance the interest of locality, on a larger scale than that of community. The interrelation of such processes if explored should, in future studies, serve to guide and to challenge our understanding of regional structure and change.

Finally, it is interesting to note that in 1964 Professor Nicholls visualized a new shift in the South's development:

> The non-economic factors which historically have shackled the South's economic progress are at last in full retreat. The recent sound and fury emerging from the South can easily be misunderstood. It clearly represents the death throes, not the renaissance of those Southern traditions which are inconsistent with the region's industrial-urban development. In the process, the South is finally creating the environment needed for it to achieve full economic parity with the rest of the nation.[17]

Thus, in Weber's terms he sees the civilizational process as dominant and economic development as the locomotive of social change in the South.

III

For much of the last century the South pursued the goals of quantity—not enough jobs, not enough capital, not enough goods, not enough services, not enough schools, certainly not enough money. None but the few well-to-do could pursue a search for quality. Before the region could ask of anything: "Is it good enough?" it had to ask: "Is there enough?" This chapter has been written with a future reference, seeking out a context and framework for research to come. As the South turns to the achieving society it must face the transition from the goals of quantity to quality in its culture and demography.[18]

Again, economic development points the trend. From the opening wedge of the poor man's industry—cotton textiles in the gray goods stage, to new fabrics, new mixtures, and high styling; from unassembled

17. In *The American South in the 1960's*, p. 40.

18. State studies are few, but the Virginia Academy of Science with the support of the Virginia Chamber of Commerce sponsored an analysis of the state's population structure. See Roscoe D. Hughes and Henry Leidheiser, Jr., eds., *Exploring Virginia's Human Resources* (Charlottesville: The University Press of Virginia, 1965). Chapters iv to ix treat occupations, skills, fertility, and physical and mental health, in the attempt to assess "the productivity and creativity" of Virginia's people.

kitchen tables and chairs in High Point's new industry to the reproduction of antique furniture—industrial development has moved to higher quality of product and the attainment of a new industrial mix. The movement to quality has involved the abandonment of a certain element of quantity production. From its excess capacity in 1929, the textile industry has lost six million spindles.

In wartime, industry moved South, not because Southern workers were cheap, but because they were of higher quality than those then available in industrialization elsewhere. In this process Southern workers were found capable of higher skills, and the movement has continued.

In education the first need was schools for the masses. This movement is now being expanded to bring high school training within the reach of all able to benefit thereby. Technical institutes and community colleges will add two years of education, while Southern colleges and universities face the problem of expanding their capacity. Southern Negro youth now have a better chance of getting college training than white Englishmen.[19]

Throughout the whole range of occupation the South's working force is rapidly being upgraded. Domestic servants, farm laborers, and the unskilled drop out of the statistics decade by decade. Skilled operators, foremen, technicians, clerical workers, salesmen, managerial and the professional and semi-professional workers show large scale increases, many over 40 to 50 per cent in the last two decades.

In the long run, population growth may well come to mean fewer people, better prepared. The demand for high quality manpower has brought the small family pattern to the region's expanding middle class. As the family seeks more training for its children, it limits its numbers. Even the baby boom, now declining, is thought to represent the middle-class family's reactions to better chances for their better educated children. Changing occupational distribution is bringing more components into the Southern middle class, thus affecting demographic structures. Rural fertility continues to decrease, and there are now indications that the non-white birth rate is turning downward.

Finally, in economics, improved product meets with better taste in an expanding market, raising the question of a better appreciation of the products of high culture and a more favorable climate for creative talent. Here the dominance of the marketplace and the mass media has led to the conflict between mass culture and high culture which apparently exists throughout the world. The South might well stabilize its population increase

19. Richard L. Wilson in "The U. S. Isn't as Sick as We Think," *Look*, Feb. 8, 1966, p. 39. The original calculations were done by C. A. Anderson of the Department of Education, University of Chicago.

as it meets new demands for quality in its culture, social conditions, and demography.

Interaction between processes now ongoing in society, civilization, and high culture furnish materials for manifold studies of a region in the midst of things to come. Challenge and response, however viewed, are moving across the South in its approach to the achieving society.

Transition and social change, it is apparent, do not issue from apathy; nor has the South, whatever it has been, been a center of apathy. While the South has been called a history without a country of its own, it can no longer be called an underdeveloped society. It, too, has heard the cry "Cargo!" and the region now knows whence cargo comes. The South is also a participant in the revolution of rising expectations. Whatever achievements this particular province has tasted, they have but whetted the appetite of people and leaders. Like Oliver Twist, the South extends its cup and pronounces that fateful monosyllable, "More," and it adds what Oliver would never have dared, "And Better."

Commentary / Gordon W. Blackwell

To understand regionalism as a process—to understand the achieving society, as Professor Vance chooses to put it—requires a combination of the theory and methodology of cultural anthropology, demography, economics, geography, history, the humanities, political science, social psychology and sociology. (I trust I have not been offensive by leaving anyone out!) Few people are so well equipped to do this as Rupert Vance.

As he suggests so subtly and yet so clearly, arguments that regionalism is passé generally miss the main point. The reason is perhaps that the critics lack the necessary preparation in the several social sciences to understand the fundamental principles of the regional approach. Most of the critics, I believe, will find it difficult to grasp the technical concepts which Vance finds necessary for his discussion—concepts such as developing economy, economic productivity, social process, social adequacy, social change, capital accumulation, take-off stage in industrialization, economic growth, intergenerational diffusion, and civilizational process, to mention a few. Yet all of these concepts, if carefully formulated in operational terms, can be helpful in understanding regional society with respect to quantity, quality, and change.

As Professor Vance points out, even social psychologists have studied the achieving society. Their perspective suggests the necessary ingredients if a society is to avoid being fettered by the bonds of cyclical change. Can man do something about guiding social change? Is Spengler's cyclical theory inevitably applicable to all societies, or is it possible to straighten out the cycle and extend the curve line of development in an ascending direction?

John Gardner, formerly a psychologist, has suggested a research tool for such an inquiry—the concept of *societal renewal.* He has developed a theoretical framework for the understanding and achievement of a renewing society.[1] (Parenthetically, this concept is not unrelated to that of *novelescence* as developed by Dr. Daniel Blain, a psychiatrist.) Just as Vance notes the place of innovation in the achieving regional society, Gardner has given prominence to this factor in the renewing society. As he puts it: "In the ever-renewing society what matures is a system or framework within which continuous innovation, renewal and rebirth can occur" (p. 5). And again: "If a society hopes to achieve renewal, it will have to be a hospitable environment for creative men and women . . . but renewal—of societies or of individuals—depends in some measure on motivation, commitment, conviction, the values men live by, the things that give meaning to their lives" (p. xv). If he were to focus his attention upon the southern United States and, I might add, if he were not in his present politically sensitive position, he would probably ask how much the South still has of "the dry rot produced by apathy, by rigidity, and by moral emptiness," which, he maintains, thwarts societal renewal.

Gardner has set down certain conditions of societal renewal, and we may note that too frequently the South of the past has been found wanting in these. I shall merely list the conditions: existence of freedom expressed through alternative choices; pluralism in decision-making points; dispersal of power and restraints on power among many groups and individuals; flexibility as evidenced in a willingness to entertain diverse views; fluidity in movement of individuals laterally and vertically in the social structure; testing and survival of new ideas; a tradition of tolerance and intellectual freedom with respect to differing traditions, beliefs, and intel-

1. John Gardner, *Self-Renewal: The Individual and the Society* (New York: Harper and Row, 1963).

lectual positions; acceptance of dissent and criticism; openness to systematic innovation.

In Gardner's words, "A society made up of arteriosclerotic organizations cannot renew itself" (p. 75). "The society capable of continuous renewal," he maintains, "not only feels at home with the future, it accepts, even welcomes, the idea that the future may bring change" (p. 107). Too frequently this has not been true of the South, but I believe the New South increasingly is exhibiting the attributes essential for societal renewal. And as the South changes in these respects, the region becomes more a part of the mainstream of American society.

Focus of research upon a large region necessarily relies upon either broad philosophical generalizations or detailed analyses of statistical data. In either approach it is difficult to get intimately and accurately at the fundamental nature of social process. For this reason, I hope that Duke University's new Center for Southern Studies will find a place for detailed anthropological case studies of representative Southern communities, perhaps somewhat like the series of Cultural Studies of the Modern South which were initiated at Chapel Hill in the early 1950's. For it is in the intimate, day-to-day relationships between individuals, groups, and institutions in the community setting that the basic social processes occur. Attitudes, motivation, and innovation may be directly observed in communities. Generalization from representative local communities to the larger region, I believe, can be fully as valid as generalizations derived from mass regional data, sometimes of doubtful validity and necessarily far removed from the actual lives of human beings and their institutions.

One final point. With my particular biases I would urge the Center to place emphasis upon the strategic part which education must play in the achieving regional society, especially in making the transition from goals of quantity to those of quality. Professor Vance has, of course, included a consideration of education at several points in his paper. Especially at the graduate level, education can make a tremendous difference in the maturing of the South as an integral part of the nation. Howard Odum pointed this out forcefully in the 1930's; but, with the unprecedented explosion of knowledge and increasing specialization in the decades which have followed, the role of education has considerably increased in significance. And even today one can count the truly distinguished Southern graduate schools on the fingers of one hand. It is to be hoped, that the Center will devote some attention to education, not through descriptive studies of quantity or even of quality, but in analytical inquiries into the part education plays in societal processes within a regional framework.

To conclude, it must be evident that Professor Vance has demonstrated his unusual ability to integrate concepts and theory from a number of disciplines in order to provide a framework for research on the South viewed as a region undergoing continuous change in its movement toward maturity and in its renewal processes. His paper can serve as a touchstone for researchers in their efforts to develop meaningful regional research within a significant theoretical context.

Depletion and renewal in Southern history / David M. Potter

The history of the South has flourished as one of the most intensively cultivated branches of American history for many decades. In the earliest stages of its development, it was preoccupied almost exclusively with the Southern Confederacy, the slavery conflict as a prologue to the Confederacy, and Reconstruction as an epilogue to the Confederacy. The original Southern Historical Society, chartered four years after Appomattox, had as its founders high officials of the Confederate government and general officers of the Confederate Army. For a generation, no Southerner apparently could write history without rehearsing over again a legalistic defense of the constitutional right of secession. Raphael Semmes, for instance, in his *Service Afloat*, prefaced his rousing narrative of swashbuckling adventure on the high seas with a long, arid, and tedious exegesis on the metaphysics of secession.

If the history of the South, so-called, had remained as it began, merely a recital of the valor and rectitude of the Lost Cause, it would probably have withered on the academic vine early in the twentieth century. It would hardly have become a vital component in a Center for Southern Studies, such as is being launched here at Duke University exactly a century plus one year after Appomattox. But it acquired a new dimension when Frederick Jackson Turner and others brought forward the concept of the "section" as an important factor in American history. Turner specifically repudiated the popular idea that "the word section applies only to the struggle of South against North on the questions of slavery, state sovereignty, and eventually disunion." On the contrary, he insisted, rivalries between East and West were often crucial. The United States,

> unlike such countries as France and Germany, . . . has the problem of the clash of economic interests closely associated with regional geography on a huge scale. . . . Economic interests are sectionalized. . . . We have become a nation comparable to all Europe in area, with settled geographic provinces which equal great European nations. We are in this sense an empire, a federation of sections, a union of potential nations. . . . There is and always has been a sectional geography in America, based fundamentally upon geographic regions. There is a geography of political habits, a geography of opinion, of material interests, of racial stocks, of physical fitness, of social traits, of literature, of the distribution of men of ability, even of religious denominations. . . . The significance of the section in American his-

tory is that it is the faint image of a European nation, and that we need to examine our history in the light of this fact.

Turner's formulation provided a supremely effective charter for a Southern history broadly conceived. Here was a concept which regarded the South as the faint image of a nation and which recognized that there were distinctive elements in Southern economic life, Southern social life, Southern literature, Southern religion, Southern ideology and popular attitudes and values—enough themes to provide a multiplicity of justifications for a center. Hence, any complete history of the South would embrace not only the Lost Cause, but also economic history, social and cultural history, intellectual history, and religious history, as well as the political and institutional history of a time span of more than three and a half centuries from Jamestown to Cape Kennedy. Such a view foreshadowed the broad concept of regionalism which men like Howard Odum and Rupert Vance were to develop with such fruitful effect in the 1930's. Turner himself, as the quotation has just shown, used the term "region" as well as the term "section."

Does this broader concept mean that anything which happens anywhere south of the Mason-Dixon line is within the province of Southern history? Are Southern historians entirely at the mercy of a geography which makes them responsible for all that occurs within an arbitrarily defined area? Not if they follow Turner, for his sectional or regional theory would confine Southern history to phenomena which have some kind of regional distinctiveness. This would exclude the history of things which are purely local on the one hand, or merely manifestations within the region of national phenomena, on the other. Thus, for instance, a history of the adoption of the commission form of municipal government in Galveston, Texas, would hardly seem to be a part of Southern history, unless regional conditions had impinged on the affairs of the city in a distinctive way. A good part of the experience of any community is likely to be shaped by purely local circumstances, with regional factors playing a minimal part. At the other end of the spectrum, the South now shares increasingly in a standardized national life and national way of doing things, which again reduces the factor of regional distinctiveness in certain areas to negligibility. For instance, dentistry is probably about the same in Durham as in Duluth; the use of structural steel for office buildings about the same in Winston-Salem, North Carolina, Salem, Massachusetts, and Salem, Oregon; television programs do not differ appreciably from New Orleans to Minneapolis-St. Paul. I am not sure that all these illustrations are well chosen, but it seems safe to assert that there are a good many features of

American life in 1966 which have been so thoroughly standardized or homogenized on a national basis that nothing is gained by applying a regional perspective to their study.

These features have already grown immensely, to extend over a broader and broader range within the spectrum of our lives; and the indications are that they will continue to crowd out the features of regional distinctiveness until, conceivably, regionalism may become vestigial, just as the mule and the use of chewing tobacco have already become vestigial. The diminishing prominence of regional features within the South has already induced in almost all white Southerners moments or moods of regretful nostalgia, and it has prompted Harry Ashmore to write an *Epitaph for Dixie*. Ashmore says that the historical identity of the South consisted in one peculiar institution—slavery, and in a triad of successor institutions—the tenancy system in agriculture, the one-party system in politics, and the system of caste and legal segregation in race relations. All of these, says Ashmore, are now perishing institutions, and when they have finally expired, Dixie will become historic only.

If Dixie is ultimately to disappear, it will only follow the destiny of all things in human history; meanwhile, there are other writers who tell us that no society can be understood purely in terms of its current material circumstances, but that the past lives in the present and the present will live in the future. With no specific reference to the South, Seymour Martin Lipset, in *The First New Nation*, has made this point with regard to Canada and the United States. The two countries have had very similar physical or material circumstances—the same ratios of men to land, the same high standard of living, the same frontier movement; but the United States repudiated the principle of authority and expelled the Tory elite in 1775-1776, while Canada received the Tory Loyalists who fled from New England, and absorbed them and their values into the Canadian system. That happened nearly two centuries ago, but the resulting differentials between society in the United States and in Canada still remain conspicuous. Lipset's observations on Canada might be regarded as paralleling C. Vann Woodward's observations, in *The Burden of Southern History*, upon distinctive factors in the past which may have a persisting effect in preserving a factor of Southern identity. As Woodward has suggested, the experience of military defeat in the Civil War, the long decades of poverty and stagnation in the Southern economy, the corroding psychological effects of the sense of guilt and evil which accompanied the caste system—these things were all features which other Americans did not share. Hence the characteristically American confidence of success, the shallow optimism, the bland conviction of the superior virtue and moral innocence of Americans did not strike root quite as deeply in the South. The residual survival of these attitudes might continue to make for cultural differentiation even after all the physical and material factors of distinctive Southernism have been eroded away.

I am really trying to say two things here: the first is that Southern studies, and especially Southern history, should not be concerned indiscriminately with everything that occurs within the South; rather, they should focus their analysis at points where the conditions of the Southern region differ from those of other regions and should concentrate their attention upon historical developments which are relevant to these differences. The second is that these differential factors may arise directly from prevailing natural or physical conditions at present, but they may also persist as survivals from the material or physical conditions of the past, and historians must be alert to both the continuing difference and the survival. To put this proposition into more concrete terms, the Southern historian has an anomalous job. His is the task of tracing the history of a region that never possessed clearly defined limits and only for four years possessed an organizational and structural identity as the Confederate States of America. For the rest of the time, he is dealing with an entity—the South—whose boundaries are indeterminate, whose degree of separateness has fluctuated historically over time, whose distinctiveness may be in some respects fictitious. His job in this complex of uncertainties is to identify and investigate the distinctive features of Southern society.

On the whole, this is what professional historians of the South have sought to do, and they have done it intensively and successfully for several decades now. They were quick to grasp the reality that one of the basic sources of sectional distinctiveness was the system of Negro slavery and plantation agriculture before the Civil War. After the war, the dominant tendencies lay in the bitter struggle to determine what social system should replace slavery and the continued dominance of the cotton economy, as well as the subordination of the Negro. All the while, both before and after the war and during Reconstruction, the political rivalries and battles which grew out of these conditions were also part of the essence of sectional identity.

Southern historians have recognized all of these themes and have cultivated them with an intensity which has not been paralleled in the historical study of any other American region. On some topics it has been worked to a point where diminishing returns now seem about to set in, and this is why, in the title of my paper, I have alluded to "depletion" in Southern history. Many of the golden nuggets in the streambed of Southern history have already been panned.

Some of the fields of investigation are closely worked indeed—so much so, in fact, that few of us would encourage a graduate student to embark on further intensive study. On the theme of slavery, for instance, there have been the state monographs by Jeffrey Brackett on Maryland, by James C. Ballagh on Virginia, by John Spencer Bassett and Rosser H. Taylor on North Carolina, by Ralph B. Flanders on Georgia, by Charles S. Davis and by James B. Sellers on Alabama, by Charles S. Sydnor on Mississippi, by V. A. Moody and by Joe G. Taylor on Louisiana, by Orville W. Taylor on Arkansas, by Chase Mooney on Tennessee, by Winston Coleman on Kentucky, and by Harrison Trexler on Missouri. There have also been the general works of Ulrich B. Phillips, Kenneth Stampp, and Stanley Elkins. On plantation agriculture, we have the irreplaceable work of Phillips, the magisterial volumes by Lewis C. Gray, the important monographic studies of rice by J. Harold Easterby and by Albert V. House, Jr., of sugar by Carlyle Sitterson, and of tobacco by Joseph C. Robert and Nannie M. Tilley, of hemp by James H. Hopkins, and on other aspects of Southern agriculture by J. C. Bonner, Cornelius Cathey, Avery Craven, John Hebron Moore, Edwin A. Davis, Alfred G. Smith, and others. On the political sectionalism between tidewater and frontier within the South, there are volumes by Charles H. Ambler on Virginia, John Spencer Bassett on North Carolina, William A. Schaper on South Carolina, Ulrich B. Phillips on Georgia, Thomas P. Abernethy on Tennessee, and Theodore H. Jack on Alabama, as well as Richard O. Curry's recent and notable study of West Virginia. On the secession movement, there have been studies for almost every state and more than one study for some states: Henry T. Shanks for Virginia, J. Carlyle Sitterson for North Carolina, Philip Hamer, Chauncey Boucher, Harold S. Schultz, and Charles E. Cauthen for South Carolina, George V. Irons for Georgia, Clarence P. Denman and Austin Venable for Alabama, Cleo Hearon and Percy Lee Rainwater for Mississippi, Willie M. Caskey for Louisiana, Earl Fornell and Edward M. Maher for Texas, Elsie M. Lewis for Arkansas, Walter H. Ryle for Missouri, and E. Merton Coulter for Kentucky.

It is a temptation to go on with a catalogue of this kind, perhaps too far; there are studies of state after state for the South during the Confederacy, such as those of T. Conn Bryan for Georgia, John K. Bettersworth and James W. Silver for Mississippi, and Jefferson D. Bragg for Louisiana. In addition to these, there are the broader works on the Confederacy by E. Merton Coulter, Clement Eaton, and Charles P. Roland, and many special studies of special topics such as morale, economic conditions, foreign relations, loyalty, social conditions, and so forth. There are studies of Reconstruction for literally every state. There are monographs on Populism in the South for various states, including Georgia (Arnett), Virginia (Sheldon), North Carolina (Delap), Alabama (Clark), Tennessee (Robison), Missouri (Clovenger), and Texas (Martin). On top of these, we have Noblin's life of Leonidas Polk and Woodward's revealing study of Watson. There are excellent studies of the progress of industrialization and economic change in the South by Calvin Hoover and Benjamin U. Ratchford, by Avery Leiserson, by Allen P. Sindler, by Thomas D. Clark, and by Robert B. Highsaw; and within the last year John C. McKinney and Edgar T. Thompson's wide-ranging and comprehensive collection of more than twenty scholarly papers on various aspects of Southern life and economy has appeared under the title *The South in Continuity and Change.*

But for three reasons, I must not go on with this listing: first, the recital is so long it would grow tiresome; second, if I attempted a fuller inventory, I would inevitably do an injustice to many significant studies which space prevents my mentioning. And most important, Professor Fletcher M. Green's former students have recently presented him with a *Festschrift* consisting of seventeen extensive historiographical essays which, with great thoroughness and learning, evaluate the present status of historical study in almost every phase of Southern history. Entitled *Writing Southern History* and edited by Arthur S. Link and Rembert W. Patrick, this *Festschrift* is perhaps the most searching and comprehensive inventory that has ever been made of any field of American history. It provides us with an unparalleled criterion for detecting what have been the more heavily worked and the more sketchily researched areas within the field of Southern history.

As we focus our attention upon the vast body of research which has been thus inventoried, we may be struck with a question as to how much of significance is left to be done. Or, to put it in familiarly Southern terms, we may wonder whether excessive historiographical "cropping" has "worked out" the soil still available to other historical cultivators. No doubt there are important areas in which it has. Where these exist, we should be glad of them, not regret them. But what I should like especially to suggest here is that, along with the depletion in some areas, there has been a recognition or discovery of other areas, so that the tasks of Southern history still present a wide range of opportunity for the historian. Very often, the completion of research at one level has simply exposed the need for work at another, deeper level. Work in one area has provided a new perspective on the problems that need to be worked out in another area. There is a saying that the increase in the diameter of our knowledge also increases the circumference of our ignorance, or, as the frontiers of our knowledge are pushed back, new contiguous areas, which have not been explored, are brought within the range of our inquiry.

This interplay between depletion of opportunity at one point and renewal at another is suggested at many points in Southern history. For instance, consider the theme of slavery. Our earliest monographic studies of slavery by men like James C. Ballagh and John Spencer Bassett, coming out of the school of history at Johns Hopkins, dealt with slavery in institutional terms, but did not seriously explore its economic aspects. The depletion of institutional studies paved the way for studies which were primarily economic (such as those of Ulrich B. Phillips, Lewis C. Gray, and Ralph B. Flanders), and for the numerous writers who have recently analyzed the question of the profitability of slavery. By the time that most of the economic possibilities had been worked out, other aspects in turn came into focus. Chase C. Mooney recognized the importance of demographic analysis, and he explored important questions of slave distribution which had never previously been analyzed. Clement Eaton and Richard C. Wade perceived that a focal point in the modification of the slave system was the employment of slaves as the equivalent of wage workers in the towns of the South. Hence they, and especially Wade, wrote about slavery in the cities. Kenneth Stampp and other modern writers insisted that it was not enough merely to ask how slavery worked as an economic system; we must also ask what it meant to the slave. But scarcely had they formed their answer in social and material terms before Stanley Elkins came forward with the contention that what slavery meant to the slave in terms of physical hardships, major or minor, was less important than what it meant in terms of psychological dependence and impairment of personality. Thus, the depletion of any one aspect of the topic of slavery has, up to now, always brought new aspects into focus.

Sometimes, as in the study of slavery, the development of one aspect has prepared the way for moving on to another. But also, sometimes changes in our basic outlook have created a need for us to rework subjects which we once felt had been completely examined. About four decades ago, for instance, there was scarcely any subject which seemed to offer less promise for a new investigation than Reconstruction. There was a complete battery of monographs—one for every state, all fully documented, and all reflecting a strong political emphasis and a point of view that was either inspired by or sympathetic to the interpretation of William Archibald Dunning. As a field for historical investigation, Reconstruction seemed entirely depleted. But in 1932 Robert H. Woody and the late Francis B. Simkins showed how many latent possibilities still remained in the study of Reconstruction. In effect, their massive book on *South Carolina during*

Reconstruction demonstrated, without asserting, that all the older studies of the so-called "Dunning school" were at least partially out of date. Then, between 1938 and 1940, A. A. Taylor, Francis B. Simkins, and Howard K. Beale all published papers in which they called for a revision of the traditional interpretation. The field of Reconstruction had again become one of the most fruitful areas for research.

Although the need was agreed upon, the actual work of revision was a long time in gestation. As David Donald has recently said, "Except for works on Tennessee by T. B. Alexander (in 1950) and on Texas by W. C. Nunn (in 1962), no full-scale study of the postwar era in any Southern state has been published in the last twenty years." Roger Shugg in 1939 and Garnie McGinty in 1941 filled some of the gaps for Louisiana, and Vernon L. Wharton's study of the *Negro in Mississippi, 1865-1890* (1947), did something of the same sort for the Magnolia State; but the shelf of state studies of Reconstruction is still mostly where the Dunning school left it, although this school is now widely regarded as obsolete.

It is true that we have had a notable and quite recent harvest of significant books on Reconstruction in general, or on particular aspects of Reconstruction, including those by W. R. Brock, La Wanda and John H. Cox, Eric L. McKitrick, James C. MacPherson, Kenneth M. Stampp, Willie Lee Rose, and David Donald. These studies have given new vitality to what had become a stereotyped theme, and they have intensively explored a number of important topics. But the late Vernon Wharton observed that "for the Reconstruction period there has been no general study of Southern Negroes, carpetbaggers (including Negro carpetbaggers), scalawags or Southern 'redeemers.'" David Donald remarks that "There are no good books on the politics of any Northern state during Reconstruction. . . . A study of the Federal Army in the postwar South is badly wanted, as is a major work on the constitutional issues of the whole period. Andrew Johnson still lacks a good biographer, and there is no perceptive account of Grant's presidency."

This last point seems to me especially salient, for the works of Brock, the Coxes, McKitrick, MacPherson, Stampp, Rose, and Donald all concentrate heavily on the period of Lincoln and Johnson, with little attention to the period of Grant. Yet the Grant administration spanned nearly two-thirds of the so-called era of Reconstruction. The overthrow of the Carpetbag regimes and the activity of Southern resistance organizations such as the Ku Klux Klan took place almost entirely during the Grant regime. Much of the period of Reconstruction has not been revised by the "revisionist" historians, even a quarter of a century after the doctrine of revisionism won acceptance at the ideological level. The brilliance of Vann Woodward's treatment of the electoral contest of 1877 in his *Reunion and Reaction* does not really qualify this statement. It is true that we have had some recent publications on the Ku Klux Klan, but Carl N. Degler, in a recent review, concludes by asserting that we still lack an adequate history of the role of the Klan, not to mention other similar organizations, during the later stages of Reconstruction.

A paper such as this is hardly the place to attempt to summarize what it took seventeen authors to recapitulate in *Writing Southern History*. My discussion of the literature of slavery and of Reconstruction has been intended rather to illustrate how the traversing of one subject leads us to the threshold of another, and how the apparent depletion of historiographical opportunities at one point is followed by a renewal of such opportunities at another. But in using these illustrations, I have fallen back to a consideration of the traditional themes—the themes of the prologue and epilogue of the Lost Cause—the very themes which Turner said we ought not to allow to narrow too much our recognition of the total sweep of the region as a realistic unit for the study of all kinds of social, cultural, and even if you please, psychological phenomena.

The distinctiveness of the South may have been rooted, as U. B. Phillips asserted, in the biracial system, and it may have manifested itself with maximum visibility in connection with the slavery conflict, the Civil War, and Reconstruction, but it has also appeared in a multitude of other forms. Southern populism, as we all know, was unlike Western populism; Southern Democrats have frequently been at odds with Northern Democrats on a multitude of issues other than civil rights. Southern attitudes on prohibition, Southern attitudes on women's suffrage, Southern attitudes on immigration restriction, Southern responses to the question of child labor, Southern attitudes toward intervention in World War II prior to December, 1941, Southern responses to modernism and secularism in the church have all been conspicuously different from the responses of other regions. Of course, as we all recognize, some of these differentials may reflect the simple fact that the South is more rural than other regions and we should try to avoid confusing ruralism in general with Southernism in particular. But the real point here is that the opportunities for the historian of the South are as broad as the social, cultural, intellectual, and economic differentials of the region. Here let me revert again to Turner's sweeping statement that there is a geography of political habits, of opinion, of material interests, of racial stocks, of physical fitness, of social traits, of literature, and even of religious denominations. Let me also suggest again that wherever there is a distinctive or formative geography, there is material for a distinctive history of each of these elements which Turner mentioned, and for others which he could have mentioned if he had chosen to extend his list.

The field of Southern history still presents many and fundamental challenges, and these challenges remind us, in a sense, of how little we know with certainty, despite all the scholarly labor that has been devoted so intensively to research. In this connection, I will say nothing about the continued and apparently insoluble differences in point of view about slavery; but let me suggest how far we are from agreeing about so basic a question as the nature of ante-bellum society. To some writers it was an aristocratic enclave in a democratic republic—a region dominated by planter grandees, few in number, but great in wealth and influence. These planters monopolized the best acreage, set the social tone, and imposed their leadership upon the only truly deferential society which existed in the United States. Their ownership of other human beings, as slaves, confirmed and sanctioned, as it were, their ascendancy, and committed the South to conservative and traditional modes of life and thought. For these writers Calhoun was the symbolic Southerner. Yet to other writers, including notably the late Frank L. Owsley and Chapel Hill's own distinguished Professor Fletcher M. Green, the Old South partook rather fully of American democracy. The planters were only cotton farmers on a larger scale; their fortunes rose and fell; they gained political leadership only by displaying affable and democratic manners; and they held it only by a steady sequence of concessions to democracy in matters of the franchise, banking, land policy, and the like. The Whiggish party of the gentleman was ever on the defensive against the Democratic party of the common man. There was as much bumptiousness as there was deference, as much landgrabbing and speculation as there was tradition and gentility. Jefferson—not Calhoun—was the Southerner *par excellence*. The Negro slave was not the representative symbol and essential feature of a system of hierarchy and fixed status, but a great and unfortunate exception, the only person excluded from the benefits of democracy in a society which was essentially democratic.

Confronted by a choice between two such diverse images, both upheld by eminent authority, how shall we picture the Old South? We have, I believe, some scholarly work to guide us. Fabian Linden, in a long and much neglected paper in the *Journal of Negro History*, has shown that there was a considerable amount of euphoria in Professor Owsley's statistics (something which Rupert B. Vance also suggested more briefly). Moreover, we all know that the democratic manners of political leaders are not an infallible proof of democratic purposes. Yet, even if these qualifications are accepted and allowance is made for them, the interplay of aristocracy and democracy in the Old South remains a subtle problem, and all the simple answers seem suspect.

Another dimension of the intricacy of this problem has been most effectively pointed up by Eugene D. Genovese's recent book, *The Political Economy of Slavery*. Genovese rejects two interpretations of the Old South which have won wide acceptance, and he offers a third, which is a most arresting intellectual construct, though it would require a great deal of testing before we could accept it with confidence. In sum, says Genovese, we have customarily been presented with an option between two explanations of the Old South. One explanation, fairly well represented by the Owsley version, says that the agrarian factor dominated—the South was a land of small farmers who lived primarily by producing their own subsistence, and for whom money income was a subsidiary, though, of course, an essential factor. This was the South of the Jeffersonian dream, and, of course, even a large plantation might be a subsistence plantation, with much of its activity devoted to production for use. Such an image of the Old South subtly discounts the importance of the slave, and that is perhaps why many Southerners, embarrassed by slavery, have accepted it; it is also why Genovese, convinced of the focal importance of slavery, rejects it.

The alternative view has been put forward chiefly by the more stringent critics of the slavery system, of whom Kenneth Stampp is the best known, but by no means the harshest. These writers tend to minimize both the agrarian and the feudal aspects of Southern life and to insist that the antebellum Southern agricultural system was an integral part of the American capitalist economic system—more folksy, more rural than industrial capitalism, but just as committed to production for the market, just as preoccupied with money income and credit facilities, just as impersonal in its mechanisms, and, of course, just as exploitative in its quest for cheap labor. This view minimizes the cultural distinctiveness of the South and reduces the region to not much more than an area of agricultural specialization, producing one particular market commodity—cotton—by the techniques of one particular mode of labor exploitation—slavery—all within a capitalistic orbit.

Genovese rejects this view also. To him, capitalism is, as I read him, a whole cultural system, an attitude toward the relationship between production and other life values. Therefore, the fact that a society produces for the market, uses a money and credit economy, or exploits its labor, is not an adequate index to the degree to which it participates in the capitalist culture. As he suggests, Saudi Arabia, India, and other countries have adopted many capitalistic devices without being culturally capitalistic. The diagnostic feature of life in the Old South, as he sees it, is neither agrarianism nor cotton capitalism, but the stark, unqualified direct relationship of mastery and dependence that inhered in the system of slavery. Such a system had a paradoxical double effect. It gave to the slaveholder a sense of responsibility which the employer might never feel, and at the same time, it released in the slaveholder the impulses which absolute power may generate, and which, again, the employer never knew.

Again, if I may construe Genovese further, I think he is saying two things especially. First, the South really did not care about capitalism in its dynamic and mobile aspects—the aspects that transform a society. It cared only about those features of capitalism necessary to the perpetuation of the cotton-based society. Southern banks, he says, were not trying in an innovative way to stimulate all kinds of economic expansion; they were trying to service the cotton economy. If this is true, it should lend itself to testing. If it is verified, it should sharpen our focus upon the Old South. Second, the system of psychological relationships in a society depends upon the institutional and operative relationships. The institutional and operative relationships of a slaveholding system were wholly different from those of a wage-labor system, and the South therefore operated under a wholly distinctive system of psychological relationships. This system must not be sentimentalized as an agrarian system, which it was not, nor categorized simply as a peculiarly brutal form of capitalism, which it was not either; it must be understood as something very distinctive, in terms of its own.

It is, of course, not in order for me here to attempt to weigh the relative validity of any of these conflicting views. What I seek to point out is this: the opportunities of study in Southern history cannot have been very seriously depleted when we are still debating the basic questions, and when the essential character of Southern society still presents different appearances to different viewers. The tasks of Southern history are constantly being depleted and renewed at the same time, and this fact stands true even without reference to the immense and even revolutionary changes of the twelve years since *Brown* v. *Board of Education.* Parenthetically, I would mention that a student of mine, Hugh D. Graham, has written a thesis on the attitudes of the Tennessee press toward desegregation and related questions during these years, and his thesis suggests to me that there are many, many opportunities for study in this period, especially if we firmly reject the stereotype of the South as a monolith and recognize the importance of newspapers as well as legislatures, church bodies as well as political parties, and differences between urban and rural attitudes, as distinguishing features within the framework of the almost universal reluctance of the white South—which ought not to be denied—to accept desegregation.

This observation, in turn, leads me to one final comment on the present tasks and opportunities of Southern history—a comment which seems especially applicable to the establishment of an interdisciplinary center. We have come into an era when, in the profession generally, historians are increasingly dissatisfied with the adequacy of their traditional methods, and are concerned to bring to bear upon history the knowledge now at the command of other disciplines. What do sociologists know about the social structure of classes which historians might utilize in their study of specific conflict between groups? What do economists know about the factors conducive to rapid development or to stagnation which historians need to know in order to understand the prolongation of poverty in one country and the sudden recovery from economic reverses in another? What do psychologists know about human motivation which will enable historians to understand what impels human action? There is much evidence today that the important frontiers of Southern history are interdisciplinary frontiers. There are a number of comments by the authors of *Writing Southern History* which corroborate this view: For instance, Bennett H. Wall says, "The most intellectually stimulating and challenging essays on slavery in recent years have been written by historians interested in sociology and economics and by economists. One of them, apparently little known and rarely cited, is Edgar T. Thompson, 'The Natural History of Agricultural Labor in the South.' " Herbert Doherty observes that one can learn more about the history of the Negro church from Benjamin Mays, a sociologist, than from the formal history by Carter Woodson. George Tindall points out that for future historians the mid-twentieth century should be a "happy hunting ground in terms of the history of changes in race relations." With some spirit, Tindall asserts that there is much deficiency along with the achievements in Southern history. He mentions a number of neglected political topics, and then continues;

> Business and labor history offer infinite possibilities, and Negro institutions of all kinds—social, economic, educational, and religious—provide ground that is not yet even plowed. Folk history may be too exotic for the common academic drudge, but is there no writer who can do for Southern Negroes what Howard Odum did for Southern white folk in his *American Epoch*, or Wilbur Joseph Cash in his *The Mind of the South*? Is there none who can do for the Negro migrant what Handlin did for the European in *The Uprooted*?

Handlin, it may be noted, is a historian, but in *The Uprooted* he is not writing quite as a historian would usually write. Odum and Cash were not historians at all. What Wall and Doherty and Tindall are all asking for is history written with an infusion of what related fields of learning may impart. When the historian studies the poverty of the six decades after Appomattox and the relatively rapid economic growth of the South today, he needs to know not only about the New Deal and twenty-odd years of a war economy, but he must be able to apply what economists know about what retards some economies and enables others to become airborne. To deal with the history of Negro-white relations—the changes and the slowness of change—he must know not only about slavery, and Appomattox, and Reconstruction, and *Plessy* v. *Ferguson*, and Booker Washington's Atlanta Address, but he must know what a psychologist can tell him about the sources and nature of prejudice. He must, in fact, ask questions which up to now have been asked by social scientists but not by historians. To what extent does the rigidity of the segregation system arise from personal insecurities in members of the Southern white population? Do such insecurities have a higher incidence statistically among segregationists than among those who are not rigid about segregation? This is a tricky question, for, on the face of it, it seems unlikely that the people in one whole block of states would have greater personal insecurity than people in another whole block. To what extent is segregation supported not primarily because of "prejudice," or specific attitudes toward Negroes, but because of a desire, shared by all people everywhere, to do what their community, or at least what their reference group in the community, expects of them? To what extent, in other words, has the support of segregation been, for many Southerners, merely a peculiarly compulsive type of conformity? To what extent is it rooted in sheer psychic inertia, to what extent in the fact that men who treat other people badly need psychologically to believe that these others deserve to be treated badly, to what extent in the fact that it is entirely realistic for men to fear those whom they have wronged? But also, to what extent is the impulse of separateness related somehow to the sense of identity, wholly apart from any animus against the group toward whom separateness is maintained? And are minorities, whose identity seems less secure than that of majorities, more sensitive about this identity? The white South has seen itself as a minority since almost two decades prior to the Civil War, and it almost lost its identity at Appomattox. The fierceness of the resistance of Southern whites to Reconstruction was partly the result of a desperate sense that their identity inhered partly in their Southernism and their whiteness and that this identity must not be lost. Is the bitterness of resistance to desegregation perhaps in part an aspect of this same identity concept?

Questions like these lie ahead of us, and the historian can hardly do justice to his themes if he avoids these questions. Viewing the problem in these terms, it seems safe to say that while several decades of intensive research in Southern history have yielded a vital and extensive body of knowledge, they have not depleted the field, but have left the investigator of today with two challenges in which he may rejoice. First, they have left him with a number of vital questions still to be resolved; second, they have confronted him with the need, in handling these questions, to work in a broader context of sharing what other disciplines have to offer both in the way of answers, and also of questions. This is to say that he needs to work in just such a context as a well organized and well integrated center for Southern studies both in the social sciences and in the humanities would be able to offer. The history of the South is more suffused with these interdisciplinary questions than, perhaps, most other fields of history, and historians of the South should welcome the establishment of an interdisciplinary center proportionately. Through such a center, they might more readily find means for vitalizing many depleted themes in the study of Southern history.

Commentary / George Tindall

I must acknowledge first that, as a professional Southerner, I read Professor Potter's paper with a growing sense of relief. It is heartening to have reassurance on good authority that the soil one is tilling has not been exhausted, that Southern historians have effected a working system of crop rotation. While we cultivate a rich harvest in one field, others lie fallow, renewing their strength for the coming seasons. The Southern historian need not, after all, join the flight from the land.

Those of us who have a vested interest in regional studies, however, have been haunted recently by the thought that the ground we are working is perhaps in danger not so much of exhaustion as of erosion, of being swept away altogether in the deluge of change. The erosion of Southern distinctiveness, if indeed that is what we are witnessing, of course is less ominous to the regional historian than to those working in fields more immediately involved with current problems. If the South should some day become one with Nineveh and Tyre, unquestionably there would still be ancient historians to pursue its past; in fact, there are now anthropologists engaged in digging up a vanished South that once belonged to the Indians.

Yet, for the time being, perhaps the remarkable thing is not the dissipation of regional distinctiveness in the twentieth century, but its stubborn persistence. And one may reasonably conjecture that regional distinctiveness might continue not simply in the kind of residual factors that Professor Potter suggests in citing Seymour Lipset's thesis about Canada. Regional distinctiveness might assume new and unexpected forms in the course of historical evolution. It would not be the first time that has happened in the successive stages of Southern history. To cite a contemporary example, who could have predicted two decades ago that the Bible Belt would produce a Martin Luther King?

I would suggest, moreover, that the very processes of change in our own time promise not depletion but renewal in regional studies. The very fact of change serves to bring into focus things that otherwise would remain blurred. As far back as the 1920's it was the consciousness of change that quickened the imaginations of a cultivated and sensitive minority, giving us the Southern Renaissance in literature. The peculiar historical consciousness of the Southern writer, Allen Tate has suggested, "made possible the curious burst of intelligence that we get at a crossing of the ways, not unlike, on an infinitesimal scale, the outburst of poetic genius at the end of the sixteenth century when commercial England had already begun to crush feudal England."

One thing that strikes me in the catalogues of past studies Professor Potter presents, and in the fields and subjects he suggests for future studies, is that Southern history need not be, and in its most vigorous areas is not, an exercise in antiquarianism. It is vitally relevant to live issues. Merely to mention the first Reconstruction is to suggest this obvious point. The new reconstruction that we are experiencing has manifest parallels in the first, and deep roots there—especially in the Thirteenth, Fourteenth, and Fifteenth Amendments. The revisionist historians of our generation are clearly influenced by the climate of their own times, just as the historians of the Dunning school were influenced by the climate of theirs—the period of disfranchisement and the passage of Jim Crow laws at the turn of the century. As Professor Potter demonstrates, even the reinterpretation of slavery assumes new relevance in the light of our own times. And the later period of Negro history, after Reconstruction, in which the situation seemed so static, now assumes the aspect of a period in which the forces of change were gathering.

There seem to be two major themes in the regional transformation of our own times. The new reconstruction is one; the process of economic development is the other. The second is not so dramatic, but it is at least as live an issue. Yet except in the study of agriculture, it is one of the most neglected areas of historical study in the South. Industrial history, corporate history, labor history, the history of economic policy, of state and community efforts to encourage industry, of the processes by which the South is emerging from poverty to affluence—these have relevance not only to the present South; they have relevance to a world in which the revolution of rising expectations in underdeveloped areas has become a major focus of concern. The South is one underdeveloped area that has made—or is making—the transition.

The relevance of regional studies to a time of change is a major part of the rationale for the Center for Southern Studies and for this symposium. And Professor Potter has valuable suggestions for other pertinent themes that may be pursued through the cross-fertilization of historical study with concepts derived from other fields of the social sciences—and we might add, of the humanities. He mentions the fruitfulness of the regional concept developed by Odum, Vance, and others in the 1930's. An important part of that concept is regionalism as a context for interdisciplinary study. Historians clearly have something to offer and something to derive from those engaged in other disciplines.

In dwelling so much upon the theme of relevance and live issues, I do not propose to argue that history must take a purely presentist approach. Knowledge for the sake of knowledge itself is not an unworthy goal. And one can never predict what kinds of relevance knowledge may achieve. The interdisciplinary approach suggests certain possibilities. The secession movement, for example, would seem to be about as dead as any issue can be. But one historian has proposed a joint historical-psychological study of secession in South Carolina as an important means to the understanding of mass behavior. Relatively little has been done on this theme for the period after the Civil War. A recent publication offers an example of other potentialities in such an approach: Alfred O. Hero's *The Southerner in World Affairs.* Written by a man trained in both political science and psychology, it is a rewarding study which in exploring Southern attitudes on foreign policy becomes involved also in the study of attitudes on domestic issues and the effects of regional factors in determining the Southern outlook on the world.

Let me turn now, however, to another of Professor Potter's points. On this I want to express a cautionary word. Southern studies, he says, "should define wherein the conditions of the Southern region differ from those of other regions and should concentrate their attention upon historical developments which are relevant to these differences." While this may be acceptable as a general rule of thumb, we should guard against it as an absolute. It poses a danger of distortion. For Southerners have not only been distinctive in certain respects; they have been Americans as well, and involved in the universal human destiny. The literature of the Southern Renaissance has assumed significance not because of its addiction to the delicate fragrance of local color but because of the universality of its themes.

We must not lose sight of the interplay among regional and national and universal factors. Frederick Jackson Turner in his essay on the significance of sections, which has been cited here, dwelt particularly upon the interplay of sections in American politics.

Another vital issue involving the interplay of regional and national factors is that of the new federalism, the relationship of state and local governments to the national, the whole matter of joint programs, grants-in-aid, and the like. What might the historian have to offer to an understanding of how we have arrived where we are in this respect? There was a time earlier in the twentieth century, down through the early years of the New Deal, when the idea seemed fairly well established that the Southern region stood to gain more from the expansion of federal programs than any other. What happened to that idea? It is not dead, of course, but certainly it is not one of the accepted staples of political rhetoric.

The theme of regional interplay might be pursued in realms other than politics. For many years, until very recently, the South served as a kind of seedbed of the nation, but where are the historians of interregional migration, narrating and analyzing the experience of those who have left the region? Intellectual history offers similar possibilities in the recognition of cultural interplay. William Taylor's *Cavalier and Yankee* demonstrates one approach, by posing the archetypal figures of the Cavalier and the Yankee as different facets of what the American was or wanted to be. Another area that still awaits exploration is the myths or stereotyped images in which people saw the "true" identity of the South: such patterns as the plantation myth, the Confederate myth, the benighted South, the visions of a New South, and so on. And there is that peculiar phenomenon of the twentieth century which expresses sectionalism in terms of nationalism, by envisioning the South as the most American region of them all, because of the native composition of its population in contrast to the immigrant hordes elsewhere.

But I, too, must avoid further catalogues. Professor Potter already has outlined a program for a generation of scholars, and I must not add unduly to the burden of Southern historians. Happily the field remains a fertile one, with prospects for renewal that stretch indefinitely into the future.

Southern literature and Southern society / Willard Thorp

In representing the scholars who have encouraged study and research in Southern literature, I feel rather like an interloper, though I will not be called a carpetbagger. After all, Harold Dodds, Emeritus President of Princeton, used to boast of Princeton as the northern outpost of Southern culture.

There are many better qualified for this task than I am. One can start down the coastal states, round the Gulf, and come up into the midland states, naming names: Charles Anderson, Floyd Stovall, Jay B. Hubbell, Arlin Turner, Clarence Gohdes, and Louis J. Budd; their neighbors at Chapel Hill, C. Hugh Holman and Arthur Palmer Hudson; John C. Guilds and James B. Meriwether; Albert E. Stone, Jr., Floyd C. Watkins, and Edd Winfield Parks; Eugene Current-Garcia; Scott Osborn; Milton Rickels, John Q. Anderson, Robert Jacobs, Earl Rovit, and Richard Beale Davis. I have inadvertently omitted some names, I feel sure, but I have not forgotten Louis D. Rubin, Jr., whose commentary on this paper will surely be gentle—but firm.

To these men, their colleagues and disciples, we owe a great debt. Year by year they have explored the literary materials, published and unpublished, and in the course of their work they have rewritten the literary history of the South.

I wonder if the social scientists know that the major part of this job of resurveying, reassessing, and rewriting has been accomplished during the lifetime of the scholars I have named. The study of American history was respectable in the time of Bancroft and Parkman. Professors of political economy began discussing the American economy as soon as their subject became an academic discipline. But when the study of literature in English was established in the graduate curriculum around 1890, philology, meaning Anglo-Saxon, Gothic, and Old High German, was queen. Over on the literary side only the earlier English authors, Chaucer, Shakespeare, Spenser, and Milton, were deemed worthy of serious study. Anything "modern" was looked on with suspicion. American literature was conspicuously modern. It was also American. At best it could be considered an inferior imitation and extension of English literature. Not until the 1920's did this intellectual condescension begin to abate. The turning point came, I believe, when the American Literature Group of the Modern Language Association was founded. This inner society, which has been since the mid-twenties the most active group in the Association, has sponsored many admirable projects in American literary scholarship. Our professional journal, *American Literature*, published at Duke since 1929, still carries the notice "published with the co-operation of the American Literature Group."

I have made this historical excursion to show how recent are the origins of the scholarly study of American literature. When its independence was declared only forty years ago, the scholars, North and South, had to start almost from scratch. The so-called "standard" texts of our American writers were imperfect. Biographies were inadequate or non-existent. Writers who had sunk into oblivion had to be rescued. Unpublished manuscripts and letters, hoarded by proud descendants and thus fortunately preserved, had to be tracked to their hiding places. It is difficult to say whether there was more to be done in the North than in the South, though I am inclined to believe that the scholars who devoted themselves to Southern literature had the harder time of it. At any rate, the achievements of these scholars have been remarkable. I should like to dwell on them for a moment. To do so will help us to see where we may go from here.

Of primary importance was the matter of texts. The first American author to be published in a complete scholarly edition was Sidney Lanier. These ten volumes, prepared under the general editorship of Charles Anderson and issued by the Johns Hopkins Press in 1945, furnished a model to other editors. We have now, at last, *The Letters of William Gilmore Simms*, issued in five volumes by the University of South Carolina Press. A scholarly edition of some of the work of Simms is on the way. The center for this edition is at the University of South Carolina. The university has committed itself to fifteen volumes. The editors would like to be able to add ten more. At the University of Virginia Professor Stovall has just completed his much-needed *Poems of Edgar Allan Poe*, with variant readings and textual notes. The works of Henry Timrod are now available in scholarly editions, E. W. Parks having published the *Essays* in 1942 and (with Aileen Parks) the *Collected Poems* in 1965.

The record in biographical research and publication is even more impressive. I cannot stress too strongly how much we needed these studies. Many Southern writers had not been given the benefit of a biography. Much of the biographical writing done before the new age of American literary scholarship was sentimental or partisan or prudish and, in most instances, pitifully thin and inaccurate. At last we are on solid ground in this area. It gives me pleasure to count off the authors and titles: Charles H. Bohner's *John Pendleton Kennedy, Gentleman from Baltimore* (1961); S. Foster Damon's *Thomas Holley Chivers, Friend of Poe* (1930); Curtis Carroll Davis' *Chronicler of the Cavaliers, A Life of . . . William A.*

Caruthers (1953); Grant C. Knight's *James Lane Allen and the Genteel Tradition* (1935); Lewis Leary's *The Literary Career of Nathaniel Tucker* (1951); Robert C. MacLean's *George Tucker, Moral Philosopher and Man of Letters* (1961); E. W. Parks's *Henry Timrod* (1964); Arthur Hobson Quinn's *Edgar Allan Poe* (1941); Arlin Turner's *George W. Cable* (1956); Harvey Wish's *George Fitzhugh, Propagandist of the Old South* (1943). Especially gratifying have been the efforts of the biographers to give the Southern humorists the acclaim they deserve. The pioneering work was John Donald Wade's *Augustus Baldwin Longstreet* (1924), prepared under that steady champion of Southern writing, W. P. Trent, then living in exile at Columbia University. Recently, in succession, we have had W. Stanley Hoole's *Alias Simon Suggs, The Life and Times of Johnson Jones Hooper* (1952), John Q. Anderson's *Louisiana Swamp Doctor, The Writings of Henry Clay Lewis* (1962), and Milton Rickels' *Thomas Bangs Thorpe, Humorist of the Old Southwest* (1962). Professor Rickels is also the author of the George W. Harris biography in Twayne's United States Authors series.

I shall not linger over the writing which has been concerned with the Southern authors of this century. It has been gratifyingly abundant. Two reasons can be offered to explain why there has been so much of it. In the first place the authors who brought on the Southern literary Renaissance are eminently worth writing about. Further, in this present age in which younger students prefer writing criticism to scholarly digging, these authors, in many instances, seemed to call for exegesis and explication. Who, among such students, would not prefer spinning theories about Faulkner's symbols and archetypes to grubbing in the archives in order to prepare a definitive biography of John Esten Cooke? We can leave the modern writers to take care of themselves. If my count is accurate, there are now eighteen studies of Thomas Wolfe and thirty-six of Faulkner.

You must not infer from what I have said in praise of the work thus far completed that the end of the labor is in sight. One has only to read the bibliographical essays in Professor Hubbell's *The South in American Literature, 1607-1900* to learn how much remained to be done when that monumental work was published, only twelve years ago. The efforts since that date have accomplished much but there are many gaps to be filled in. Biographies are lacking for several Southern humorists, notably W. T. Thompson, creator of Major Jones; Joseph Glover Baldwin, author of *Flush Times of Alabama and Mississippi*; and Charles Henry Smith ("Bill Arp"). Enough new material has been turned up to call for the writing of new biographies of William Byrd[1] and Sidney Lanier. There is no biog-

1. I believe Marion Tinling and Louis B. Wright have in preparation a full-length study of Byrd.

raphy of Joel Chandler Harris to supersede the familial *Life and Letters,* published by his daughter-in-law in 1918. In due course these and other deficiencies will be remedied because the literary scholars are fully aware of them.

I should like to dwell for a moment on how all this activity has altered our view of the condition of Southern literary culture in colonial times and in the nineteenth century. An account of Southern literature written in 1920 would have gone, in outline, something like this:

> There was little colonial writing of any importance aside from a few interesting journals, some letters, an abundance of political tracts, and some historical works. In this respect the South differed little from the North except that the quantity of writing was greater in the North. In the early national period [so the account would go], there was in the North a determined effort on the part of the writers to break from England, now that political independence had been secured, and create a national literature worthy of the potential greatness of the new nation. Such writers as Irving, Cooper, Emerson, Thoreau, Whitman, and Melville were self-conscious and deliberate in this matter. A few writers, Longfellow and Lowell among them, deplored this literary chauvinism, as they felt it to be. Nevertheless, by the time of the Civil War there was a literary tradition in the North, and Europe had begun to take notice.
>
> [Our hypothetical account would then explain how very different the situation was in the South during this period.] Few literate Southerners cared whether the region produced any writers or not. Indeed there was hostility to the idea of creating a Southern school. Edward W. Johnston voiced this in the *Southern Review* for August, 1831. "We do," wrote Johnston, "in the name of the good people of the planting states, utterly disclaim having even the humblest part, which is assigned us, in a separate school of writers, dignified with the title 'American.' " To Johnston, American literature was still a part of English literature and should be proud to remain so.
>
> Under such opprobrium [so the account would go], the Southern writers who ventured poems and novels were severely limited. Few of them could afford to be full-time professionals. They earned their living in other ways and wrote on the side. Caruthers, the novelist, was a busy physician. William Wirt and J. P. Kennedy were lawyers. George Tucker retreated to a professorship at the University of Virginia. When the Civil War loomed ahead, some in the South ing chiefly *Uncle Tom's Cabin.*
> regretted that it had not bred up a race of writers to counter effectively the barrage of anti-slavery propaganda from the North, mean-

Such, then, was the accepted view of the Southern literary tradition (or the lack of any such thing) before scholars began to examine the image. Has their work altered this image? Very markedly, I believe.

In the first place figures who were hidden in the shadows of history have been brought out into the light. I am thinking of such a writer as Nathaniel Tucker (1750-1807), to whose name Lewis Leary attached a life in the biography he published in 1951. William Byrd of Westover was not a shadowy figure but his inner life was revealed to us only with the recent publication of three portions of his secret diary. Many writers, like Byrd, about whom something was known, have been made substantial. Their unpublished works have been uncovered, so that at last their whole careers are known. In spite of the limitations imposed on them, the Southern writers did create a tradition in defiance of such cavilers as Edward Johnston. This the scholars have proved. Meanwhile the folklorists and ballad collectors recorded, before it was too late, the rich oral literature of the South, richer by far than that of any other region in the country.

All this scholarly activity is restoring to us the literary life that was. Students of literary culture have, I think, a curious blind spot. We tend to believe that the state of writing in any country, in any period, is healthy if all the genres are represented—poetry, drama, the novel, criticism. Something was askew in eighteenth-century English literature because only one poet of high rank emerged, Alexander Pope. (Blake is sometimes remembered at the last moment.) And something was wrong with the literature of the nineteenth century because, struggle as they might, the poets could not turn out any actable poetic drama. In short, we tend to complain about things lacking while overlooking unexpected and unorthodox excellencies.

By showing us what Southern literature really is, the scholars and critics will persuade us to enjoy it as it is and not ask for what does not exist. If there is no Southern Dickens, there are the creators of Simon Suggs and Sut Lovingood. If there is no Southern Burns, there are "Barbey Ellen" and "Old Smoky," "Go Down Moses," and "Steal Away to Jesus." It is thought to be a fine thing that we are to have in print all the letters of Horace Walpole and all the journals of James Boswell. I should prefer to own the seventeen volumes of the *Papers of Thomas Jefferson*.

When the canvas is completely filled in, we shall discover that aside from the work of such excellent writers as Poe, Simms, Cable, Wolfe, Faulkner, Welty, Tate, Warren, Ransom, O'Connor, Porter (how the line lengthens!), the glory of Southern writing is to be found in letters (such as Jefferson's), diaries, oratory, political writing, ballads, and folklore. I would add another kind of writing of which there has been an abundance. Southerners have loved their land and have written lovingly of it. I have no name for this kind of writing, but you will know what I have in mind when I instance such works as William Elliot's *Carolina Sports by Land and Water* and William Alexander Percy's *Lanterns on the Levee*. The English equivalents would be, possibly, Walton's *Compleat Angler*, White's *Natural History of Selborne*, and Cobbett's *Rural Rides*.

I have been thinking a great deal lately about new areas of investigation which the Center might open up, as the other members of this symposium have also been doing. In reporting on some of my speculations I shall say little about projects which have to do solely with literature. As I have noted, the study of Southern literary culture is in good hands and will go forward. What I prefer to talk about is the sort of project which will best be carried out as an interdisciplinary effort. The five possible projects I shall speak of briefly are listed at random. There is no natural order among them.

1. We should know a great deal more than we do about North-South relations from colonial times to the present. Too much writing about the South—in almost every field—has tended to stress the differences and the animosities. The memory of the Civil War still haunts us and we find it hard to believe the extent to which the two regions have been interdependent except for the tragic four-year break. A study of these relationships would involve all manner of sub-subjects: trade between the Northern and Southern coastal cities; political and military co-operation in the time of the Revolution; the migration of artists and writers from one region to the other; the carpetbaggers who had legitimate business in the South and stayed on to help rebuild the Southern economy; the movement of Negroes from the rural South to the urban North; the brain drain from the South to the North; the extent to which the flourishing Southern textile industry has diminished the economy of New England. I have one subproject here which I should like to get on the agenda: the relationships between Southern writers and their publishers in the North and their fellow-writers there. A collection of the letters which passed in both directions before and after the Civil War would tell us much about the literary life, North as well as South.

2. After spending several hours looking at the collections housed in Princeton's Bureau of Urban Research, I have concluded that we need comprehensive historical accounts of the major cities of the South. In his *Cities in the Wilderness* Professor Carl Bridenbaugh proved spectacularly that the colonial coastal cities were the transmitters and originators of culture on the edge of the frontier. But cities continued to serve this function even in the agrarian ante-bellum South. The plantation received its books and music and furniture from Charleston and New Orleans. No colleges were planted in the cotton patch. In the present time of rapid urbanization the city provides many important new services for its region. Books about cities written in the past seem to have been of three kinds: the patriotic tract assembled to satisfy local pride; the dry statistical study which forgets that people *live* in cities; and the colorful, gossipy account written by literary folk more interested in Mardi Gras than manufacturing. There is no study of a Southern city which equals in depth and comprehensiveness Constance McLaughlin Green's two-volume *Washington, Village and Capital, 1800-1878* and *Washington, Capital City, 1879-1950*. We should have some matching studies of Southern cities to go on the shelf beside this work.

3. I note with pleasure that one of the papers in this symposium is concerned with religion in the South. We already have for use the excellent chapter by Professors Fichter and Maddox in *The South in Continuity and Change*—"Religion in the South, Old and New." I surmise from these facts that the Center may undertake studies of the religious life of the South. So I shall say nothing about this area of investigation except to note how backward we have been in exploring it. Certainly the South is the region where the church and the clergy have had, since colonial times, the most influence in people's lives. We need to know in detail the nature of this influence and how pervasive it has been.

4. I shall be stepping way out of my own province in making my next suggestion, but it needs to be made. In the plans for the work of the Center, so far as they are adumbrated in this symposium, the only one of the arts which is recognized is the art of writing. There is no hint that studies of Southern architecture, painting, and music will be needed. The developments in architecture have been fairly well treated, but such studies as we have of Southern music and painting are meager, and they are usually pervaded by a sense of discouragement. I wonder if, again, we are not suffering from myopia, from a failure to look in the right places. In accounts of music in the South there are the expected allusions to opera in New Orleans; the St. Cecilia Society in Charleston; the birth of Gottschalk, the great pianist, in New Orleans; the two-year sojourn of Frederick Delius in Virginia and Florida; and Dvořák's use of Negro melodies. In these accounts and in the older general histories of American music only the expected and hoped-for phenomena are treated, such as symphonies, choral works, string quartets, orchestras, and choral societies. Yet Europe, since the 1920's, has considered that the greatest and possibly the only contributions America has made are jazz and the blues. George Pullen Jackson, a professor of German at Vanderbilt, revealed another place to look for the music that was (and still is) when he began his studies of the white spirituals and the music of the Sacred Harp singers. It is gratifying to note that in the most recent comprehensive history of American music, Gilbert Chase's *America's Music from the Pilgrims to the Present* (1955), an entire chapter is devoted to "the fasola folk." It could not have been written if Professor Jackson had not shown the way. Consider another place where looking resulted in an amazing discovery. In the Moravian Archives are upwards of ten thousand musical compositions, including some lost works by European composers. This musical archive comprises the largest collection of indigenous American music composed between 1760 and 1860. Only in the last few years has the richness of this treasure been known. You can now play records of eighteenth-century Moravian anthems and chorales for your friends and entice them into asking, "Is that Haydn you're playing?" John W. Molnar looked in another Southern place where music once flourished, in his study of the musical life of colonial Williamsburg ("Art Music in Colonial Virginia," *Institute of Southern Culture Lectures at Longwood College, 1960*). He had to dig for his facts, but he found them in abundance, down to the last violin owned and songbook borrowed.

I suspect there is a great deal yet to be written about the art of painting in the South. I know of *one* place where there should be some looking. Almost no attention has been paid to Southern primitive painting. Yet there must be quantities of it. Where are the primitive portraits and landscape paintings hiding out? Someone ought to go to work.[2]

5. My last proposal has to do with Negro life in the South. It is a sad thought that millions of Negroes lived and died in slavery times without leaving a trace behind, not even a letter or a document. And there were few of their own race, freedmen or escaped slaves, to speak or write for them. Except as seen indirectly in the words of white men, we know little about the inner life of the slaves. A slave is only a statistic. Things were better after the Civil War, of course, but most Negroes with literary ability, from 1865 to the present, left the South as soon as they

2. Is it not ironic that the most comprehensive study of the art produced by the American Negro, South and North, should have been written by a Eurasian, born in Calcutta and educated at the University of Edinburgh—Cedric Dover's *American Negro Art* (1960)?

could. In consequence there are few novels about Negro life in the South written by Negroes. Many white novelists have depicted Negroes as accurately as they could—for instance, Du Bose Heyward, Julia Peterkin, Lyle Saxon, and William Faulkner. But what they have written hardly compensates us for what we have lost.

What can be done at this late date, especially for the time of slavery? The situation looks hopeless. If the writing is not there, how can we find it? Something does remain, however, and use should be made of it. Herbert Aptheker collected a few items from the ante-bellum period in his *A Documentary History of the Negro People in the United States* (1951). There may be more documents to be found. We know a fair amount at first hand about the free Negro, yet, as John Hope Franklin notes in *From Slavery to Freedom*, there is no general history. When it is written, let us hope the writer or writers stumble on documents the equal of the vigorous diary of William Johnson, free Negro of Natchez. The Slave Narrative Collection of the Federal Writers' Project, tapped by B. A. Botkin in compiling *Lay My Burden Down*, would be an invaluable source. Materials have also been accumulating in *The Journal of Negro History* and *Phylon*. If the Center undertakes projects in this area, the help of Negro historians, sociologists, and authors will be needed. Indeed, such projects would appropriately be put in their hands.

Since I have already got myself pretty deep into the business of suggesting research projects which the Center might wish to encourage, I may as well go deeper. What I wish to discuss next are some activities which the Center might well engage in itself.

My first practical suggestion calls for a close follow-up on the doctoral dissertations concerned with Southern writers and writing. Such dissertations are one of the main sources of new information and amended judgments about Southern literary culture. Fortunately, the listing of dissertations in this area has gone on for many years, and information about current research is presented in each issue of *American Literature*. But information about publication has not been available in recent years because of the labor which would have been required to obtain it. I hope that the Center can keep a record of published dissertations and the prospects for publication of others not yet printed.

We all know how much dissertation research rusts unused. The author's interests are diverted; or he finds no way of getting his dissertation published, usually because he cannot find a subsidy; or he reached his limit when he completed his dissertation and wishes to forget about research. Settled in some safe academic post, he is now cultivating his garden. For several reasons, therefore, it would be helpful to literary scholars if all the dissertations in the area of Southern literary culture were available on film at the Center. I do not think the cost would be prohibitive.

I have another proposal to make in this connection. I should like to see it put into operation for all dissertations on American literature. But I realize that "all" is too big a proviso, when all means the whole country. It would not be if my proposal were limited to all dissertations on Southern writers. The young scholar who has just completed his graduate training is in a tight situation. The institution that engages him wants him to be a good teacher and spend much of his time helping his students. It also wants him to be a productive scholar—immediately. The hot breath of publish or perish is on his neck. Consequently he flounders for a time, getting into print scraps of scholarship until he can find support for a major effort. Yet he has produced in his dissertation a work which shows, presumably, the best he could do at that time. Why should he not be told by an authority in his field just how good it is?

My proposal is that the Center should undertake to review these dissertations just as if they were books. In effect they *are* books. They may be read by other scholars, quoted from by permission, and used as the basis for further work. I can imagine what a boon such a review by Floyd Stovall or Arlin Turner or Edd Parks would be to a young scholar—if the review were favorable, of course! He could show it to his department and ask for a little time to catch up. And might not such reviewing diminish the flood of hastily done, inconsequential articles which are turned out in desperation to insure promotion?

My next practical suggestion is that the Center organize a mighty hunting expedition in the brakes and brackens of libraries, museums, and historical societies. We know that quantities of unused and unpublished materials are hiding out in such institutions, waiting to be flushed into the open. One could cite case after case to show how many lacunae in American literary history have been filled in because scholars were good hunters. One of the most notable instances in the North was the recovery of a major poet of early New England, Edward Taylor. His descendants gave his poetical manuscripts to Yale in 1883. They lay undisturbed there until Dr. Thomas Johnson uncovered them in 1939. A similar instance of recovery in the South is the fascinating story of the finding of three portions of William Byrd's secret diary, one portion of which had migrated to the Huntington Library. Do other portions of the diary exist? If so, where are they hiding?

The success of such hunting expeditions, North and South, convinces me that the Center might well, in the literary fields at least, undertake to compile and keep up to date a census of literary manuscripts and allied materials. If my suggestion makes you see hundreds of scouts searching through thousands of manuscripts, I can put your imagination at rest. Excellent beginnings have already been made. The bibliographical essays in Professor Hubbell's *The South in American Literature* are a rich mine of information. Most useful, also, would be *American Literary Manuscripts, a Checklist of Holdings,* published under the auspices of the American Literature Group in 1960. This compilation surveys the holdings in 270 American libraries and lists materials relating to 2,350 writers. The category symbols indicate the whereabouts of literary manuscripts, journals, letters, and even books containing marginalia. Southern writers have not been slighted.

It may seem that for any scholar doing research in Southern literature this volume will be all he could desire as a guide to manuscripts. The Center could, if it wished to, provide additional assistance. A book such as this goes no farther than the year of its publication. Where do we look for information about new acquisitions? I can cite one illustrative fact: since 1960 the Princeton Library has acquired three archives containing materials relating to Southern authors. Again—not to speak in derogation—*American Literary Manuscripts* relied, perforce, on what the co-operating libraries reported. Some libraries—very few, in fact—have the staff to calendar every letter and scrap of a first draft. Others can only report "extensive holdings" or "special collection." The Committee on Library Resources which supervised the compilation of *American Literary Manuscripts* did have a "field" worker, but he could not go very far behind the returns. Since the volume provides a listing of manuscript holdings by author only, rubrics are not there which would be most useful to a student of Southern literature. I am thinking of such categories as "The Fugitives," "Poetry Society of Charleston," "Carolina Playmakers."

In one other way the Center could enlarge our knowledge of manuscript holdings. It could find out something, at least, about manuscripts in private hands. Acquiring such information would require tact and ingenuity, and the results of the inquiry would be haphazard. Nevertheless I think the attempt ought to be made. So far as I know, no listing of this kind has been attempted in this country for any field. It has been done successfully in England. In 1945 the Historical Manuscripts Commission set up the National Register of Archives to maintain and keep up to date a collection of typescript reports on privately owned manuscript collections. To view the materials indexed in the National Register, one must apply to the Registrar, never directly to the owner. Thus the owner is protected from intrusion, if that is his desire.

I should like to suggest next that the Center consider what it might do to increase the publication of Southern materials. I am not proposing that the Center become a publisher itself, except in certain limited areas which I shall speak of in a moment. But it should be, I believe, a powerful encourager of publication. To this end, a survey of what has been published by the university presses in the South (and the North, too, for that matter) and of what is promised for the future might well be undertaken. I have looked into this situation cursorily myself, and what I find is encouraging. State university presses have obligations to their states and region, but they must also aid scholarship in diverse fields. I think the presses in the South have kept the balance admirably.

Some of the Southern presses publish Southern materials for learned societies, such as the American Dialect Society, the Texas Folklore Society, and the Virginia Historical Society. The national movement to print *in extenso* the papers of our statesmen has received co-operation in the South. The University of South Carolina Press is issuing the papers of John C. Calhoun and of Henry Laurens. Rice University plans to publish the Jefferson Davis Papers. Several notable series have been undertaken, such as the Floridiana Facsimile and Reprint Series; Dominion Books of the University Press of Virginia; Southern Literary Studies, recently inaugurated at Louisiana State University Press; and the Southern Historical Publications of the University of Alabama Press.

The showing is a good one, and it might seem that the publishing of books about the South is going along well enough. I doubt if the directors of these presses would agree. If they were called together and asked what they would like to do further in this area, the Center might receive more calls for assistance than it could take care of in a decade. At least it would possess some valuable information about publishing needs. The Center may wish to establish, eventually, a series of its own. One might say, indeed, that a beginning has been made with the publication of *The South in Continuity and Change.*

I have two modest publishing projects in mind which ought to be undertaken by one of the Southern presses, possibly under the sponsorship of the Center.

We should get into print again a number of Southern works which are referred to frequently but are now scarce and will soon be unobtainable in the early editions. I made up a brief list of such works, selected at random, as I was thinking about the Center's future. A publishing venture like this one I propose already exists in the John Harvard Library of Harvard University Press. There were fifty-three titles in this series by 1965. Only six of them are "Southern." It will take the John Harvard Library a half-century to get to all the titles we might propose. Here is my sample list.

E. C. L. Adams, *Nigger to Nigger*, 1928
William J. Grayson, *The Hireling and the Slave, Chicora and other Poems*, 1856
Twelve Years a Slave: Narrative of Solomon Northup, a Citizen of New York, Kidnapped in Washington City in 1841, and Rescued in 1853, from a Cotton Plantation near the Red River, in Louisiana, 1853
J. K. Paulding, *Letters from the South*, 1817
James Ross, *Life and Times of Elder Reuben Ross*, 1882
Edmund Ruffin, *Anticipations of the Future, to Serve as Lessons for the Present*, 1860
John Taylor, *The Arator: Being a Series of Agricultural Essays, Practical and Political*, 1813
George Tucker, *A Voyage to the Moon*, 1827

Included in this series should be several works of scholarship which are out of print. I have in mind such books as John Spencer Bassett's *The Plantation Overseer* (1925) and E. L. Tinker's *Les Écrits de la Langue, Française en Louisiane au XIXe Siècle* (1932).

In suggesting that the Center arrange for the re-publication of such works as I have listed I am not thinking only of the needs of students in the South. New colleges and universities are coming into existence all over the country. They are building libraries, but where are they going to get such impossible-to-find books? We ought to think, too, of the needs of libraries in various places around the world where the study of American civilization is a new and thriving discipline.

My second publishing proposal calls for a book of readings for use in the colleges. It should be organized to accord with our present view of what the best and most interesting Southern writing is. The making of such an anthology should not be turned over exclusively to the literary folk. Anthropologists, folklorists, and historians should assist. They will know where good Southern writing is to be found which the literary scholars may have overlooked.

We may take it for granted, I am sure, that the Center will organize conferences and symposia to investigate various aspects of Southern culture. I wish to suggest that some of these be organized in such a way that a well-planned, carefully integrated, definitive book will be the end-product. To make this possible, contributors of individual chapters should work in concert, seeing one another frequently to comment on the study as it progresses. Those of us who have participated in the American studies movement have learned to work together in this way. In any area study, no matter what the subject, the economist has something to tell the literary scholar, and the anthropologist contributes to the studies of the art historian.

In this connection, I should like to digress for a moment to speak of the state of American studies as a discipline in the Southern colleges and universities. I do this because the Center will be able to count on help from the seventeen programs or departments already established.[3] Most of the programs are flourishing; a few could do more if they had the necessary financial support. The four Southern branches of the American Studies Association are active, each holding at least one well-attended meeting a year. Three of them send out newsletters. Joint sessions are always held with the Southern branches of AHA, MLA, and a number of other societies. One journal, the *Mississippi Quarterly*, is trying to do on a regional scale what the *American Quarterly* attempts for the national scene. Members of these programs and regional associations will be able to say what kinds of beneficial co-operation may be expected between their organizations and the Center for Southern Studies.

My last practical suggestion may seem far too impractical to be considered, but I shall mention it just the same. I think there should be writers—novelists, poets, critics, writers of that kind—at the Center from time to time. I have two reasons for believing this would be a good thing. Not so long ago the presence of a poet or novelist in a department of English would have been thought an absurdity; scholarship and literary creativity could not mix. Today a department that does not have a Writer in Residence is conspicuously behind the times. To have a poet on the premises stimulates the scholars, pulls them away from their preoccupation with historiology, and puts them in contact with writing as it is written. The presence of a creative writer at the Center would have this kind of fecundating influence.

I have another reason. For what ends does the Center exist? Not solely, I should suppose, to illuminate our knowledge of Southern life in all its aspects, though that is a high aim. But do we not hope that what the economists discover in working at the Center will benefit the Southern and the national economy? That the explorations of the political scientists

3. If we count Maryland as a Southern state and Washington as a Southern city, the number is twenty. We should note also that of the sixty-odd summer programs in American studies organized last year, sixteen were conducted on Southern campuses.

will improve the administration of government in the South? If this is the case, then should the Center not do something for Southern writing beyond taking account of it, measuring and weighing it?

Commentary / Louis D. Rubin, Jr.

It is kind of Mr. Willard Thorp to suggest that I could set him straight on the condition of Southern literary scholarship, and it is also unduly modest of him, for of course I could not do any such thing. There is little that I can add to his excellent account of what has been done, save for what knowledge I have of the series of Southern Literary Studies that I am editing for the Louisiana State University Press. For example, a quite interesting and adequate biography of Joel Chandler Harris is now in the final stages of revision, and I can also report that several projects are under way which should help to fill what Professor Thorp rightly says is a great lack, the study of Southern-Northern literary relations. Another way of putting this would be to say that what we need are some studies of nineteenth-century Southern writers in their role as men of letters—which is to say, studies of what it cost them and meant to them to be writers in the Old South, and what their relationships with the publishing centers in the Northeast were. We also need, I might add, a good overall study of Southern magazine journalism in the nineteenth century and I am glad to add at once that Mr. Robert D. Jacobs plans to write such a study.

So I can't provide any detailed comment on what I think is an admirable survey of what might (and what certainly should) be done to put the field of Southern literary scholarship in a shape whereby it can better help to tell us what the South was, is, and can and will be.

Instead, I should like to venture a few observations on what might be done to improve the way in which we go about the study of Southern writing. For here it seems to me is the problem. I agree thoroughly that we need better biographical accounts of some of the neglected figures in Southern literary history, that we need authoritative texts and editions, and better and more detailed research into precisely what was involved in Southern literature in the eighteenth and more importantly the nineteenth centuries. And surely Mr. Thorp is right when he notes that fortunately we do have the definitive overall historical and biographical (and bibliographical) guide to the study of the men and the time in Jay B. Hubbell's magnificent *The South in American Literature*. This master work is the starting point, as well as the point of reference, for anyone who would examine writing in the South before 1900. He has charted the way for all of us.

But is what Mr. Thorp suggests all that we need, and is it the principal way to go about it?—I mean of course more extensive biographical studies, more detailed and thorough historical monographs, better texts. I would suggest that there is another very great general shortcoming in the study of Southern literature past and present, one that so long as it is allowed to go unremedied will seriously limit and handicap anyone who wants to use Southern literary scholarship to understand Southern life. It is the need, I think, to understand the *meaning* of the cultural milieu and the history of the nineteenth-century South, and especially to view the Southern writers as related to and as affected by that cultural milieu. It seems to me that precious little has been attempted along this line—precious little, that is, of an interpretative, analytical sort. We hear a great deal about Simms in Charleston, for example, and Poe in Richmond. But how little we know about what as writers they were really up against! How little we know of their true imaginative relationship to their society. And how much we need to know.

One of the most harrowing literary accounts I have ever read is that in Mr. Hubbell's fine study of the last years of Henry Timrod: his struggle, which was not successful, to feed himself and his family in wartime and devastated South Carolina. Now we might blame that on the war. But *why*, for example, should a gifted man such as William Gilmore Simms have proposed as an epitaph for himself those words to the effect that here lies one who, after a long lifetime of unceasing labor, left all his best books unwritten?

And Simms did precisely that, I think we ought to admit. The conditions of nineteenth-century Southern life did not permit him to cultivate whatever there was of talent with the intense and uninterrupted devotion that makes talent into great literature. His energies were necessarily squandered and diverted, just as Poe's energies went into magazine journalism because he had to earn a living. And Timrod never became the poet he might have become had he lived in New England; he had a gift at language second to no American poet of his time save Walt Whitman, but he lived and he died a second-rate writer. *Why*?

It has only been in the twentieth century, and in the last four decades at that, that our writers have been of important enough stature to be read the world over. Until then, we have been considered pretty unimportant in the literary scene, and justifiably so. Mr. Thorp has it about right when he remarks that "If there is no Southern Dickens, there are the creators of Simon Suggs and Sut Lovingood." Precisely. That is what there are. No Dickenses, and no Melvilles and Hawthornes and Whitmans or even Emersons and Thoreaus. And Mr. Thorp is also right when he says that "the glory of Southern writing is to be found in letters [such as Jefferson's], diaries, oratory, political writing, ballads, and folklore." It is indeed, and it is pretty tarnished glory at that. There are not novels and poems and stories and plays of national and international importance; speeches and letters do not provide what major literature provides and nothing else can provide for a culture: the image of its meaning.

Again, I ask why this was so. Where does the answer lie? I know the usual reasons that are proposed: the agricultural economy, the lack of urban centers, the absence of publishing outlets, the refusal of Southerners to buy and read Southern magazines and Southern books, the channeling of the region's chief energies into the sectional fight for political and economic survival. But I am not satisfied with these answers. They all seem to me to be either rationalization, or more often symptoms of something else.

I should like to know what this something else was, and why somehow it ceased to function along about the time of World War I. But I am not likely to find the answer, nor are you, until we get in the study of nineteenth-century Southern literature something that has thus far been, with only a few exceptions, conspicuously absent: a genuinely evaluative and critical approach to the relationship of the literature to the society out of which it evolved, an approach neither blinded by chauvinism nor encased in undue pedantry.

As Mr. Thorp suggests, we have had a surfeit of critical, evaluative, thematic studies of some of the modern writers, and we could do with a little less straining for symbols and theme-hunting. But at the same time, what we have had in the study of the nineteenth century is, I think, equally incomplete, and that is, either a pathetic chauvinism that tries to make a Thomas Holley Chivers into a Ralph Waldo Emerson, or else a kind of non-critical, non-evaluative, non-questioning historical fact-collecting that neither importantly relates a writer to his times nor goes beyond the most superficial and surface discussion of his works.

The worst part of this is that while allegedly historical, what this kind of approach does is quite unhistorical. For surely the essence of the study of history is to know how to relate individual actions and individual people to larger actions and larger groups, in order to understand the full meaning of a time and place. This has not been done with the writing of the nineteenth-century South, and we therefore have very little idea of what Poe, Simms, Hayne, Lanier, Harris, and the others have to tell us about what the South used to be.

It is time that we began this task. It is time that we encourage our young scholars not only to assemble, but to relate; not only to praise, but to understand. We need works in nineteenth-century Southern literary and intellectual history of the same kind as Matthiessen's *American Renaissance,* as R. W. B. Lewis' *The American Adam,* as Perry Miller's brilliant work on Jonathan Edwards and on the Transcendentalists, as Henry Nash Smith's study of Mark Twain's literary development. All we have is W. J. Cash's *The Mind of the South,* a brilliant book but hardly thorough enough or careful enough. We need in Southern literary scholarship the kind of critical insight that Rupert Vance, Howard Odum, George Tindall, C. Vann Woodward, Francis Simkins, Clement Eaton, and others have brought to Southern historical and social studies. We need in Southern literature scholars who can tell the difference between the work of Thomas Holley Chivers and that of William Wordsworth. The only thing that I know that has been attempted along this line by a thoroughgoing scholar is William R. Taylor's *Cavalier and Yankee*—a splendid beginning, but so far it stands quite alone.

In other words, I agree with all that Mr. Thorp has to say about the need for more solid research and more accurate texts, but I think too that the primary job has hardly been begun, and that job is importantly critical and interpretative. Of course we need both facts and their evaluation and interpretation. But if this Center for Southern Studies can serve to encourage and to instigate more penetrating and more imaginative inquiries into what the literature of the South really means about the South, we shall all be in its debt.

Needed research in Southern dialects / Raven I. McDavid, Jr.

With a sub-Potomac accent now enunciating the national policies, the time is fair for examining what we know about Southern speech and what we need to learn. Whatever Southerners may feel about Mr. Johnson's policies, none of them can deny that his presence has made people in other regions less patronizing toward Southern speechways, and has removed at least this cause of Southern defensiveness. There has never been a more opportune occasion for assessing objectively our speech and its implications.

Since Cabell Greet's overview of the subject in Couch's *Culture in the South*, there has been much solid evidence gathered on Southern ways of talking, and a fair amount of scholarly publication. Yet except for my own updating of Mencken's *The American Language*,[1] a work whose fundamental structure limited the amount of new material that could be included, almost none of the new evidence has been included in works designed for *l'homme moyen intellectuel.* Even the textbooks, which should have made special efforts to discard timeworn myths for new-won facts, are little improved over those of the 1930's; though the ghost of the mythical "General American" should have long ago been laid, it still returns to haunt us, sometimes under its old label, sometimes under such new disguises as "consensus English" or "network English," neither of them very palatable in a region where locally identifiable ways of speech are cultural traditions, as soon to be denied as the legitimacy of one's descent.[2]

The distinctive characteristics of Southern speech—at least, those which outsiders judge as distinctive—have been attracting attention ever since the Reverend John Witherspoon delivered his castigation of the national idiom in 1781; but the appraisal of them has generally been casual, impressionistic, unstructured, and uninformed. Among the characteristics most often noted[3] are:

1. New York: Alfred A. Knopf, Inc., 1963. There is extensive bibliographical information in the footnotes to chap. vii, sec. 4, "Dialects."

2. "Consensus English" has been used by Priscilla Tyler of the University of Illinois; "network English" by William Stewart of the Center for Applied Linguistics, Washington, D. C. The diversity of educated accents to be encountered on the streets of Atlanta or New Orleans suggests that we are still far from even a "consensus Southern."

3. This is an *ad hoc* list, based on popular notions. A more accurate—and more diffident—summary, first put together by Atwood with the help of other workers on the Atlas project, is to be found in W. Nelson Francis, *The Structure of American English* (New York: Ronald Press, 1958), pp. 513-527.

1. The so-called "Southern drawl."
2. *You-all* as a plural, and allegedly as a singular.
3. To *tote* groceries from the store.
4. To *carry* a mule to the barn or a young lady home from a party.
5. The loss of post-vocalic /-r/ in such words as *barn, beard, board.*
6. A so-called "Brooklyn diphthong" [ɜi] in *bird* and *turn.*
7. The positional alternation of "fast" and "slow" variants of the diphthongs /ai/ and /au/, giving [əi] in *write* but [a·ɛ] in *ride*, [əu] in *house* but [æ·o] in *houses.*
8. The appearance of a monophthongal [a·] for /ai/ before voiced consonants and finally, but not before voiceless, giving [a·] in *ride* but [ai] in *write.*
9. The appearance of /ai/ as [a·] in all positions, as in *nice white rice*, a well-known social shibboleth in much of the South.
10. The alleged falling together of /ai/ and /a/, so that *blind* and *blond* become homonyms.
11. The alleged falling together of /ai/ and /æ/, so that *right* is indistinguishable from *rat.*

Some of these assumed features, like the two last, seem to be noticed only by outlanders. Some of them, like the two last again, simply do not occur.[4] Some of them contradict others, as with 7, 8, and 9, or with 10 and 11. None of the list is actually universal in the South, however the region may be defined—whether as the territory of slaveholding states before the Civil War, that of the seceding states, or that in which the plantation system was dominant. To take one feature, the drawl: there is no evidence that Southerners on the average talk any more slowly than Midwesterners, and much evidence that some varieties of Southern speech—notably that of the Charleston area in South Carolina—are much more rapid than the varieties of speech in the Middle West. But the myths persist, largely because the evidence is unpublished or confined to scholarly articles and treatises that are seldom noted.

The evidence at hand is of three kinds: (1) detailed phonetic transcription by trained field investigators, on which is based the project of a Linguistic Atlas of the United States and Canada (in this instance, transcriptions are found in two regional surveys, the Atlas of the Middle and South Atlantic States and that of the North-Central States); (2) a corre-

4. The monophthongal [a·] is identified with the vowel of *father* when that vowel is somewhat fronted in Northern speech; with the vowel of *rat* when that vowel is lowered. Needless to say, the Southern speaker makes the contrast; the falling together is in the perception of the Northerner.

spondence survey, involving vocabulary questionnaires, for the interior South, conducted primarily by Gordon Wood of Southern Illinois University; (3) a series of more localized studies, using field work or correspondence questionnaires or sometimes a combination of both methods.

The Linguistic Atlas of the Middle and South Atlantic States, launched by Hans Kurath in the late 1930's, comprises about eleven hundred field interviews of over seven hundred questions each, with responses elicited by professional investigators from identifiable local informants and recorded in finely graded phonetic transcription. The area investigated is roughly that of eighteenth-century settlement, as far west as the Altamaha Valley, with four communities as outposts in northern Florida. The field records, originally at Brown and later at Michigan, are being edited at the University of Chicago, with the first volume scheduled to go to press in 1968. Although the passage of time has dated many of its cultural details, this Atlas nevertheless constitutes an indispensable baseline. Out of its archives have come many articles, several dissertations, and three broad-gauge summary volumes,[5] issued by the University of Michigan Press:

Hans Kurath, *A Word Geography of the Eastern United States* (1949).

E. Bagby Atwood, *A Survey of Verb Forms in the Eastern United States* (1953).

Kurath and Raven I. McDavid, Jr., *The Pronunciation of English in the Atlantic States* (1961).

Like most scholarly books, these were printed in small editions, with limited publicity and consequent limited distribution;[6] as *particeps criminis* I note with somewhat wry amusement that the *Pronunciation* evaded detection by the survey of scholarly books issuing from university presses. The *Word Geography* appeared before there was full evidence in hand from the South Carolina Low-Country and eastern Georgia; my summary, "The Position of the Charleston Dialect," in *Publication of the American Dialect Society* No. 23 (1955), is brief and cursory, without accompanying maps. Popular and pedagogical discussions of the dialects of the older South usually stem from summaries by Kurath and Atwood and me, notably my chapter in W. Nelson Francis, *The Structure of American English* (New York: The Ronald Press Company, 1958). The Atlas of the North-Central States, with duplicate sets of field records at Chicago

5. The method of the Atlas project is summarized in Francis, discussed at length in Kurath, *Handbook of the Linguistic Geography of New England* (Providence, R. I.: Linguistic Atlas of the United States and Canada, 1939).

6. The *Word Geography*, for some time out of print, has recently been reissued in paperback format; the *Pronunciation* will also be reissued in the near future.

and Michigan, touches the South only in Kentucky; its evidence, also, has been presented largely in scholarly articles and dissertations.[7] The vocabulary of Kentucky has also been investigated through correspondence questionnaires by Mrs. Christine Duncan Forrester; her master's thesis (Kentucky, 1954) is unpublished.

The survey of the Interior South by Wood has been discussed in a series of articles in American and foreign journals.[8] For Texas there is one first-rate work, Atwood's *The Regional Vocabulary of Texas* (Austin: University of Texas Press, 1962); it was based on field investigations of vocabulary only, undertaken by graduate students over a period of years. Several good local studies by Atwood's students—notably by Arthur Norman in the Beaumont region and by Mrs. Janet Sawyer in San Antonio—are accessible only in articles or on microfilm. The field records for Oklahoma are being edited by W. R. Van Riper, of Louisiana State University, who is also custodian of some hundred field records made by students of the late C. M. Wise—uneven in quality but providing a basis for choosing communities intelligently when more highly trained investigators can be sent into the field. In Alabama there have been two studies of parts of the plantation area, by James B. McMillan and Mrs. Madie Barrett; neither has been published. Linguistic Atlas field work in Missouri began during the summer of 1966. Frederic G. Cassidy, of the University of Wisconsin, has several investigators in the South, gathering material toward a Dictionary of American Regional English, a project complementary to the Atlas as well as significant in its own right; one of the investigators will provide the first solid evidence on local variations in Mississippi.

The most significant study of Negro speech is Lorenzo D. Turner's *Africanisms in the Gullah Dialect* (Chicago: University of Chicago Press, 1949). Miss Juanita Williamson, of LeMoyne College, Memphis, has completed a dissertation on the Negro speech of Memphis (Michigan, microfilm, 1961); Saunders Walker, of Tuskegee Institute, has done one on the folk vocabulary of the Eastern Alabama Negro (Western Reserve, MS, 1956). There have been several studies of Louisiana Negro French,

7. See Virginia McDavid, *Verb Forms in the North-Central States and Upper Midwest*, diss. (microfilm), University of Minnesota, 1956; Raven I. McDavid, Jr., and Virginia McDavid, "Grammatical Differences in the North-Central States," *American Speech*, XXXV (Feb., 1960), 5-15; Albert H. Marckwardt, "Principal and Subsidiary Dialect Areas in the North-Central States," *PADS*, XXVII (April, 1957), 3-15.

8. "An Atlas Survey of the Interior South," *Orbis*, IX, No. 1 (1960), 7-12; "Word Distribution in the Interior South," *PADS*, XXXV (April, 1961), 1-16; "Dialect Contours in the Southern States," *American Speech*, XXXVIII (Dec., 1963), 243-256.

most recently by Raleigh Morgan.[9] Other French dialects, in Louisiana and elsewhere, are relatively unstudied. The same may be said for other colonial languages, though Spanish settlement dates from 1565 and German settlements, beginning in the early eighteenth century, dot the historical South from western Maryland to southern Texas, while Czechs settled in Texas soon after San Jacinto.[10]

The information now at our disposal should give us a far better picture of Southern dialects than we encounter in most popular summaries, but it needs to be made more accessible if we are to have a better understanding of the varieties of English (not to say other languages) now spoken in the South. And in addition to making better use of the data which we now have, we need to fill in many gaps and to undertake other studies—some of a radically different design—that will enrich our knowledge and will enable us to cope more effectively with the practical problems confronting the student of Southern speech, the demographer, and the classroom teacher of English, whether in a Southern school or elsewhere.

The highest priority should go to the editing and publication of the data already recorded, classified, and filed. Fairly clear plans were laid down by Kurath at the time the Atlas archives were transferred from Brown to Michigan; they are as applicable now as they were twenty years ago, and developments in typewriter design should make it possible to prepare list manuscripts for printing at a fraction of the cost of the hand-lettered maps of the traditional linguistic atlases. Although the exact date will depend on how much financial support is available, it should be possible to publish all the evidence from the Middle and South Atlantic States and from the North-Central area within the next decade; the first volume or so will naturally be the most difficult to edit, with the others following easily once the pattern is established. Along with these two surveys, one should push to publication Van Riper's evidence on Oklahoma speech. Although Oklahoma is a recently—and suddenly—settled part of the United States, it may provide valuable insights for linguistic geographers everywhere on what happens in newly settled territory, and thus may enable us to understand what went on when Englishmen of various origins established themselves in North America, when the Angles and Saxons spilled across the Channel into Britain, or even when the Germanic tribes moved westward in the fifth century; it is an excellent laboratory example, since this time

9. "The Lexicon of St. Martin Creole," *Anthropological Linguistics*, II (Jan., 1960), 7-29.

10. The German dialect of the New Braunfels, Texas, area has been studied systematically by Fred Eikel of Maryland State College (Princess Anne, Maryland); it has received little attention and is not in many university libraries.

we know in some detail where the settlers came from and we have evidence on the kinds of English they brought with them. Along with these three studies we might put the completion and editing of the Missouri survey, since it is assured competent direction and field work and needs only time and money.

Once we are assured of the publication of the data we have, the highest priority should go to completing the Atlas survey—a first round survey, it should be emphasized, without prejudice to follow-up projects—from the Altamaha to the Sabine, and from Missouri and Kentucky southward to Key West (Atwood's successors at Texas can be counted on to follow up his work on vocabulary with comparable work on pronunciation and grammar). As early as this area was settled, it is practically untouched by serious and systematically comparable investigations. Part of the explanation has been the sheer poverty of the region, which has not generated enough wealth to afford the luxury of extensive research; part has been the inability of the genteel tradition of Southern humanistic studies to focus seriously on everyday speech, and the parallel failure of social scientists to concern themselves with language. However, the territory is not excessively large, nor is the population history uncharted; using the same scale as was adopted in the North-Central States, one could complete field work in the region with some 450-480 interviews—about four years' work for a single trained investigator, proportionately less if more went into the field. Here one would hope that liaison could be established with the Dictionary of American Regional English, so that investigators would not duplicate each other's work, and so that the greatest amount of data might be made available to all serious scholars. As the Dictionary moves into the regions already surveyed for the Linguistic Atlas, one would further hope that its investigators would also be interested in charting the changes in speech patterns that the last generation has brought. Industrialization, urbanization, and mass education—important social forces in America since 1620—have noticeably altered the patterns of Southern dialects since 1930. Even the most informal observations will reveal that /-r/ in words like *barn* and *beard* is being pronounced in communities and among people where it would not have been heard before the Hoover Depression, that /ju/ is giving way here and there to /u/ in *tube, due, new, student,* that *morning* and *mourning* are becoming homonyms.

Even without the incentive of Cassidy's dictionary, it would be necessary to see what changes have taken place. A new survey on the scale of the original Atlas might be hard to defend, since rural ways of life have so often given way to urban, so much of rural life itself has altered, and so many rural customs and the words describing them have become obsolete. But it would be feasible to survey much of the same area with a shorter questionnaire, perhaps focused a bit more on city life, designed to elicit all the phonetic contrasts that could be established in the original investigation (and perhaps a few more)[11] and much of the same information on grammar. We may concede that Northerners set the fashion in the southern half of Florida, and that Virginia diphthongs—especially the centering beginning of /ai/ before voiceless consonants, as in *ice*—are no longer prestigious around Washington, but we need to know the limits of this attrition, as well as the possible expansion of Southern speechways in other regions.

In any future work in Southern dialects, it would be desirable to include detailed investigations of urban and metropolitan areas. At the moment, the only city south of the Ohio that has been adequately studied is Louisville, though Atlas evidence is available for at least the first stage of studies in Charleston, Baltimore, Savannah, Richmond, and Atlanta. Nothing is known about the white speech of Memphis, almost nothing on Washington or New Orleans, nothing on Dallas or Houston or Nashville or Chattanooga or St. Louis or Charlotte or Birmingham or Mobile or Miami, to take a few cities at random. For each city an investigation should cover pronunciation and grammar and vocabulary of various ethnic, age, and educational groups. The research design should indicate the traditional differences between cultivated, common, and folk speech in the community—in Frances Patton's terms, the difference between "representative" people and those who are not; it must then indicate the traditional differences between the speech of the community and that of the surrounding countryside; finally, it must assess the differences that have been wrought by the passage of time—whether by mass migration from other areas (particularly important in Washington or Miami), or by the normal centripetal processes of industrialization and urbanization and mass education, which may be most important in the textile centers of the Piedmont. In each of these cities we must determine whether the older type of "elegant" Southern is losing its prestige, and whether or not speech varieties associated with particular castes or classes are becoming more or less alike. A striking index of the growth of racial tensions in Chicago is the fact that the speech of twenty-year-old Chicago-born Negroes differs sharply from that of contemporary Chicago-born whites, while there are sharper differences among the seventy-year-olds of each race than there are between the two races where that generation is in-

11. For instance, additional items might show whether there is a two-way or a three-way contrast (or any at all) involving such words as *had, sad, bad,* or whether there is a contrast between the stressed vowels in such pairs as *scissors/schism, sister/system, ribbon/ribbing.*

volved. It would not be surprising if social differences in language had decreased in the South at the same time they were increasing elsewhere, but only systematic investigation can give us the answer.

But not merely the cities deserve intensive studies to show the effects of cultural change and the passage of time. The South has possessed some of the most striking relic areas in the English-speaking world—areas where the lack of a focal city has prevented the outward spread of local forms, but where geographical or cultural isolation or a combination of these has preserved many older forms that have been lost in other regions. Appalachia comes first to mind, though the mountains are of more recent settlement and of less sharp isolation than lower Delmarva, Albemarle Sound and the Outer Banks, or the Sea Islands. Are relic forms disappearing, or will some remain? And is it possible that the pronunciation of Appalachia will be the Standard Southern of tomorrow? As the sons of families of high fertility leave lands of low fertility and move into the cities, they will have economic and educational opportunities their fathers never dreamed of; their sons in turn may well be the new élite. The cold facts of Southern demography are that the increase in white population, and in the college population, will come from the foothill and mountain areas and not from the plantation belts. Even now the Appalachian monophthongal /ai/ in *nice white rice* is heard and accepted where it would have been unthinkable before 1930 —but this does not yet go for the homonymy of *fire* and *far*, of *tired* and *tarred*. Perhaps other forms, once substandard, are becoming a part of cultivated Southern speech. It would be useful—not only from the point of view of the pure scientist but from that of the practical teacher—to sort out the changes that are in progress, so that there will be a minimum lag between the facts of change and the myths that are perpetrated and perpetuated in the classroom.

A more intensive study of Appalachian speech is also desirable from the point of view of the Northern cities to which so many Southern rural whites have migrated in recent years. The rapid growth of Akron following the establishment of the rubber shops was due chiefly to West Virginians; in Cuyahoga County (Cleveland), Ohio, it was estimated that 150,000 West Virginians had arrived in the decade following World War II;[12] in Detroit, Southern rural whites are one of the largest cultural groups on the automobile assembly lines; from eastern Kentucky there is constant migration to the aircraft industries of southern Ohio, and in

12. The estimates for Cleveland are informal ones; for Akron there are fairly detailed statistics, and some suggestions why official figures may underestimate the immigration, in Gerald Udell, "The Speech of Akron, Ohio: A Study in Urbanization," diss. (MS), University of Chicago, 1966.

Chicago there is a sizable island of Southern mountaineer settlement on the Near North Side in the vicinity of the Newberry Library. The attempts of well-meaning schoolmarms to bulldoze out the characteristic Southern vowels in the name of correctness and elegance have too often encouraged resentment of the condescension implied and apathy toward schoolwork in general—among a group less than fully habituated to the necessity of long-term schooling. The urbanization of the mountaineer cannot succeed unless his speech is better described than it is now, and unless the school program is directed not toward eradicating a regional accent but toward the replacement of indubitably substandard forms with standard ones.

But as important as is the study of the speech of relic areas, and especially of Appalachia, the study of Negro speech is far more urgent for teaching programs in all parts of the United States. Not only in Chicago and New York, but in cities as far apart as Boston and Las Vegas, Portland, Oregon, and Miami, Milwaukee and Los Angeles, the Negro population has swollen tremendously during the past two decades. In many Northern cities, Negroes constitute a majority of the school population; in Washington they are more than 85 per cent. In all of these cities the habitual language patterns of the Negro—a heritage of his status and education in the South, compounded and reinforced by the residential patterns in the North—set him off strikingly from the local white middle class and constitute serious obstacles to his economic and educational and social advancement. Such grammatical forms as the uninflected third-person singular present (*it make, he do*), or the omission of auxiliaries (*they done dead, she been talking about it*), which are heard widely in the South from uneducated whites as well as from Negroes, are identifiable in Chicago as "Negro forms," by which an unsophisticated teacher can consistently tell the race of the author of a theme. And the same situation is repeated in Oakland and Cleveland and dozens of other cities. Confronted with grammatical problems that will not yield to the conventional middle-class-oriented correction exercises, the Northern teacher either attempts—and usually unsuccessfully—to eradicate the home dialect completely or gives up in despair; in either event, the language practices of Northern urban Negroes are one of the principal reasons why Negro unemployment and the consequent relief load remain high, despite a growing number of jobs for skilled labor and for service employees. Nothing short of a better-designed teaching program, based upon accurate knowledge of Southern Negro speech, will suffice; for as fast as a description of Harlem or the South Side is established, new migrants come in to disturb the pattern.

Here is our greatest lack of data. Both Gullah and Louisiana Negro-French are rather special cases; and the available description of Gullah is so skewed in the direction of African survivals that much of its structural system has to be inferred. The Memphis study of Miss Williamson, on the other hand, deals only implicitly with the norms of local cultivated white speech. In the Atlas survey the sampling of Negro speech was far coarser than that of white speech—all told, perhaps fifty informants. This sampling would probably be enough to show whether there is any consistent structural difference between Negro speech and white, since each of these interviews is paired with one for a Southern white of comparable education and social status; yet such a comparison is still to be undertaken.[13] But one should not rest satisfied even with such a study; it would be desirable to make intensive studies of Negro speech in a variety of communities, Northern and Western as well as Southern, with particular attention to unguarded conversation. In such studies many hypotheses could be tested. Some observers have recently asserted that American Negro speech has a different "deep structure" from that of white speech, and they would derive it from an underlying *Gemeinnegrischpidgin.* To a naïve social scientist, what is generally known about the operations of the domestic slave trade should be sufficient to refute such an argument; the variety of Negro accents heard in Woodlawn and Englewood (in Chicago) make one wary of simple explanations. Nevertheless, since the arguments have been so plausibly put, by linguists with serious credentials,[14] it would be well to have enough data, from a wide enough spectrum of communities, to sort out fact from fancy.[15]

One would also like to see a fuller record of language data in those communities where non-English dialects are still spoken, or where speakers of such languages have migrated heavily in recent years. Of rather high priority in the first category are the Spanish-Americans of the Southwest and the Cajans of Southern Louisiana. In 1940, when I was teaching in Lafayette, Louisiana, it was locally estimated that there were three or four hundred thousand native Louisianians for whom French was the native tongue; the inadequacy of the U.S. census reports—the 1960 census asked only for the mother tongue of the foreign-

13. Such a comparison has been proposed, as a dissertation at the University of Chicago, by Vernon S. Larsen.

14. Notably Beryl Bailey of Yeshiva University, herself a native speaker of Jamaican Creole, who has written extensively on varieties of Jamaican English. Her dissertation on the syntax of Jamaican Creole has just been published.

15. The grammatical problems of uneducated Negro speech, of course, are of such an order that standard English needs to be taught by the techniques commonly associated with the teaching of foreign languages; but the same could be said about many varieties of white speech.

born—gives us barely 1200 speakers of French in Louisiana. Though it is possible that even the Cajan birthrate cannot compensate for the erosion of their way of life, native speakers of Cajan French are still numerous in Louisiana; furthermore, the conditions under which English is normally acquired in the older French communities of Louisiana are likely to produce dialects little more than *de facto* pidgins. Having struggled with Cajan graduates of Louisiana high schools, many of whom brought to college four years of official exposure to English but an inability to read, write, speak, or understand a standard English paragraph, I would feel that an investigation of Louisiana French, and of the English spoken in areas of French colonization, is still needed. I would feel the same for border Spanish and for the English of Southwest Texas, in spite of the valuable evidence in Mrs. Sawyer's study of San Antonio; in such cities as Miami, where two or more Spanish-speaking groups have settled in recent years, the problem is even more complicated. And though native speakers of German or Czech or Cherokee are not numerous statistically, an examination of Southern dialects of those languages, and of the English spoken by those groups, could teach us much about the problems of language contact.

Along with the study of Southern speech, English and otherwise, in its multifarious varieties, we should undertake studies of the other aspects of face-to-face communication, even though the exact description of their phenomena is yet to be worked out. We know that language signals alone are not enough; we often comment, "What he said was all right, but I didn't like the way he said it." The way a person says his message involves a number of modalities: *proxemics,* or spatial relationships, including the distance at which communication becomes possible; *haptics,* or matters of physical contact; *kinesics*, or gestures and other bodily movements;[16] *paralanguage*, or such modulations of the stream of speech as give unusually high or low pitch, unusual loudness or softness, drawl, clipping, nasality and rasp. And coming back closer to the essential phenomena of English, no one has yet worked out a systematic comparison of the way dialects differ in stress and pitch and transitions between syllables. Yet these differences are felt so intuitively in the South that by them one can often place an inhabitant of the Coastal Plain within a few miles of his home—even if, as with some clergymen and other public performers, he has taken pains to conceal his origins.

16. Ray L. Birdwhistell, *Introduction to Kinesics* (Louisville, Ky.: University of Louisville, 1954); Robert E. Pittenger, Charles F. Hockett, and John J. Danehy, *The First Five Minutes* (Ithaca, New York: The Martineau Press, 1960); William M. Austin, "Some Social Aspects of Paralanguage," *Canadian Journal of Linguistics*, XI (1965-66), 31-39.

Finally, we need studies of reactions to particular kinds of dialect differences. No region escapes petty ethnocentrism in this respect. A test administered to middle-class white Chicagoans discloses that they consistently interpret the speech of urban-reared white Southern college professors as that of rural uneducated Negroes: the educated Southerner has all the superficial characteristics that Chicagoans associate with Southern Negro speech, notably the loss of postvocalic /-r/ in *barn* and the like.[17] But to redress the balance, there are many Southern professional men who wonder why the educated Northerner sounds so much like the uneducated Southerners: here they are prejudiced because the strong postvocalic /-r/ associated with the Middle West is heard in the South most often from mountaineers, from textile workers, and from marginal farmers in the sand hills and pine barrens. Both reactions are visceral, rather than intellectual; sufficient publicity for both would help to break down the notion that one dialect is inherently better or worse than another, and would strengthen the American tradition of cultural pluralism, by which the best speech for a person to imitate is simply the educated speech of his own community.

It is clear that the amount of work to be done on Southern dialects—as indeed on the dialects of any American region—is staggering; but it is also clear that established methods make it possible for us to get very far toward our objectives if we could only have a modest amount of money and a few competent investigators in addition to those already available. The cost of the full set of projects here proposed would perhaps come to a million dollars; an intelligent application of the knowledge to be obtained could probably save that amount in one year in the city of Chicago alone.

17. See Lee Pederson, "The Pronunciation of English in Chicago: Consonants and Vowels," diss. (MS), University of Chicago, 1964.

Anthropology and the study of culture, society, and community in the South / J. Kenneth Morland

Anthropological studies of contemporary American culture, including its manifestation in the South, have been comparatively limited in number. A recent publication by the American Anthropological Association of a bibliography of 1,714 books and periodicals considered basic in the undergraduate teaching of anthropology lists only 40 volumes under contemporary North America, while it lists 179 under aboriginal North America, 80 under Oceania, 175 under Africa South of the Sahara, and 264 under Asia.[1] Although this list of basic books does not purport to be a general bibliography of anthropological writings, it is safe to say that it does reflect the far greater attention given by anthropologists to cultures other than that of the United States.

The relative neglect of the United States by anthropologists is understandable when it is remembered that the primary concern of cultural anthropologists has been the study of entire cultures. Consequently there has been a concentration on the description and analysis of the patterns of life in relatively small, isolated, slow-changing, homogeneous folk societies. United States society is so large and heterogeneous and its culture so varied and multi-faceted that to study them as entities has not been generally considered to be feasible. Also, cultural anthropologists have been busy studying as many folk societies as possible in order to have a broad enough basis to develop generalizations about the nature of culture. There has been a certain urgency in observing these varying ways of life before they are transformed by contact with Western urban societies and cultures. In utilizing folk societies as their "laboratories," anthropologists have developed methods of investigation particularly suited for the study of small, homogeneous, isolated groups practicing a common way of life. As a matter of training, most students of anthropology are sent out to live in and observe such remote societies in order, as Margaret Mead states, "to be exposed to ways of behavior quite different from our own, so different in fact that no effort of mind will work that simply redefines the new ways in terms of the known old ways."[2] Furthermore, sociologists have been concentrating on industrialized, urban societies and

1. David G. Mandelbaum, Gabriel W. Lasker, and Ethel M. Albert, eds., *Resources for the Teaching of Anthropology*, Memoir 95 of the American Anthropological Association, 1963.

2. *Male and Female* (New York: Morrow, 1949), p. 25.

have developed methods suitable for doing research on such large, heterogeneous populations. It might be said that a form of division of labor has emerged between anthropologists and sociologists in their study of human societies.[3]

Contributions of past studies

In developing generalizations about the nature of culture, anthropologists have increased the understanding of cultures and societies everywhere, including the United States. But the direct studies of American culture by anthropologists, although limited in number, have also made contributions in their own right. Let us look at some of these contributions, particularly in the studies made of the South. Of the forty books listed under contemporary North America by the editors of *Resources for the Teaching of Anthropology* some nine deal with the South, almost all of which are studies of small communities in the region. The first of these studies were carried out in the 1930's and include *Caste and Class in a Southern Town* by John Dollard,[4] *Deep South: A Social Anthropological Study of Caste and Class* by Allison Davis and the Gardners,[5] and *After Freedom: A Cultural Study of the Deep South* by Hortense Powdermaker.[6] A major contribution of these studies was to provide greater knowledge of American social structure, particularly of caste lines and of social classes within castes. By employing participant observation as the chief research method, the authors, particularly of *Deep South*, demonstrated variations in the perception of social classes by different strata in the society, thereby questioning whether or not a single, overall structure existed, or whether there were many "structures," depending on who was doing the viewing. A recent summary of research on social

3. It should be noted, however, that anthropological research has been utilized in dealing with problems of human relations in modern societies, especially through the Society for Applied Anthropology. The journal of the Society, *Human Organization*, has included articles on research in United States culture that deal with such practical problems as the mental health of factory workers, union-management relations, planned change in industry, the relation of American Indians to United States society and culture, and the role of physicians in hospitals.

4. New Haven: Yale University Press, 1937.

5. Chicago: University of Chicago Press, 1941. It is of interest to note that William Lloyd Warner directed this study. Warner's later findings on social class in America, derived largely from studies of communities in Massachusetts and Illinois, are of fundamental importance to the field.

6. New York: Viking Press, 1939. Powdermaker and Dollard studied the same Mississippi town.

class uses the findings of *Deep South* as an illustration of the "interactional concept" of social class, indicating the lasting value of the study.[7]

Another study in this period, *Children of Bondage: The Personality of Negro Youth in the Urban South*,[8] by Allison Davis and John Dollard, dealt with the relation of culture to personality development, showing how the caste system affected the personalities of Negro adolescents in two Southern cities. This study contributed to greater understanding of the impact of culture on behavior and personal development in the region.[9]

The next important group of anthropological studies of the South came in the late 1940's under the direction of John Gillin and through the Institute for Research in Social Science at the University of North Carolina. Five communities representative of different subcultures were chosen for study. They included a plantation community in the Alabama Black Belt, a Piedmont community in South Carolina where three different studies were made—of the "town," mill, and Negro sections—a piney woods community in Alabama, a mountain community in North Carolina, and a coastal fishing community in North Carolina.[10] Field workers entered each community to obtain an overall description of the way of life found there. They used participant observation as the chief data-collection technique, and supplemented this with interview schedules, available statistical data, Rorschach tests, and questionnaires. The researchers drew largely upon a theoretical framework of culture developed by Gillin,[11] and they were guided in the collection and organization of data by the Yale University Department of Anthropology *Outline of Cultural Materials*.[12] From a content analysis of these studies, Gillin, with the aid of Emmett J. Murphy, made a list of the distribution of some 198 traits characteristic of the region, thus giving a preliminary summary of the manifestations of American culture in the South.[13] Gillin also drew upon these studies in comparing the South with other regions of the United States

7. Thomas E. Lasswell, *Class and Stratum* (Boston: Houghton Mifflin, 1965), pp. 64-65.

8. Washington, D. C.: American Council on Education, 1940.

9. A follow-up study of these youth was made by J. H. Rohrer and M. S. Edmonson, *The Eighth Generation: Cultures and Personalities of New Orleans Negroes* (New York: Harper, 1960).

10. Three of these studies were published by the University of North Carolina Press: *Plantation County* by Morton Rubin, 1951; *Blackways of Kent* by Hylan Lewis, 1955; *Millways of Kent*, by John Kenneth Morland, 1958.

11. Contained, for the most part, in *The Ways of Men* (New York: Appleton, Century, Crofts, 1948).

12. New Haven: Yale University Press, 1945. A third revised edition appeared in 1950.

13. John Gillin and Emmett J. Murphy, "Notes on Southern Culture Patterns," *Social Forces*, XXIX (May, 1951), 422-432.

in regard to cultural values.[14] Values dominant in the nation as a whole were first summarized, and then the special emphases and special values for the various regions were discussed.

Numerous other uses of these field studies of the modern culture of the South have been made. For example, in gathering data for his *The Southerner and World Affairs*,[15] Alfred O. Hero, Jr. chose the Alabama Black Belt "Plantation County," and the South Carolina Piedmont town of "Kent" as two of the ten places in which he conducted interviews, largely because of the studies that had been done there by Gillin's students. Thomas E. Lasswell in his *Class and Stratum*[16] drew upon the two published studies of Kent in order to illustrate how social class could be viewed from cultural perspective. Robert Blauner utilized the study of Kent's mill-village sections in his research on factory workers in various industries, published as *Alienation and Freedom*.[17]

Another contribution to knowledge of the South, as well as to anthropological methodology, came with the employment of "event analysis" by Solon T. Kimball and Marion Pearsall in their research in Talladega, Alabama.[18] Kimball and Pearsall and their associates observed how the people of Talladega proceeded with the task of organizing and carrying out a community survey of health needs. From their observations they were able to delineate basic social and cultural characteristics of the community, including the types of influence, class divisions, roles of organizations, and the relationship of existing traditions and social conventions to the problem of carrying out the survey. Their study increased understanding of what is involved in social process, while revealing at the same time fundamental culture patterns of this Southern town.

Pearsall's study of an impoverished neighborhood in the Southern Appalachian Mountains[19] not only increased knowledge of the operation of culture under such conditions but also gave insight into what is involved in carrying out anti-poverty programs, now under way in that area. In her "natural history" framework, she viewed Little Smoky Ridge in relation to its physical surroundings, its internal structure, and the surrounding communities. She also dealt with factors promoting change.

So much for some of the past contributions of cultural anthropology

14. "National and Regional Cultural Values in the United States," *Social Forces*, XXXIV (Oct., 1955), 107-113.

15. Baton Rouge: Louisiana State University Press, 1965.

16. Boston: Houghton Mifflin, 1965.

17. Chicago: University of Chicago Press, 1964.

18. *The Talladega Story: A Study in Community Process* (University, Ala.: University of Alabama Press, 1954).

19. *Little Smoky Ridge: The Natural History of a Southern Appalachian Neighborhood* (University, Ala.: University of Alabama Press, 1959).

to an understanding of the culture traits, the social structure, the basic values, and personality development in the South. Where does the discipline go from here? What special contributions can it make to the Center for Southern Studies? Before discussing the "what," that is, the content of anthropological research in the South, it is necessary to deal directly with the "how," that is, with the research method. As has already been indicated, the matter of research method has been and continues to be a special problem for cultural anthropology in its study of United States society; and future contributions to the study of the South require further clarification of research procedures. Such clarification is not only important for the discipline itself, but it is also crucial to the kind of relationship anthropology develops with the other social sciences in the Center, particularly with sociology.

The problem of research method

The difficulties of applying anthropological research techniques to the study of heterogeneous, fast-changing urban society have been recognized from the time when anthropologists first began the task of studying culture, society, and community in the South. Both anthropologists and sociologists have raised questions about the suitability of participant observation and related techniques for studying entire communities in modern society. This is seen, for example, in the review of Hortense Powdermaker's *After Freedom* by Willard Waller in the *American Anthropologist:*

> Since anthropological techniques are here applied to a problem which has often been attacked by conventional sociological procedures, a question arises as to whether anything has been accomplished by the new procedure that has not already been done. As to this, the verdict must be inconclusive . . . . One cannot say how much of the merit of the book is due to the anthropological technique and how much to the skill of the writer in organizing and presenting materials. There is little in the book that is startlingly new; there is much that is thrown into new perspective, better interpreted, better said than before.[20]

Sociologists have expressed outright skepticism about anthropological attempts to obtain a summary view of an American community through participant observation. T. Lynn Smith, writing in the *American Sociological Review* about John Dollard's *Caste and Class in a Southern Town,* was strongly critical of what he saw as an attempt to make too many gen-

20. XLII (July-Sept., 1940), 504-505.

eralizations from too few facts.[21] Robert Schmid, also writing in the *American Sociological Review*, criticized *Deep South* by Davis and the Gardners in the following way:

> To this reviewer it seems unquestionable that the project bit off more than it could chew. "Old City," Mississippi is not just another collection of native huts on the banks of the river; it is a tremendously complex segment of a culture so vast that one wonders at the audacity of the four men and women who seek to comprehend it and indeed to generalize about it after mingling with the inhabitants and taking copious field notes for two years. There is a certain bravery in attempts like these, but in science as in war discretion is the better part of valor. In the long run social scientists will learn more from the modest pursuer of a single spoor, who sharpens his knives as he goes, than from the valorous fellow who hurries out with inadequate weapons to try to capture the whole wolf pack.[22]

No one has been more aware of the problems involved in trying to apply traditional anthropological research techniques to the study of American culture than have cultural anthropologists themselves. John Gillin has dealt explicitly with this matter on at least two occasions.[23] He has recognized the difficulties for anthropological research posed by large populations, large territory, heterogeneous customs brought about by culture contact and immigration, regional variations, the presence of many large and administratively complex organizations, and the rapid change that is a built-in feature of modern civilizations. At the same time he feels that these difficulties have been exaggerated and certain advantages overlooked. Gillin argues that anthropological methodology can be successfully applied to modern civilizations if there are sufficient funds, enough trained research personnel, and the co-operation of anthropologists with specialists in the other sciences concerned with human behavior. However, he recognizes that in the study of modern cultures the anthropologist has to give up the traditional practice of personally investigating and learning all aspects of the way of life in a community. Rather, he will have to rely on materials provided by scholars in other areas and interpret them in terms of their function and integration in the particular setting. Gillin's emphasis on the necessity for the co-operation of disciplines in the study of modern communities has special relevance for the Center for Southern Studies.

21. II (Oct., 1937), 796-797.
22. VII (April, 1942), 263.
23. "Methodological Problems in the Anthropological Study of Modern Cultures," *American Anthropologist*, LI (July-Sept., 1949), 392-399; "The Application of Anthropological Knowledge to Modern Mass Society: An Anthropologist's View," *Human Organization*, XV, No. 4 (Winter, 1957), 24-29.

Kimball, like Gillin, sees the major problems in the anthropological study of American culture to be the magnitude and variability of American life.[24] Such problems have no comparability in tribal studies or even in studies of predominantly agrarian societies. Kimball acknowledges the need for anthropologists to modify their sampling techniques in working in modern cultures, but he also recognizes the dilemma that arises in utilizing statistical procedures. While increasing the reliability and validity of generalizations, such procedures negate the basic approach that cultural anthropology has employed and through which it has made its main contribution, namely, the method of studying human behavior directly in its actual setting, rather than in terms of statistical abstraction. He believes that a technique compatible with the naturalistic approach and one that can serve as an alternative to statistical abstraction is "event analysis," discussed earlier in this essay. He points out that event analysis has been used in the study of group activity in small, isolated societies and in small-group behavior research in modern society. He believes that it can likewise be utilized in the study of American communities to find the interconnections of behavior in a specific environmental setting. He and Pearsall conclude their argument for the use of event analysis as a means of studying communities in the following way:

> It is our experience that event analysis may be combined with taxonomic principles as an effective and efficient method for delineating both small and large social systems and their interrelationships within community. We were fortunate in having an event of community-wide importance [the community health survey in Talladega] as the focus of our observation. However, there is every reason to believe all on-going events, irrespective of the magnitude of relationships or depth of values affected, are amenable to this type of analysis. In fact, the future development of this approach should permit social scientists to build a typology of events and equations of process as a basis of community characterization. This could well represent a long step forward in our knowledge of community.[25]

Arensberg has pointed out methodological difficulties in studying modern communities in this way:

> It is nowhere really clear what a community is, in size, organization or other characters, or how the relationship between community, culture, and larger society is to be treated. That the method should

24. Solon T. Kimball, "Problems of Studying American Culture," *American Anthropologist*, LVII (Dec., 1955), 1131-1142.

25. Solon T. Kimball and Marion Pearsall, "Event Analysis as an Approach to Community Study," *Social Forces*, XXXIV (Oct., 1955), 63.

> run into problems as it develops is no surprise, of course . . . there seems to be general agreement that what is needed is a better unification of concepts and a better building of models.[26]

Arensberg himself has moved to deal with these difficulties in a discussion of the community as an object of study in itself and as a sample of something larger than itself.[27] He suggests ways to determine how "representative," how "complete," how "inclusive," and how "cohesive" a community is. The basis for determining these characteristics is what Arensberg calls "the table of organization" or the personnel that incorporate the major demographic variations of the culture. Specifically,

> If the culture knows two sexes, several ages, several classes, several sects, several ethnic groups, including majority and minority ones, several or many professional or full-time specializations, of occupation or technical and economic function, then the community we choose must have some at least of all these people, enough to man at least minimally their roles and statuses.[28]

There must also be, according to Arensberg, a "temporal" dimension, in that the table of organization has personnel giving "a continuity in depth, uniting the lives of the people of the table, repeating or reiterating, in the main, their experience from generation to generation."[29]

Anthropologists who have studied American culture have been acutely aware of the problems involved in sampling. They feel that misunderstandings have arisen from anthropological methods of establishing generalizations about a culture or a society or a community. Thus, Margaret Mead states that anthropological sampling is not a poor imitation of sociological sampling; rather, it is a different kind of sampling.[30] She points out that the validity of the sampling depends not so much on the number of cases as on the specification of each case in terms of a large number of relevant variables, like sex, age, and family background. Within such specification each case becomes "a perfect example, an organic representation of his complete cultural experience."[31] She compares this procedure with that in medicine in which numerous measurements are made on a small number of cases. Mead further argues that the anthropologist is

26. Conrad M. Arensberg, "The Community-Study Method," *American Journal of Sociology,* LX (Sept., 1954), 121.

27. "The Community as Object and Sample," *American Anthropologist,* LXIII (April, 1961), 241-264.

28. *Ibid.,* p. 255.

29. *Ibid.,* p. 256.

30. Margaret Mead, "National Character," in *Anthropology Today: An Encyclopedic Inventory,* prepared under the chairmanship of A. L. Kroeber (Chicago: University of Chicago Press, 1953), pp. 642-667.

31. *Ibid.,* p. 655.

interested in the delineation of patterns in a way that is different from that of the sociologist. The anthropologist is looking for basic aspects of the structure of a culture; the sociologist for the distribution of the behavior involved in that structure. In dealing with cultures, according to Mead, the anthropologist makes the assumption that he is dealing with a system which can be delineated by an analysis of a small number of very highly specified examples. She states that this is what the linguist does in the study of a language. A pattern, says Mead, is not established by asking "how much" but rather by examining enough specified cases to find out when consistency begins to appear. This is different from the social survey which is designed to establish exact proportions.

David Mandelbaum questions whether Mead's analogy to linguistics is appropriate for aspects of culture that are less "compulsive" or "imperative," since the function of communication is overriding in language and does not allow for much variation.[32] While such restricted patterns are important to describe, he argues, there are other patterns with greater variability. The extent of such variation can be ascertained only through sampling that is representative of the population in question. Thus, according to Mandelbaum, the measurement of consistency in behavior (i.e., the establishing of patterns), and the ascertaining of how much variation are not two independent operations but rather are related steps in a single research operation. The only way to be sure that observations constitute a valid pattern is to test to find out if it recurs under a range of various kinds of observation. "Unless the range and incidence of occurrence is ascertained, the perception and formulation of pattern is left as a potentially useful notion rather than as a verified and documented datum."[33]

These discussions of the problems of research method give directions anthropology can take in the study of culture, society, and community in the South. Combining points made by Gillin and Mandelbaum, we can arrive at the first guiding principle, namely, the necessity for the co-operation of cultural anthropologists with those in other disciplines. Gillin has long advocated this, pointing out that the practice of the lone participant observer absorbing the way of life of a community must be surrendered in modern civilization and that the anthropologist must co-ordinate his efforts with those of other social scientists. Mandelbaum implies the same thing when he speaks of the necessity of delineating patterns as a first step and of measuring the extent of variability as a second. At least this co-op-

32. David G. Mandelbaum, "On the Study of National Character," *American Anthropologist*, LV (April-June, 1953), 174-187.
33. *Ibid.*, p. 183.

eration seems to be called for in the study of large urban societies. Anthropologists would have as their chief task the delineation of consistencies or patterns of behavior, while those in other disciplines, especially sociology, would utilize careful sampling as a means of noting variability and of testing the validity of patterns. This sort of co-operation between cultural anthropology and sociology, especially, is very much needed to delineate more fully the basic characteristics of culture in the South. Such co-operation is long overdue, in the author's opinion. Therefore, it is disturbing to hear of new moves that act to separate cultural anthropology from other disciplines rather than to promote needed co-operative, coordinated efforts. For example, a recent New York *Times* article announced that New York University has established a Department of Urban Anthropology.[34] The announcement pointed out that the new department would use New York City as a laboratory to study man in urban societies. "Unlike sociology," according to the announcement, "which is concerned with a descriptive and statistical analysis of society, anthropology centers on man in his environment. It attempts to determine how environment—physical, social, and linguistic—affects his development as a human being and his mobility or, more frequently, his immobility."[35] The article acknowledged that anthropologists had traditionally devoted themselves to the study of small, remote societies and had paid little attention to the cities. However, since more and more people are living in cities, and since small, remote societies are being urbanized, anthropologists are turning their attention to the study of urban problems. Anthropology can make a unique contribution to the study of urban problems, as will be pointed out in a moment; however, in the author's opinion, it can make this contribution most effectively in co-operation with other disciplines, especially sociology. Such co-operation can avoid proliferation of effort and assure depth of study, and the Center for Southern Studies can help to make this possible in research on the South.

A second guiding principle that emerges from the discussion of the application of anthropological method to the study of the modern South concerns the unique contribution cultural anthropology can make. While anthropologists may differ about certain aspects of method such as sampling, they are in agreement that fundamental in the anthropological approach is the study of human behavior in its natural setting, a study of behavior "in the round." Arensberg, in reference to anthropological studies of communities, has stated it in this way: "It [community study] is the study of human behavior *in* communities; that is, in the natural contexts

34. New York *Times*, March 11, 1966, p. 29M.
35. *Ibid.*

made up of natural and full human cooperative living, of living intergenerational and intersexual relationships, of ongoing cultural and interfamilial communication and transmission."[36] He calls this method the study of behavior and attitudes "in vivo" through observation and comparison, as opposed to study "in vitro" by means of isolation and statistical abstraction. There is, of course, no claim that anthropology alone uses the techniques of observation and comparison; rather these are focal points in anthropological method, providing an overview of the cultural setting and stressing the relationship of one aspect of the culture to another.

The studies of the South Carolina Piedmont town of Kent illustrate in a limited way how co-operative–co-ordinated, "in vivo" research may be carried out. The initial studies were made by cultural anthropologists who delineated the chief patterns of community life as found in its three major social and geographical divisions of town, mill, and Negro. Then came specialists in psychological testing and child development who worked with those doing the basic research to make studies of manifest personality traits and child-rearing practices, utilizing a random sample of respondents.[37] Ten years after the initial studies, a follow-up study was made of the mill-village sections of Kent to determine the extent of change in certain aspects of village life and to compare the occupational and educational aspirations of town and mill children.[38] These special studies provided statistical measures of variability in the patterns, and they could then be interpreted in terms of the culture patterns of the community. The initial participant-observation studies gave a foundation for the more specialized studies, which in turn gave additional meaning to the culture patterns. Greater depth of understanding of the community could have been gained if additional co-ordinated studies had been made by other social scientists, including those in economics, education, political science, and religion. Again, the Center can provide for such co-ordination of research.

There could well emerge from anthropological concentration on the culture patterns and variations in the South an area specialty in the field

36. "The Community-Study Method," p. 120.

37. Results of the child-rearing study of a sample of mill-village mothers were not only drawn upon in the writing of *Millways of Kent* but are also reported separately in Barbara Chartier, "Weaverton: A Study of Culture and Personality in a Southern Mill Town" (unpublished M.A. thesis, University of North Carolina, 1949).

38. Published as J. K. Morland, "Educational and Occupational Aspirations of Mill and Town School Children in a Southern Community," *Social Forces*, XXXIX (Dec., 1960), 169-175; and J. K. Morland, "Kent Revisited: Blue-Collar Aspirations and Achievements," in A. B. Shostak and William Gomberg, eds., *Blue-Collar World* (Englewood Cliffs, N. J.: Prentice-Hall, 1964), pp. 134-143.

of anthropology. Just as there are anthropologists who specialize in the cultures of Pueblo Indians, Plains Indians, Melanesians, Australian Bushmen, and the like, there could also be those who specialize in the South as a regional variation of United States culture.[39] Such a specialist would not only acquire detailed knowledge of behavior patterns in the region but would also utilize a methodology that could enable co-operative and coordinated research to be carried out with those in other disciplines.

Periodical studies of selected communities

Since the fundamental contribution of anthropological studies to furthering understanding of the region lies in studies "in vivo," it is to be assumed that these studies will be made of particular groups of people in particular settings. This assumption means that research will be carried out in selected Southern communities or sections of communities when such sections are distinctive. Therefore several communities in the South can be chosen for intensive, periodical study, with each study in a community utilizing and building upon preceding ones. Initial or base-line studies can delineate the chief patterns of behavior, while subsequent studies can measure specific aspects of behavior in greater depth.

The advantages of a series of studies of the same community are many. Such studies afford the opportunity to relate all sorts of behavior to the natural setting; they provide for the checking of the accuracy of previous research and interpretations; and they make possible the measurement of change. There are, at the same time, risks involved in studying the same communities over a period of time. The studies themselves might affect the responses of the members of the community in subsequent research. Also, publications about the community might hamper later studies. For example, the unfavorable reaction of some members of the community of "Springdale" in New York to the depiction of their town in *Small Town in Mass Society* shows how difficult a follow-up study of that community would be.[40] At the same time, one is reminded that the initial reactions to the Lynds' *Middletown*[41] by citizens of that city were mixed, but that when the research staff returned to make a follow-up study the city was

39. The name of "Southernist" for such a specialty has been suggested by Edgar Thompson of Duke University.

40. The book was written by Arthur J. Vidich and Joseph Bensman (Princeton, N. J.: Princeton University Press, 1958). Some of the reactions are discussed in an editorial, "Freedom and Responsibility in Research: The Springdale Case," *Human Organization*, XVII, No. 2 (Summer, 1958), 1-2.

41. Robert S. Lynd and Helen Merrell Lynd, *Middletown: A Study in Contemporary American Culture* (New York: Harcourt, Brace, 1929).

found to be "friendly and cordial, with perhaps just a note of caution,"[42] and the necessary co-operation was given to make this second study possible. These incidents suggest that the proposed periodical studies call for the exercising of great care by the researchers, both in their relations with the community and in the handling of their publications, to make repeated visits possible.

Just how many communities can be studied depends on the factors that Gillin has mentioned, as cited above, namely the availability of funds, the number of anthropologists willing to enter such research, and the co-operation of other disciplines in joint undertakings with anthropologists. The more communities that can be studied, the more valid will be the generalizations to the entire South, provided these communities are "representative." Also, the more communities selected, the greater the number of comparative studies that can be made of various parts of the South. In the selection of the communities, criteria similar to those used by Gillin might be employed.[43] Indeed, some of the same communities might be chosen. Kent, with its three-way investigation of town, mill, and Negro sections already recorded, offers a good possibility. So does the Mississippi community studied by both Dollard and Powdermaker. In the selection, as well as in the studies of behavior in the community, Arensberg's "table of organization" could be used to help assure representativeness. But just how "typical" of the South the selected communities are need not be of major concern. All human beings studied in their natural setting reflect general principles of behavior and can add to our knowledge of human behavior in general and of behavior in the South in particular.

As has been indicated, the first step in the study of these selected communities would be the delineation of the chief patterns of behavior, belief, and attitudes. Such study would involve ascertaining class lines and salient characteristics of family, economic, political, religious, educational, and leisure-time practices. The Yale *Outline of Cultural Materials* and the Arensberg outline, "Gathering and Analyzing Data for Community Studies,"[44] could serve as guides for the content of base-line studies. Event analysis could be employed as a means of further clarifying the social structure and behavioral patterns. Of course the carrying out of base-line studies is itself an ambitious undertaking requiring considerable effort, time, and expense, as the series of studies directed by Gillin proved. Also, these studies have been criticized as having no particular focus, as not being

42. Robert S. Lynd and Helen Merrell Lynd, *Middletown in Transition: A Study in Cultural Conflicts* (New York: Harcourt, Brace, 1937), p. xiii.
43. Described in Gillin and Murphy, *op. cit.*, p. 422.
44. "The Community-Study Method," pp. 115-118.

guided by a theoretical problem.[45] However, it is difficult to see how studies of specific aspects of behavior in the community could be made and related to other aspects from an anthropological, "in vivo" perspective unless the salient aspects of the culture were known. Otherwise we deal with "bits and pieces of behavior" as statistical abstractions without reference to their natural setting. Perhaps base-line research could be carried out at the same time that a specific problem was being studied, but, in any event, a base-line study should be made. Also one is reminded that the largely descriptive studies made by cultural anthropologists in the South have found wide utility in illustrating cultural perspective on social class, in showing how caste-like lines operate, and in strengthening theories of "alienation" among factory workers. Finally, base-line studies might seem to conflict with the contention of Arensberg that anthropological community study is not the study of *entire* communities but rather the study of behavior *in* communities.[46] He emphasizes that community study is a method, a "tool of science," not a "subject matter." However, Arensberg states that as a method, community study uses the community as "a setting for the exploration, discovery, or verification of interconnections among social and psychological facts and processes."[47] Since the setting is composed of the interrelated patterns of behavior in the community, it is to be assumed from the viewpoint of this writer that the patterns must be delineated, either in a separate study, or as an initial part of a study of a specific aspect of behavior in the community.

Suggested specific research undertakings

In addition to the base-line studies already suggested, there are many other possibilities for anthropological research in the selected Southern communities. The research topics mentioned in this section of the essay are offered as suggestions and are presented largely through raising questions; no organized program is proposed. Since it has been stressed that anthropological research should be carried out co-operatively with people in other disciplines, it is understood that those who co-operate will have a part in determining the selection and formulation of research projects. The following, then, are meant to be illustrative of the possibilities, an exploration of some of the things that might be done.

The sorts of research undertakings suggested, as will be seen, include

45. See, for example, Gerhard Lenski's review of *Millways of Kent* in the *American Journal of Sociology*, LXIV (May, 1959), 645.
46. "The Community-Study Method," pp. 110, 120.
47. *Ibid.*, p. 110.

those of both a theoretical and a practical nature. The study of the South as a region can be carried out with the aim of furthering theory or of contributing to the solution of practical problems or of doing both. It is assumed by the writer that the fundamental task of cultural anthropology is to develop sound theory about the nature of culture—how it varies, how it changes, how it unites a society, and how it affects personality development. The South offers a laboratory in which theories of culture can be tested. At the same time, anthropological study of the South can be devoted to the solution of non-theoretical problems, and in a sense the setting up of a Center for Southern Studies implies that problems peculiar to the South, that is, practical problems, are among those to be studied. Theoretical and practical problems are not unrelated, for soundly based theory is of crucial importance in the solution of practical problems, while the study of practical problems can lead to hypotheses and thereby stimulate further research to develop and test theory.

Southern values. All anthropological studies of communities, including the base-line studies mentioned above, would reveal some aspect of shared values. It can be assumed that no group could hold together without basic agreement on what is considered to be of worth—in terms of objects ("value entities"); or of personal traits ("character values"); or of forms of institutions, like monogamous marriage or political democracy ("dominant values"); or of recurrent, underlying emphases that characterize the institutions ("value themes").[48] Such agreement is necessary for effective co-operative effort and for similarity of outlook and interpretation. While there is some disagreement among anthropologists as to whether or not the anthropologist himself makes value judgments in his work, there is no disagreement that values as a field of study are a legitimate part of anthropology.[49] This point of agreement is the basis for the research suggestions offered here.

Gillin's articles on Southern culture patterns and on national and regional cultural values, referred to earlier, can be used as a starting point. He laid down what he called "a tentative check list" of traits and values that could serve to stimulate further research. The values he lists as those

48. A classification of values has not been "standardized" in anthropology. The one used here relies heavily on that given by Ethel Albert, "The Classification of Values: A Method and Illustration," *American Anthropologist*, LVIII (April, 1956), 221-248.

49. See, for example, "Values in Action: A Symposium," *Human Organization*, XVII, No. 1 (Spring, 1958), 2-33. Illustrations of differences in views come from statements by Robert Redfield that "anthropologists do in fact draw value deductions from their science—even when they claim the impossibility of doing so," and by Conrad Arensberg that "morals and values, *unless one is examining other people's as third party neutral observer*, are inseparable from sentiments and emotions," and are therefore not subject to scientific validation or invalidation.

emphasized in the Southeast and the values that are suggested as special to the region could be checked in each of the communities, and comparisons made and related to differences between communities.

Gillin mentions the emphasis in the South on freedom for the individual from "non-Southern" interference. He also notes a special value of "regional cultural chauvinism," which is expressed in the attitude that the South can solve its problems if "outsiders" will not interfere. Related to this is the notion that the South is different, with a way of life uniquely fitted to it, and that this way of life should remain as it is. Research could be carried out to discover how prevalent this value emphasis is in the selected communities and how it is related to feelings and actions toward, for example, the federal government. Funds for urban renewal, teacher institutes sponsored by the United States Office of Education, and federal aid to education are being rejected in some communities for fear of what is termed "federal control." Research in this area of values could also help to throw light on feelings and behavior toward unionization, particularly opposition to unionization.

Gillin points out the special emphasis in the South on family relations, including the extended kinship grouping. It was clear in the study of the mill-village sections of Kent that kinship ties were a basic factor in the unity of the sections and that loyalty to kin was fundamental in promoting security and a feeling of belonging. Research could relate this value emphasis to values that are promoted in religion, economics, and politics, and in the status and power systems. It would also be instructive to explore the relation of the emphasis on individualistic values to what Gillin terms "Protestant morality."

Sociocultural change in the South. The South might be characterized as a formerly distinctive region that is fast losing its distinctiveness. It has been different from other American regions in its caste-like system of race relations, its agriculturally based economy and its relatively slow industrialization and urbanization, its fundamentalistic religion, and its feeling of separateness from the rest of the nation. All of these characteristics are probably being altered as culture traits and patterns throughout America become more similar. Many social forces are contributing to what can be called greater standardization of culture in United States society. The Civil Rights Acts of 1964 and 1965 are culminations of the moves toward the elimination of legally sanctioned racial segregation; thus they spell the end to the South's traditional handling of the relations between the races. The 1960 census revealed that for the first time in census history more Southerners were living in urban than in rural areas. Industrialization has increased rapidly while agriculture has declined. Rapid transportation and extensive migration are breaking down the separateness of the region. Standardization from mass production and mass communication has meant that Southerners are using, seeing, reading, and hearing the same things as all other Americans. The South, therefore, offers an excellent setting for observing change and testing theories of change. It also provides an opportunity for studying stability and continuity amid change, for the Southern values mentioned earlier are likely to continue for some time, although modified in form. Numerous questions regarding change could be raised and studied in the selected communities.

There are questions related to the consequences of the expansion of industry. What happens to high-status families when new industry enters a community? Do these established families help to bring in new industry, or do they oppose it? What conditions are associated with support or with opposition? Does the new industry and the "outside" personnel it frequently brings present a challenge to the existing attitudes and beliefs? Do the established families take the newcomers into their churches, their clubs, their social circles? Or do the newcomers develop parallel and separate organizations and social lines? What factors in the several communities are associated with variations in how newcomers are treated? There are Southern communities, like Kent, in which these matters could be studied historically. There are other communities, like Lynchburg, Virginia, into which two large industries, along with highly educated managerial staffs, have recently moved, in which these issues could be studied currently.

Another area of change concerns what is happening to the pattern of race relations under the impact of federal legislation, industrialization, standardization, and mobility. Every community in the South now offers ongoing situations in which the speed of desegregation and alterations in racial attitudes can be ascertained and related to culture patterns in the community and to outside forces. Has *de jure* segregation been replaced by *de facto* segregation? How extensive has integration become in schools, in housing, in churches, in clubs? What factors appear to be associated with the rate of integration? Is there support for the hypothesis that the elimination of racial segregation is a necessary condition for the reduction of racial prejudice?

What happens to political attitudes and behavior as such changes as reapportionment and the removal of restrictions on voter registration take place? Do office-seekers change their approach? Is there a change in the outlook of those who have been politically inactive? Most Southern communities have experienced drives to register Negro voters. These drives and their effects could be studied and related to any alterations in political campaigns, the organization of local political parties, and legislation enacted in the community. In some communities and counties in the Deep South there are now more registered Negro than white voters. What happens politically under these circumstances? What happens to race relations?

Urbanization tends to bring with it a secularization of belief in which reason plays a greater part in outlook and behavior and tradition plays a lesser part. Does this tendency hold in communities where unquestioned religious traditionalism is strong? Anthropologists could join with sociologists and those in the field of religion to see whether modifications in belief occur among traditionalists in the community, whether sermons and church-school teaching are modified, whether the status and role of ministers change. There are challenges to religious traditionalism in mass media and mass education. Do these challenges penetrate to the communities being studied? If so, how are they handled? The Kent mill-village sections, for example, would provide a fertile field in which to look for these types of change. The author found that religion in the villages was highly traditionalistic and characterized by a literal belief in the Bible. As new ideas and new people come, are these traditional ideas modified or are the new ideas rejected? What factors are associated with modification or with rejection?

What happens to family unity and kinship ties, mentioned earlier as having great strength in the South? What sorts of modifications occur in the security that the extended kindred group has given in the past? How much mutual help among kin remains? How significant are family lines in status and prestige under the impact of change? And what happens to the racial caste line so far as marriage is concerned? Does it hold firm amid other changes? Are social class lines within races crossed, or do these lines continue to regulate marriage?

Finally, what changes occur in the forms of recreation and the beliefs about what is proper recreation under the impact of industrialization? Gillin speaks of the special emphasis in the Southeast on "non-commercial recreations of the 'folk' type."[50] What happens to this emphasis as communities become more urbanized? How are changes in recreational pursuits related to changes in religion, which in the Kent mill-village sections rigidly regulated what church members could do in their leisure time? As the communities change, is time away from the job looked upon as a chance for self-improvement and advancement or as a time for enjoyment? Does the drive to get ahead increase in a community that is becoming more industrial?

50. "National and Regional Cultural Values in the United States," p. 112.

Cultural transmission. The continuation of a culture or subculture is dependent upon passing on established customs and attitudes to the young. Studies of how "Southern" ways are passed on, even as they are being altered, can contribute to theories of learning and personality development. Knowledge derived from such studies can also be of practical use, especially in the area of education.

One aspect of cultural transmission that might be studied concerns the learning experience of migrants to the South from other regions. We spoke earlier of persons from other parts of the United States brought in by new industry to fill managerial positions. How much modification of ideas occurs among these persons? How much of the Southern way of life is transmitted to them and especially to their children? How much do those from other regions transmit ideas and behavior that are different from those found in the South? It has been claimed that a number of migrants from other regions become more "Southern" in their views than Southerners themselves. Is this actually the case? What does take place, and how?

What is the learning experience of those in the communities who might be termed "culturally disadvantaged"?[51] These "disadvantaged" are so designated because they are not prepared to compete successfully in school and consequently for the better jobs. Their school drop-out rate is high, and they end up in low-status, low-paying jobs or among the chronically unemployed. Studying disadvantaged children in their natural setting would lead to a clearer understanding of environmental forces and their consequences. Behavior can be related to attitudes inculcated and rewards received. Since the disadvantaged are the object of numerous government programs, including the Headstart Program, the Upward Bound Program, the Job Corps, and others, further understanding of the cultural transmission involved in what the disadvantaged learn can be of practical help to those involved in these programs. Attempts to change the behavior and outlook of these children so that they will succeed in school and in jobs must start with an understanding of where these children are and what motivates them.

A third area in which cultural transmission in the communities could be studied would be the area of how notions of race and the significance attached to race differences are learned. Research shows that both Negro and white children in the South, at very young ages, learn to prefer and to identify with whites, and that white children learn to make correct racial

51. The term "culturally deprived" has sometimes been used instead of culturally disadvantaged, for example, in Frank Riesman's *The Culturally Deprived Child* (New York: Harper, 1962). However, anthropologically speaking, these children are not "deprived" of culture; rather, the culture patterns they have learned are not those that help them to succeed according to dominant standards.

recognition at an earlier age than Negroes.[52] Furthermore, preference and identification have been found to be unrelated to the ability of very young children to recognize race differences, which suggests that ideas about race are "absorbed" from the cultural setting before racial designations can be verbalized. Theoretical contributions of such research can lead to further understanding of how children acquire concepts of many sorts. Practical contributions can be made to those whose job it is to help young children develop self-acceptance and consequent achievement in terms of their ability.[53]

Educational programs. Knowledge gained from cultural transmission can be utilized in co-operation with those in the field of education to examine aspects of the school program in the communities under study. The Center can provide much-needed exchange between cultural anthropologists and educators. The field of the anthropology of education is a rapidly developing one,[54] and co-ordinated studies in the South can contribute to its development.

A number of questions can be pursued in this area. To begin, how closely related is IQ testing to the actual experience of the children under study? How accurately does the testing show the potential of children as compared to what they learn in their family and community setting? The author found, for example, that mill children learned and were skilled in a number of things not considered by tests given in school. They learned a great deal about playing mill-village games, about hunting and fishing, about ways to become "saved" at revival meetings, about living in a small and crowded home, about the work-shifts at the mill, about obligations to family and kin, and about other matters with which they had to deal each day. Can tests of what is learned in coping with actual surroundings be made in order to reveal more clearly the ability to learn?

What relationship does the use of achievement tests and standardized tests have to the motivation and self-concept of children in the selected

52. H. W. Stevenson and E. C. Stewart, "A Developmental Study of Racial Awareness in Young Children," *Child Development*, XXIX (1958), 399-409; J. K. Morland, "Racial Recognition by Nursery School Children in Lynchburg, Va.," *Social Forces*, XXXVII (Dec., 1958), 132-137; J. K. Morland, "Racial Acceptance and Preference of Nursery School Children in a Southern City," *Merrill-Palmer Quarterly*, VIII (Oct., 1962), 271-280; J. K. Morland, "Racial Self-Identification: A Study of Nursery School Children," *American Catholic Sociological Review*, XXIV (Fall, 1963), 231-242.

53. Wilbur Brookover and David Gottlieb, *A Sociology of Education*, revised ed. (New York: American Book Co., 1964), pp. 468-480, cite evidence to show that self-concept of ability is a significant variable in the learning process.

54. Helpful volumes in this area include: George D. Spindler, ed., *Education and Anthropology* (Stanford, Calif.: Stanford University Press, 1955); Theodore Brameld, *Cultural Foundations of Education* (New York: Harper, 1957); and George Kneller, *Educational Anthropology* (New York: John Wiley, 1965).

communities? Studies in the Southern communities could be related to the series of studies being carried out under the auspices of the Russell Sage Foundation to measure the social consequences of standardized intelligence, aptitude, and achievement testing in the United States.[55] The treatment in depth of the social consequences of ability testing in particular community settings could provide case studies that would illustrate and check the broader generalizations of the Russell Sage series.

What ideas about culture and race are held by school teachers in the communities, and what transmission about these concepts is made to pupils? Anthropologists have developed a large body of knowledge about culture and race and are especially suited to work with those in education in these areas. What kind of direct teaching about the nature of culture and of race can be effective with children in these Southern communities? The introduction of scientific notions about culture and about race, particularly, would be difficult at pre-college levels because of social, political, and religious attitudes. However, as the anthropology of education develops and as traditional Southern views are modified, such teaching might become more feasible.

Conclusion

In conclusion, then, cultural anthropological studies of the South can yield knowledge about the region that can contribute to the development of the theory of culture and to greater understanding of practical problems. Studying the behavior of Southerners in the natural setting of communities can provide a dimension of comprehension that is required for full, rounded knowledge of what the South is like and where it is headed. While it is granted that cultural anthropologists face special difficulties in applying techniques for studying behavior "in vivo" in comparatively large, mobile communities which are parts of a highly complex society and culture, these difficulties are surmountable. Part of the solution lies in the co-operation of cultural anthropology with other disciplines. The Center for Southern Studies can provide the opportunity for such co-operative, co-ordinated studies of Southern life.

55. This series of studies, under the direction of Orville G. Brim, Jr., David A. Goslin, and David C. Glass, has support from the Carnegie Corporation of New York and the United States Office of Education, as well as the Russell Sage Foundation. One of the publications in the series is *The Search for Ability: Standardized Testing in Social Perspective* by David A. Goslin (New York: Russell Sage Foundation, 1963). Altogether, six volumes are projected for publication by 1968.

Research potential in Southern folklore / Edwin C. Kirkland

The folklore of the South has been collected and studied as a distinct and separate subject since the beginning of the present century; but long before 1900 creative writers and artists used folk ways, and such disciplines as anthropology and sociology gave a part of their study to folklore. Although much has been done in folklore research, much remains to be investigated in practically all geographical areas, in various types of folklore, various ethnic groups, and in particular professions and occupations. Now scholars have the option of approaching this study and research from a number of different points of view, such as those of anthropology, sociology, literature, art, musicology, linguistics, folklore, and perhaps others. Co-operative efforts are needed from all of these and other fields, rather than efforts that are entirely and forever isolated from all others.

Folk literature and folklore in the works of literary authors have been the object of some research, but the potentialities for further research are almost limitless. Such scholars as Francis James Child and Francis B. Gummere have recognized the literary quality of certain folklore genres and have made provocative comments such as the following:

> The great poems of the world are far greater than the greatest [folk] ballads; but no poet has ever had the power to compete with popular tradition on its own ground. Art can create far beyond the beauty of sea-shells, and on occasion can exactly reproduce them; but it cannot fashion or imitate their murmur of the sea.[1]

What are these qualities which Gummere has reference to? The aesthetic and literary qualities of the folksong and other folk literature, such as the folktale, proverb, riddle, and rhyme, need to be studied and co-ordinated with the findings of research on these types in non-folk literature. Practically no studies of this kind have been made, although they are urgently needed and would be most valuable for the understanding and appreciation of folk literature. Conflict—dramatic conflict—is an important and essential part of great drama and much narrative literature, and it is present in folk literature. Conflict in all kinds of folk narratives, ballads, tales, etc., could be profitably examined to determine how it is present in folk literature and how it is similar to, or different from, conflict in non-folk literature. "Sir Patrick Spens" has been found in the oral

1. Francis B. Gummere, *The Popular Ballad* (New York: Dover, 1959), p. 321.

tradition in America only twice, once in Virginia[2] and once in Tennessee.[3] Sir Patrick Spens has a conflict within himself. Shall he be loyal and obedient to the orders of the king, or shall he be loyal to the sailors on his ship and save them from almost certain disaster? Is this old ballad a tragedy in the same way that a great literary drama is tragic because the protagonist cannot resolve the conflict but is engulfed by it? What other literary techniques and characteristics are found in folk literature? How are they presented and developed, particularly in comparison to their use in non-folk literature? A vast area lies open for investigation which should throw light on both folk and non-folk literature.

Folklore in the works of literary authors has been the subject of considerable research; for example, ancient myths in Faulkner have been studied,[4] and folklore in Joel Chandler Harris,[5] Mark Twain,[6] and Jesse Stuart.[7] This area is the happy hunting ground for those looking for subjects for masters' theses or doctoral dissertations; however, the area is still wide open for sound research. None of the following authors has been completely studied for the use of folklore; some have not been considered at all: William Gilmore Simms, Edgar Allan Poe, Thomas Wolfe, Marjorie Kinnan Rawlings, Julia Peterkin, Ambrose Gonzales, George Washington Harris,[8] Irwin Russell, Elizabeth Madox Roberts, Robert Penn Warren, Harper Lee, Mary Justus, Andrew Lytle, and Mildred Haun. The mere mention of the names of these Southern authors or writers on Southern life immediately calls attention to the vast amount of folklore in their works.

Art history has largely neglected folk art in the South, although it has been extensively studied for some countries. Musicologists have done little on the technicalities of folk music in the South, although such outstanding musicologists as George Herzog, Allan Seeger, and Sam Bayard have made significant contributions to areas outside the South. George Pullen Jackson, in numerous books on the Sacred Harp and the white spirituals, covered rather extensively some of the phases of this folk

2. John Powell, "In the Lowlands Low," *Southern Folklore Quarterly*, I (March, 1937), 1-12.

3. Edwin C. Kirkland, " 'Sir Patrick Spens' Found in Knoxville, Tennessee," *Southern Folklore Quarterly*, I (Dec., 1937), 1-2.

4. Lennart Björk, "Ancient Myths and the Moral Framework of Faulkner's *Absalom, Absalom!*," *American Literature*, XXXV (May, 1963), 196-204.

5. Stella Brewer Brookes, *Joel Chandler Harris, Folklorist* (Athens: University of Georgia Press, 1950).

6. Victor Royce West, *Folklore in Mark Twain* (Lincoln: University of Nebraska Press, 1930).

7. Mary Washington Clarke, "Jesse Stuart Reflects Kentucky Lore of Tokens and Ghosts," *Kentucky Folklore Record*, IX (July-Sept., 1963), 41-46.

8. *The Lovingood Papers*, edited by Ben Harris McClary, has been recently published by the University of Tennessee Press, 1962.

music. Much of the folk music of the South has been recorded and published in many collections, and a few articles have appeared;[9] however, much more research is necessary.

Linguistic scholars have given a little attention to folk speech[10] and its use by creative writers.[11] What has been done on folk speech needs to be much expanded.

One of the methods of research under the discipline of folklore is the Finnish, or historical-geographical, method; it is not the only one by any means, but is very sound when it is understood and carried out as it should be. Two excellent examples of this method which serve as models are Walter Anderson's study[12] and Holger Nygard's.[13] This method was designed primarily to examine traditional narratives and give the life history of the narrative, including as far as possible the origin and paths of transmission. The method includes both written and published texts as well as oral ones, and is therefore a complicated study demanding training in both literature and folklore. A rather brief example of the use of this method on Southern folklore is a study of tale type 922.[14] Actually this study should have been titled "The Southern Redaction of Tale Type 922," since practically all of the variants were recorded from the South. The changes which took place in this tale when it traveled from Europe to the South reveal an adaptation to Southern mores and customs. Instead of the King of the European form who metes out severe punishment, frequently death, to a courtier or one who frequents the court, the tale has been adapted to its new environment by having a schoolmarm mete out a once-not-infrequent whipping to a schoolboy. Folk narratives which have a number of variants in the South should be studied by some acceptable method to determine what the Southern form is, how it differs from the form in other locations, how its form came about, and how it was influenced by, or reflects, Southern customs. Some of the narratives found in the South perhaps do not have a distinct Southern form but do have a distinct position in the development of the tale. "Brer Rabbit and the Tar-

9. Linda Traywick, "Some Contemporary Builders of the Sacred Harp," *Tennessee Folklore Society Bulletin*, XXX (June, 1964), 57-61; Joan Moser, "Instrumental Music of the Southern Appalachians: Traditional Fiddle Tunes," *North Carolina Folklore*, XII (Dec., 1964), 1-8.

10. Joseph D. Clark, "Folk Speech from North Carolina," *Southern Folklore Quarterly*, XXVII (Dec., 1963), 300-325.

11. Mary Washington Clarke, "Jesse Stuart's Writings Preserve Passing Folk Idiom," *Southern Folklore Quarterly*, XXVIII (Sept., 1964), 157-198.

12. *Kaiser und Abt*, FF Communications, no. 42 (Helsinki, 1923).

13. *The Ballad of Heer Halewijn* (Knoxville: University of Tennessee Press, 1958).

14. Edwin C. Kirkland, "The American Redaction of Tale Type 922," *Fabula*, IV (1961), 248-259.

baby," found in the oral tradition of Florida,[15] has been recorded in many parts of the world including ancient India, where it is 55 in the *Jataka*, traditional stories of Buddha's other births.

Oral transmission is a distinct characteristic of folklore, and we do not know enough about how it operates or what effect it has on the folk literature. Reed Smith in *South Carolina Ballads*[16] has a chapter on "The Road Downhill." Here he presents evidence to indicate that oral transmission may cause deterioration or improvement. Other studies give some evidence to support the idea that oral transmission produces improvement.[17] Is it possible for oral transmission to be a creative process and to produce folklore by changing and developing a narrative originally the work of one person? Is this a process in which the folk become the author, and in which instead of the spontaneous and instantaneous communal creation seriously proposed by scholars we have slow, gradual communal creation—or perhaps not so slow if the material is handed on rapidly from one person to another? Although Reed Smith opened up important questions on oral transmission, its nature and its effects, practically no research has been given to it in Southern folklore.

Before this much-needed research can be done, adequate collecting and recording must be carried out. The scholar who comes to do research on Chaucer, Shakespeare, or Milton has the problem of getting a proper text, and if he has had adequate training he has the skill to get an adequate text; for some authors this may be quite simple while for others it is a most complicated piece of research in itself. Scholars who come to research on folk literature must also get an adequate text, or rather adequate texts, because a song, a tale, or a proverb in the folk tradition has not one authentic text but many, and the more there are, the better able one is to reach sound conclusions on matters such as origins, paths of transmission, and changes in details due to new environments. Unfortunately, folklore at times attracts persons who have more enthusiasm than training. Others who have the proper training in one area, such as literature, anthropology, sociology, or music, may have only their own limited area in mind and may neglect the interests of the others. For example, when the ballads were first collected, men of literature were for the most part the collectors, and they had concern only for the text of the old English and Scottish ballads as literature, completely ignoring the music, the singers, and the customs connected with the songs.

15. Recorded on tape now in the archives of the Stephen Foster Memorial, White Springs, Florida.

16. Cambridge, Mass.: Harvard University Press, 1928.

17. Edwin C. Kirkland, "The Effect of Oral Transmission on 'Robin Hood and Little John,'" *Southern Folklore Quarterly*, IV (March, 1940), 15-21.

Even in recent collecting, all the facts and details of concern to all scholars —anthropologists, sociologists, musicologists, linguists, and men of literature—have rarely been recorded. The ideal recording and collecting needs not one person but many, well organized and supported. The need for further publication of collections in the form of books or articles may be questioned in some cases; but manuscripts, sound recordings, and even sound films, accompanied by notations, will always be needed and will be useful if properly archived so as to be readily available. Also, collecting is never completely finished. There'll always be a folklore. It may not be today what it was in Bishop Percy's day or in Walter Scott's. And it may not be tomorrow what it is today. However, nothing could be farther from the truth than to suppose that folklore belongs exclusively to the primitive, the illiterate, or the rural, and that it will cease to exist when the primitive, the illiterate, and the isolated rural communities cease to exist. "Don't sell that man short," a current folk proverb, obviously comes straight out of Wall Street. Every college professor in grading his papers may not use the method which folklore ascribes to him of throwing the papers on the stairs, but if any college professor does not know what folklore says about his method of grading, he is limited in his knowledge of life around him. The professor may know that he is traditionally supposed to be absent-minded, but he may not know that folklore delightfully expresses it by telling of a professor who bought six shirts, and to guard against their loss when he sent them to the laundry got indelible ink and put his name in one and ditto marks in the other five. Collecting from a particular person or community is never finished, but at intervals the collector should go back to the same person, the same community, to record every change, every variation in the bit of folklore or its use or setting. What that interval should be has not been determined. Obviously collecting is just the beginning of research on some of the possibilities suggested earlier.

Looking at the folklore of the South from the point of view of geographical areas, we must recognize that state boundaries are not as significant as cultural areas such as the Southern Appalachians or the plantation areas of the Atlantic coast. However, such cultural areas are not clearly defined, and most of the folklore activity has been organized along state lines for societies and journals. The Virginia Folklore Society, organized in 1913 under the leadership of C. Alphonso Smith, was one of the earliest, and at first it concentrated on the Child ballads, which were published as *Traditional Ballads of Virginia*[18] under the editorship of

18. Cambridge, Mass.: Harvard University Press, 1929.

Arthur Kyle Davis, Jr. Later Davis published *Folk-Songs of Virginia,*[19] a descriptive index and classification. Some three thousand songs of all types collected by the Virginia Folklore Society were listed with significant factual details about the song, the singer, and the collector, including several hundred phonograph records of genuine folk singers. But what has developed from these excellent publications? Scholars in the various disciplines of anthropology, sociology, literature, and folklore have ample material for research according to their particular fields. The little that has been done shows some of the methods which can be used and some potentialities that lie open. In other types of folklore from Virginia, Richard Chase has collected and published much significant material on folk dance and on the Jack tales. Through the work and activity of Annabell Morris Buchanan, the White Top Festival has kept alive many of the folk traditions. This festival and others throughout the South are most important, particularly if the material is properly recorded and made available.

North Carolina's folklore society which was under the leadership of Frank C. Brown in its early years has produced under the general editorship of Newman Ivey White the monumental edition of *The Frank C. Brown Collection of North Carolina Folklore,*[20] which contains not only songs but all of the significant types, such as tales, proverbs, games, riddles, customs, etc., with a specialist editing each of the types. Duke under the tradition of Brown and White and with present-day folklorists such as Holger Nygard, and the University of North Carolina under the leadership of Arthur Palmer Hudson and Ralph S. Boggs, have long been and still are centers for folklore collecting, study, and research. Bascom Lamar Lunsford, the moving force in the North Carolina Folk Festival at Asheville, has preserved and encouraged much of the traditional lore of the region.

South Carolina has not had as extensive collections and publications as Virginia and North Carolina. In 1913 Reed Smith founded at the University of South Carolina the South Carolina Folklore Society. His *South Carolina Ballads* is a very significant work, not because of the number of the songs but because he went beyond the process of collecting (necessary and important though collecting is) and considered some of the aesthetic and literary characteristics of folksongs in his chapters on "Dramatic, Lyric, and Narrative Traits," "Communal Composition," "The Road Downhill" (deterioration from oral transmission, and its opposite, improvement by oral transmission), and "The Ballad in Literature." This

19. Durham, N. C.: Duke University Press, 1949.
20. Durham, N. C.: Duke University Press, 1952-1964.

is scholarly research that should serve as a model for future papers and books and as inspiration for new and original methods of research in the as yet vast unexplored regions of Southern folklore. Mason Brewer founded and has led the South Carolina Negro Folklore Guild, with headquarters at Claflin College in Orangeburg. One of his earliest publications was *Humorous Folktales of the South Carolina Negro.*[21] His most recent work is *Worser Days and Better Times,*[22] based on his collecting in North Carolina; as he states himself, he has reworked the material and put in something of himself. Mason Crum has added to the South Carolina material with his *Gullah: Negro Life in The Carolina Sea Islands.*[23]

Tennessee with its folklore society and its *Bulletin of the Tennessee Folklore Society*, published for some thirty years, has preserved much of the folklore of that state, a considerable portion of it from the Smoky Mountains. C. S. Pendleton of Peabody and Edwin R. Hunter of Maryville College were active in establishing the state society in 1934. Hunter and William J. Griffin of Peabody, along with George Boswell and others, are carrying on the important work of the society. Although the Tennessee society was not among the earliest ones to be started, it has been active longer than any other society and appears to be destined for a long life. Griffin has an invaluable list of folklore periodicals with pertinent details about each.[24] Edwin C. Kirkland published "A Check List of the Titles of Tennessee Folksongs,"[25] which taken along with the Virginia and North Carolina lists provides ample opportunity for studying particular songs in a number of variants, many of them for the cultural area of the Southern Appalachians. Mary Justus and Mildred Haun have, through their creative writing, recorded and made artistic use of folklore. Virginia, North Carolina, and Tennessee have more recorded folklore than any of the other Southern states.

Georgia, without any folklore society or folklore journal, has done the least of all Southern states to collect and preserve its folklore, and it therefore needs attention more than any other state. Joel Chandler Harris alone is ample evidence that Georgia has a body of folklore, and Stella Brewer Brookes in *Joel Chandler Harris, Folklorist* has a sound approach for research studies of this kind. Lem Griffith of Okefinokee Swamp is a teller of tall tales par excellence. Lydia Austin Parrish's *Slave Songs of the Georgia Sea Islands*[26] with music and an introduction by Olin Downes

21. Orangeburg, S. C.: South Carolina Negro Folklore Guild, 1945.
22. Chicago: Quadrangle Books, 1965.
23. Durham, N. C.: Duke University Press, 1940.
24. *Tennessee Folklore Society Bulletin,* XXIX (June, 1963), 42-46.
25. *Journal of American Folklore,* LIX (Oct.-Dec., 1946), 423-467.
26. New York: Creative Age Press, 1942.

is probably the most significant recent publication. *Drums and Shadows*, published in 1940 by the University of Georgia Press, has some of the WPA activity. Almost every Southern state has some of this WPA material, usually deposited at the state university. Unfortunately, much of it was collected by persons not too well trained in proper methods. However, all of the material should be examined, and some of it in all probability should be made available.

Florida has some recorded folklore. Alton C. Morris has been one of the leaders with his book *Florida Folk Songs*.[27] He has also edited the *Southern Folklore Quarterly*, which in coverage is much beyond even the South and which since 1938 has included an extensive annual bibliography. The annual Florida Folk Festival, held at the Stephen Foster Memorial at White Springs since 1951, was started under the direction of Sara Gertrude Knott and is now under the able direction of Thelma Boltin. Foster Barnes is largely responsible for recording on tape much of the lore—songs and tales particularly—and this is available to scholars. However, little use has been made of this extensive collection of Florida lore. Lillian Smith and Marjorie Kinnan Rawlings have in their creative works recorded and preserved much of the lore and traditions.

Mississippi has had no society except for one very short period, from 1927 to 1930; it was organized by Arthur Palmer Hudson and became inactive after Hudson moved to North Carolina. Mississippi has no journal and no festival, but it does have several collections in book form, among them Hudson's *Folksongs of Mississippi*,[28] with its accompanying publication *Folk Tunes of Mississippi*[29] by Hudson and George Herzog. Alabama has Byron Arnold's *Folksongs of Alabama*[30] but little else. Alabama and Mississippi, along with Georgia, have been the most neglected Southern states.

Looking at the material from the standpoint of types, we see the obvious, that ballads and folksongs have been the main concerns of most collectors and societies. Many of the major publications have already been pointed out. Others of importance are Dorothy Scarborough's *A Songcatcher in Southern Mountains*[31] and Mellinger E. Henry's *Folk-songs from the Southern Highlands*.[32] Collections of tales have been cited earlier. J. O. Sanders has a "Finding List of Southern Square Dance Figures."[33]

27. Gainesville: University of Florida Press, 1950.
28. Chapel Hill: University of North Carolina Press, 1936.
29. New York: National Play Bureau, WPA, Federal Theater Project, 1936.
30. University, Ala.: University of Alabama Press, 1950.
31. New York: Columbia University Press, 1937.
32. New York: J. J. Augustin, 1938.
33. *Southern Folklore Quarterly*, VI (Dec., 1942), 263-275.

Other types which have had some notice are proverbs, riddles, folk recipes, folk medicine and remedies, superstition, and speech. Although further research on songs and tales should not be neglected, much more is needed on the other types.

When we consider the ethnic groups, we see immediately that the Negro has had more attention than any other group outside the Anglo-Saxon heritage. The folklore of any ethnic or geographical group is not completely restricted to that group, but is intertwined with other groups in so many complex ways that when we speak of the folklore of a limited group we mean what is present at some time in that group and not what is necessarily indigenous or exclusive to that group. Numerous publications of Negro folklore have been pointed out earlier. Others are Howard W. Odum and Guy B. Johnson, *The Negro and His Songs: A Study of Typical Negro Songs in the South*;[34] Newbell N. Puckett, *Folk Beliefs of the Southern Negroes*;[35] Newman Ivey White, *American Negro Folk-Songs*;[36] Guy B. Johnson, *John Henry: Tracking Down a Negro Legend*;[37] and William Francis Allen, Charles Pickard Ware, and Luch McKim Garrison, *Slave Songs of the United States*,[38] originally published in 1867. The well-known Negro spirituals add to the extensive list of publications.

The America Indians need much further study. Some attention has been given to them by Frances Densmore. The most extensive work (some nine hundred pages) is John R. Swanton's *The Indians of the Southeastern United States*.[39] Florida has many ethnic groups, the Spanish, the Greeks, and the Czechoslovakians, to mention only a few. Other groups are scattered throughout the South, and their folklore is rapidly dying out. Therefore, collecting and preservation here are most urgent.

When we consider the folklore found in and about various professions, trades, and other occupations, we see that no extensive study has been made for any profession, trade, or occupation in the South such as is given to lumberjacks, cowboys, or miners. However, less glamorous occupations are just as important in understanding the life and culture of a region. Some of the occupations in the South are represented by a section or a few examples in collections and studies made on such types as songs, tales, superstitions, riddles, etc. Superstitions, customs, beliefs, proverbs, and anecdotes of a specific occupation would be profitable not only for the

34. Chapel Hill: University of North Carolina Press, 1925.
35. Chapel Hill: University of North Carolina Press, 1926.
36. Cambridge, Mass.: Harvard University Press, 1928.
37. Chapel Hill: University of North Carolina Press, 1929.
38. New York: Oak Publications, 1965.
39. Washington, D. C.: Bureau of American Ethnology, Bulletin number 137, 1946.

intrinsic value of the material but also for the knowledge it would give of the sociological, historical, and traditional characteristics of the group. The following anecdote illustrates some of the traditional attitudes toward religious denominations. Three men who had been drinking heavily were driving around one Wednesday night and came to a church where the usual Wednesday evening prayer meeting was in progress. They went in, and when they joined in the singing, their unnecessary loudness attracted unfavorable attention. The minister called on the congregation for sentence prayers. The men joined in, but instead of a brief prayer each held forth for a considerable time. The minister then called for the collection. Each of the three men reached in his pocket and contributed a twenty-dollar bill. The preacher pronounced the benediction quickly; the men left and drove off. A member of the congregation came up and said, "Preacher, who were those men?" The preacher said, "Brother, I don't know. They sang like Baptists; they prayed like Methodists; and they gave money like Presbyterians. But you know, they smelled like Episcopalians."

Certain political anecdotes are frequently dated and do not live long enough to warrant the designation of folklore, which implies traditional material, but other political anecdotes have a way of being repeated about different candidates or they survive because of a universal application. Certainly those which persist in oral tradition must have certain qualities, such as satire or homely wisdom, which cause them to persist, and therefore they should be studied for their intrinsic characteristics as well as for the light that they shed on politics and attitudes toward politics and candidates. Specific illustrations are hardly necessary since almost every person will be able to give several of his own. The folklore of teachers and professors, or about teachers and professors, was illustrated earlier by the anecdotes of the method of grading papers and of protecting shirts from being lost at the laundry. The life of the farmer, or rather the farmer's wife, is reflected in the riddle, "Big at the bottom and little at the top, and something in the middle goes flippity flop." The changing South in the last fifty years has moved so rapidly that few persons today, even on the farms now modernized to urban standards, can answer this riddle, which clearly describes the wooden churn, once a very common and useful object on every Southern farm.

Outside of history probably no material demonstrates the changing South more than folklore, which reflects life and thought in the ballads and songs, the tales to some extent, and the proverbs and riddles, not to mention the obvious folk customs and beliefs. An urgent need to collect according to acceptable practices always exists because, although folklore will never die out, particular aspects and characteristics will change or die out, to be lost entirely or replaced by entirely different aspects and characteristics. After the collecting comes the need for archiving, cataloguing, and preserving the material in a way that will make it as readily available as possible to serious scholars in all fields and subjects which properly study folklore and come to valid conclusions. The opportunities are so vast that they may never be fully recognized, but any advance in the directions indicated, or in directions yet to be developed, will be an advance in the understanding, evaluation, and appreciation of the culture of the South in all of its aspects.

Southern education: A new research frontier / C. Arnold Anderson

Is the South an underdeveloped nation?

The lamentations over Southern deficiencies and the prescriptions for their remedy during the past century both correspond strikingly to present-day assessments of underdeveloped countries. Incomes are low and unequally distributed and they derive disproportionately from primary industries. In the lagging sectors technological equipment is crude and human resources are poorly rewarded, for low levels of skill preclude the productive use of capital. Economic along with other aspects of social life display marked local and ecological differentials; a few localities match prosperous ones elsewhere, but others display a stubborn backwardness. There is among Southerners an attachment to what in many countries today is called "tribalism," and the now-familiar debates about colonialism and neo-colonialism find their echo in the South. Though education has been looked to as a means to bring the South into the modern world, the social milieu required to insure that schooling will yield its benefits has been attenuated and fractured.

Tempting as this analogy with underdeveloped countries may be, even Appalachia is one of the high-income places in the world. Moreover, within the South, as within other regions of the nation, local differences far exceed the contrasts with other regions. Most important of all, the South is part of a larger and unified polity and it is a specialized part of one complex economy; the boundaries of the South are vague and they are easily surmounted. Even the residents of the traditional heart of the South cannot attend to their claimed distinctiveness long enough to ward off the intrusive influences from the larger society. Southern products enter national markets unhampered by quotas or tariffs. The rest of the nation is willing to accept the South's surplus unproductive individuals, while well-educated persons can be freely imported into the South. The capital resources of the nation can be drawn on readily, even levied upon through political horsetrading. Basic private and public services are generously staffed by individuals whose competence could be questioned only in an even more affluent society.

The educational system in particular has been long established; it is on the whole adequate in scale, and its quality appears inferior only by comparison with schools in the most developed areas of the world. There need be no bottlenecks in trained manpower whenever the people of the South choose to make use of and improve the schools at hand—and they need not sacrifice the necessities of life for their support.[1] One will gain little understanding of the South, it is clear, by interpreting it in the light of events in underdeveloped countries.

Southern economic development is so advanced that we need to go beyond the conventional indexes of per capita income or employment in manufacturing. For the South it seems more appropriate to define development as "the enlargement and diffusion among the population of opportunities to widen the range of experiences and satisfactions and to participate in an ongoing national life."[2] It is poverty of mind and poverty of outlook that afflict the South; although these may be correlated with low incomes, they are a different dimension of human life.

The appropriateness of using the analysis of education as a way into an understanding of the South is strengthened by certain persisting and distinctive features of that society. Not least important is the fact that education has been close to the center of the rending controversies in Southern life for a full century. The dramatic episodes of present-day obstruction of desegregation or the ante-bellum defenses against intellectual subversion, however, are less important than the chronic apathy. Out of Southern life have emerged familiar social types that are not wholly stereotypes: poor white, slaveholder, yeoman, bourbon, mill worker, and of course Negro (including a Negro elite). Each of these has been the theme of a distinctive educational story and actor or occasion in educational controversy; certainly each has experienced a different educational fate. The complex patterns of economic regionalization before and after the Civil War were crosscut by the intrusion of "modernization" and by diverse educational influences. Neither in status nor in education has any of these different elements in Southern society been monolithic. Some members of less-esteemed groups have enjoyed privileges undreamed of by the less fortunate members of higher-ranking groups. Today, as in previous epochs of Southern history, we can use education as a diagnostic device for tracing out the changing pattern of regional life.[3]

1. John Friedman, "Poor Regions and Poor States," paper read to Society for Applied Anthropology, 1965.

2. M. J. Bowman and C. Arnold Anderson, "Interdisciplinary Aspects of the Theory of Regional Development," forthcoming in J. Mattox, ed., report of a conference in March, 1965.

3. As pointed out in the last section of this essay, and also as topics for important lines of research.

Occupations, incomes, and the diagnosis of Southern education

During the last few decades observers have watched Southern per capita incomes rise from a half to three-fourths of the national level. Gains in recent years, however, have been slight. Less often mentioned is the fact that the dollar spread between Southern and national incomes has failed to narrow. In education, likewise, the lag of the South has diminished, yet no firm base has been laid for transforming Southern economic life through schooling. One reason for this reservation is that the relationship between schooling and either occupation or income is patterned differently in the South, even among whites alone. For example, it is noteworthy that poorly-schooled Negroes residing in the North earn more than Southern whites with equal amounts of schooling.[4] Among whites, at the top of the income distribution the ratio of Southern to Northern incomes is near unity, but at the lower part the regional gap widens. Even holding schooling constant, Southern incomes diverge from Northern averages by larger amounts at the lower income quartiles.[5] Within particular occupational categories, men with extensive schooling can in the South earn as much or more than equally schooled men in the North. But among the less-educated individuals in given occupations Southern incomes lag—once more, even among whites alone.[6] As one traces out "the interrelationships between Southern tradition and Southern poverty" it is especially to the reflection of tradition within education that one must attend.[7] As we look for the distinctive characteristics of the Southern matrix of education-occupation-income, we find that the distribution of schooling among individuals and groups has some special features. Schooling in the South has in some ways different implications for the acquisition and rewarding of skills within particular occupations.

When we introduce racial comparisons, paradoxical features emerge, while some of the stark contrasts observed among whites recur among Negroes. Differences of income between whites and Negroes (even within matched categories for occupation and education) are larger in the South.[8] The increment to income associated with more schooling is

4. M. J. Bowman, "Human Inequalities and Southern Economic Development," in J. W. McKie, ed., *Education and the Southern Economy* (Chapel Hill: University of North Carolina Press, 1965), p. 87.

5. *Ibid.*, 84; see also my "Regional and Racial Differences in Relations between Income and Education," *School Review*, LXIII (Jan., 1955), 38-45.

6. Bowman, *op. cit.*, p. 95.

7. W. H. Nicholls, *Southern Tradition and Regional Progress* (Chapel Hill: University of North Carolina Press, 1960), p. 1.

8. Bowman, *op. cit.*, p. 75; P. M. Siegel, "On the Cost of Being a Negro," *Sociological Inquiry*, XXXV (Winter, 1965), 41-57, esp. p. 51.

smaller among Negroes than among whites in both regions, but that increment is proportionately larger among Southern than among Northern Negroes.[9] It is as much the poverty of the untrained whites as it is Negro poverty that is the Southern problem; the forces underlying the one contribute to the other, and the two sets of disadvantageous circumstances reinforce each other and in many contexts are indistinguishable.[10]

The South's reliance upon agriculture takes on a new dimension when we explore regional differences in the divergence in educational opportunities between urban and rural populations. Within the urban sector Southern levels of schooling are not markedly retarded. Within the North, moreover, rural men are not much more likely than urban ones to have received only a few years of schooling. But in the rural South the proportion even of whites with meager schooling is very large.[11] Today as a century ago, the roots of Southern problems lie in Southern agriculture: at median levels (even ignoring the long tail of "submarginal" farmers) the urban-farm spread of income is typically much larger in the South.[12]

The correlated structures of occupations and incomes reflect the educational history of the region and other features of the traditional way of life. Those institutional residuals also determine the future interrelationships of education, occupation, and income. Perceived occupational opportunities affect individuals' educational aspirations; racial differences in income-education relationships within occupations supply many of the more subtle cues by which persons guide their educational decisions. Racial disparities in occupational opportunities are not consistently larger in the South; neither are they tightly correlated with the percentage of Negroes in the population or with the level of prejudice and discrimination displayed by whites. Racial disparities tend to be larger within the middle range of occupations than at either extreme.[13] In some respects the distribution of occupations within the South actually favors Negroes.[14] Convergence of occupational distributions for the two races has been under

9. Siegel, *op. cit.*; Bowman, *op. cit.*, p. 87.

10. Nicholls, *op. cit.*, pp. 56-67.

11. Bowman, *op. cit.*, p. 75; and my "Inequalities in Schooling in the South," *American Journal of Sociology*, LX (Sept., 1954), 547-561. A much-needed study is to compare "discrimination" against women with that against Negroes.

12. Bowman, *op. cit.*, p. 85. There is a substantial correlation over the states and within each type of farming between output per worker on farms and value of land and buildings, resting of course in part on capacity to use superior equipment; see H. S. Perloff *et al.*, *Regions, Resources and Economic Growth* (Baltimore: Johns Hopkins Press, 1960), p. 560.

13. Siegel, *op. cit.*; N. Hare, "Recent Trends in the Occupational Mobility of Negroes," *Social Forces*, XLIV (Dec., 1965), 166-172.

14. J. P. Gibbs, "Occupational Differentiation of Negroes and Whites in the United States," *Social Forces*, XLIV (Dec., 1965), 159-165.

way for a long time and it was accelerated by wartime changes in job markets, but that convergence slowed down during the late 1950's and may have moved against Negroes in both North and South.[15]

These disparate occupational patterns are reflected in the distributions of incomes, both gross and within education-occupation categories. Southern agriculture tends to be weak as a generator of income. But within other industries or categories of occupations the specific Southern occupations are disproportionately those with low earnings.[16] Thus Southern employees are disproportionately lacking in the skills to work with the more productive types of capital equipment.

In unemployment rates, as in other features of the labor market, skill qualifications display complex relationships to race. Much of the higher level of unemployment among Negroes goes back to earlier differential opportunities to acquire qualifications for entry into less exposed occupations. During recent years, it has been estimated, two-fifths of the national white–non-white disparity in unemployment rests on differences of occupational distribution; the share of the unemployment difference thus explained is three-fifths in the South. These racial differentials are largest for the intermediate occupations and for men with intermediate amounts of schooling. Especially in the South among unskilled workers, whites are about as likely as Negroes to be unemployed, reflecting again the distinctive educational handicaps among low-status whites.[17]

Up to now I have avoided using the concept of discrimination, for it is an activity that is peculiarly recalcitrant to clear identification.[18] Many use the term to describe inequalities, generally with the implication that normally they reflect exploitation through power. For readers of this symposium, there is little need to allude to the demonstrable and acknowledged practices of discrimination, particularly in education. Indeed, a large por-

15. Siegel, *op. cit.*

16. By contrast industrial variation in composition of income among states is less important as a source of differences in state average earnings (F. A. Hanna, *State Income Differentials*, Durham, N. C.: Duke University Press, 1959, p. 192). Shifts in economic situations are not uniform among the Southern states. Of the total interstate variance in per capita income, that due to South–non-South difference has been fairly steady since 1929 at about 60 per cent; variance among non-Southern states has diminished from about 50 per cent to 30 per cent, while variance among Southern states has increased slowly but is the least important (F. A. Hanna, "Income in the South Since 1929," chap. vii in M. L. Greenhut and W. T. Whitman, eds., *Essays in Southern Economic Development*, Chapel Hill: University of North Carolina Press, 1964, p. 243). See also E. S. Dunn, Jr., *Recent Southern Economic Development*, University of Florida Monographs in Social Sciences, No. 14, 1962.

17. H. J. Gilman, "Economic Discrimination and Unemployment," *American Economic Review*, LV (Dec., 1965), 1077-1096, esp. pp. 1080, 1087-1090.

18. C. Arnold Anderson and P. Foster, "Discrimination and Inequality in Education," *Sociology of Education*, XXXVIII (Fall, 1964), 1-18.

tion of the observed imparities in employment or occupation rest not on present discrimination within the job market but on past educational discrimination. Behind much of the observed disparity in earnings, for example, lie unequal qualifications; use of the same occupational title is no warranty of parity in skill. As we turn to analysis of the educational system in less gross terms, we have to take account of subtle differences between populations in confidence in acquiring skills and in demonstration of their possession in practice. Through such analyses we can distinguish discrimination from cultural deprivation and apathy.

It is noteworthy that most of the serious analyses of these race-education-occupation-income matrices have been carried out by scholars in the North.[19] Few innovations in "economics of education," to particularize, have originated in the South, yet that is just where "necessity" should have stimulated its invention. Without anticipating later comments on higher education, it is pertinent to link this observation with another: even with large federal subsidies the Southern states have been unable to establish first-rank research centers for the principal industry, agriculture. Sustained development requires the diffusion of innovative behavior as a cultural value and the emergence of foci for innovation. Two illustrations bearing on this point have been mentioned from the sphere of higher education. Others could be cited from more humble levels of skill as explaining the weak representation of the more rewarding occupations within the Southern economy. The many Southern inhibitions on private enterprisers are frequently mentioned.[20] A South that is half-hearted about the development of education and that actively encourages apathy toward education by half its population will display little innovative behavior at any level, except possibly the political.

The outcome of schooling in any society depends not only upon the residue of the previous generation's education but also upon other qualities of the milieu that encourage innovation and receptiveness to novelty. As crude indexes of this milieu we can tally the use of libraries or attendance at PTA meetings. Alternatively we can search out the stultifying features in local environments, inhibitions that are distinct from the mere absence of stimulating qualities. As we are able to identify these aspects of the milieu separately from the simple indexes of formal schooling, we can be more definite in assigning some outcomes of improved education to technical productivity, some to heightened general

19. Our increased knowledge on many of these questions has become possible only as a result of the improved data supplied by the Bureau of the Census.

20. C. A. Hickman, "The Entrepreneurial Function," in Greenhut and Whitman, eds., *op. cit.*, chap. ii, p. 109.

alertness, and others to rising aspirations for children's education. We will then be able to penetrate behind the statistical screen of occupational and income categories to the generative factors.

Continuities in Southern education

"With its more highly differentiated and complex social organization, the increasingly heterogeneous South of today maintains a stability of behavioral form and social relationship even as new social perspectives and arrangements continue to evolve."[21] Over the broad spectrum of societal life, including education, differences among Southern subregions in 1860 remain discernible in 1960. Nicholls has shown for the Upper East Tennessee Valley that the counties today most advanced were marked off a century ago from neighboring ones. In particular, those counties that have moved ahead were then superior in agricultural production, especially for relative investment in farm capital goods, and in literacy.[22] The differing responses over the South in recent years to pressures for school desegregation and civil rights were predictable broadly from the social and educational patterns of 1860 and in detail from the patterns of 1950.[23]

As our data improve we can draw more precise maps of the Southern cultural landscape. Unfortunately we have few field studies of the localities that lead or lag in schooling and its utilization. Only the first steps have been taken to untangle the racial complexities as they take different local forms. We can start with broad contrasts: while in 1840-1860 Southern states lagged in enrolment, over that period the Western states outside the South converged rapidly to northeastern levels despite poverty and thin settlement. It is estimated that youth in northeastern and north central states in 1860 were receiving about five times as many days of schooling as were white youth in the South.[24] The Project Talent data reveal that

21. J. C. McKinney and Edgar T. Thompson, eds., *The South in Continuity and Change* (Durham, N. C.: Duke University Press, 1965), p. 3. See my "Economic Status Differentials within Southern Agriculture," *Rural Sociology*, XIX (March, 1954), 50-67; and (with Bowman), "The Vanishing Servant and the Contemporary Status System of the American South," *American Journal of Sociology*, LIX (Nov., 1953), 215-230.

22. W. H. Nicholls, "Some Foundations of Economic Development in the Upper East Tennessee Valley, 1850-1900," *Journal of Political Economy*, LXIV (Aug., 1956), 277-302; *ibid.*, LXIV (Oct., 1956), 400-415.

23. See my article cited in n. 11 and any recent annual statistical summary published by Southern Education Reporting Service.

24. A. Fishlow, "The American Common School Revival," pp. 14, 25, 31 of the mimeographed version. H. G. Richey published a more detailed analysis reaching similar conclusions: "Reappraisal of State School Systems of the Pre-Civil-War

the correlation of high-school achievement scores today with army test scores in World War I is .73 among all the states (.88 among regions), while the correlation with per pupil expenditures today is .67 (.88 among regions). Historical trends are as powerful as present effort.[25] In other respects also, the achievement scores correspond to now familiar differentials in education within the South. For example, pupils from well-off urban homes in the South receive nearly as high scores as similar pupils in Western states, but among pupils from low-status urban and from rural homes, Southern scores lag markedly.[26] In broad terms the educational situation for Negroes varies among localities as does that for whites.

Nam has pointed out that an increase of only 200,000 non-white enrollees would bring the two racial distributions together for the nation as a whole. The enrolment distributions for the two races widened from 1920 to 1940 but narrowed during the two subsequent decades; overall, there is about a two-decade lag in Negro education.[27] The persisting deficiencies of Southern rural schools show up dramatically in the proportions of young adults of both races possessing less than five years of schooling.[28] Fortunately the absolute numbers—though not percentages—of such individuals shrank substantially in the rural South after 1950. The massive migration from the rural South was made up of youth who were ill-educated compared to the populations at their destinations, but the migrants were somewhat better schooled than their fellows who remained behind.[29] Fein has estimated the aggregate loss annually from the South in "capitalized human resources value" by migration at less than .1 per cent of the Southern stock.[30] Improvements in the education of Southern youth will redound mainly to the benefit of that region.

Many features of this complex pattern of educational change can be summed up by tracing out the relation of overall trends to racial dispari-

---

Period," *Elementary School Journal*, XLI (Oct., 1940), 118-129; and *ibid.*, XLII (Jan., 1942), 358-370, and XLII (Feb., 1942), 456-463.

25. J. C. Flanagan *et al., Project Talent: A Survey and Follow-Up Study of Educational Plans and Decisions in Relation to Aptitude Patterns* (Pittsburgh: University of Pittsburgh Press, 1962), ch. 4.

26. *Ibid.*; these results are for whites only.

27. See the manuscript version of J. K. Folger and C. B. Nam's forthcoming census monograph on education, chap. v. These wave or lead-lag movements are a recurrent phenomenon among locality and status, as well as among race categories with respect to diffusion.

28. Bowman, *op. cit.*, p. 77.

29. See comments on Bowman, *ibid.*, by Alice Rivlin.

30. R. Fein, "Educational Patterns in Southern Migration," chap. v in McKie, ed., *op. cit.*; also E. M. Suval and C. H. Hamilton, "Some New Evidence on Educational Selectivity in Migration to and from the South," *Social Forces*, XLIII (May, 1965), 536-547. None of these studies using census data can make any adjustment for quality of education.

ties.[31] How these processes are manifested by subpopulations within a state goes far to determine the dynamics of education within that state.

Broadly speaking, degrees of race disparity in educational attainment reflect a combination of the stage of educational progress among a state's population in the aggregate and the extent to which the two races have distinctive subcultures. This is most readily seen by sketching three types of situations. (*a*) Where educational progress is rapid for whites but social distinctions between the races are great, high indexes of racial inequality emerge at each attainment level. While this extreme is most nearly approximated in Mississippi, the average record of that state in providing eighth-grade education for Negroes is an important qualification. (*b*) Where there has been little emphasis on education, a mass of semiliterate whites share disadvantages with the Negroes, but a white minority completing elementary and high school stands apart from the rest of the whites and from virtually all the Negroes, as in rural Louisiana. (*c*) Where racial distinctions are moderate, the value placed upon schooling extends to both racial groups, making for a smaller lag of Negro behind white progress and for smaller inequality indexes, as in Tennessee and Virginia.

Before turning to analysis of recent data on enrolments I will summarize some recent reports on school dropouts. For the nation as a whole in 1960 the dropout rates among whites at ages sixteen and seventeen were 13.4 in urban places, 19.8 in rural non-farm places, and 16.5 among farm youth; for the South alone the corresponding white rates were 16.7, 26.5, and 22.7. The disadvantage of white farm youth is about twice as large in the South. Among non-whites, regional differences were negligible.[32] Among nineteen-year-olds there are very large urban-farm disparities within the South, but also in New England.[33] The southeastern states were very diverse in respect to racial differences of dropout rates (see Table 1).

The race differences in dropout rates among nineteen-year-olds vary among these six states by a factor of 2:1, but the order among states for race disparity is not the same in both residence categories; these states are least similar for urban whites and most similar for rural Negroes. Rates for farm whites approximate those for urban Negroes, and only in Georgia are

31. From my article cited in n. 11, p. 557.

32. U. S. Department of Agriculture, "Age-Grade School Progress of Farm and Nonfarm Youth, 1960," *Agricultural Economic Report* #40, Table 15. What are called "presumptive dropouts" are not included in the figure used. The data point to neglect of Indian education by Northern and Western states.

33. U. S. Department of Agriculture, "School Dropout Rates among Farm and Nonfarm Youth: 1950 and 1960," *Agricultural Economic Report* #42, Table 7. Because of sample size, full subclassifications were given for only six southeastern states.

the urban-farm differences distinctly larger among Negroes than whites. It is important to notice, however, that urban drop-out rates (for all races combined) are higher in two north central states than for urban whites in two Southern states. Among farm youth, the highest north central rate just equals the lowest Southern-white one. The urban-farm differences in the north central states run about half as large for Southern whites, but the regional distributions of residence differences overlap.[34]

The discussion moves now to the history of school enrolments for the states of the nation; the data include both sexes and all races combined.[35] Back in 1910 the percentages of sixteen- and seventeen-year-olds enrolled ranged over the forty-eight states from 28 to 66; in 1960 the range was 69 to 90 (see Chart 1). Fourteen of the lowest seventeen states in 1960 (one tie) were Southern or marginally Southern. In 1910, however, it was Northern states also that lagged (twelve of the lowest eighteen); the lowest rates stretched westward from the northeast to Illinois, reflecting the high proportion of pupils of foreign parentage.[36] By 1930 these non-Southern states had reached higher enrolment levels; only five of the lowest sixteen were Northern. By 1950 the South was far behind; only Rhode Island made so poor a showing as any Southern state. During the 1950's a few Southern states were edging up to the level of the northeastern states.

These snapshots result from divergent trajectories between shots. The scattergram relating 1910 to 1960 enrolments displays only a modest correlation; though enrolments in 1910 and 1930 were quite closely associated, between 1930 and 1960 many states drifted out of pattern. Between 1910 and 1960, for example, Idaho along with Kentucky and North Carolina achieved an increase of 20 points; South Dakota and Virginia about 30 points; Minnesota, North Dakota, and Georgia about 40 points; Louisiana, Wisconsin, and Connecticut about 50 points of gain.

Another way of looking at the gains in enrolments is to classify the states on one dimension according to the proportion of their 1910-1960 gains that were made in the component periods (1910-1930, 1930-1950, 1950-1960) and then to divide the states into thirds by 1960 per capita in-

34. R. A. Dentler and M. E. Warshauer, *Big City Drop-Outs* (New York Center for Urban Education, 1965). Tables B-2 and B-3. A plotting of the non-white–white differentials in dropout rates for the 131 cities reported on reveals no consistent regional pattern.

35. Age-specific enrolment rates cannot be taken as fully valid measures of subpopulation differences in ultimate school attainment; they can be interpreted also as indexes to propensity to supply schooling to youth. See Beverly Duncan, *Family Factors and School Dropout: 1920-1960*, Office of Education, Cooperative Research Project No. 2258, 1965.

36. F. A. Ross, *School Attendance in 1920*, Census Monograph 5, 1925, chaps. iv and vii.

comes (see Table 2). Early progress in raising enrolments occurred in the states now enjoying high incomes; and this relationship with income is as close as that between early gains and 1960 enrolments. On the other hand, there is little correlation between 1960 incomes and enrolment levels in 1910 or even 1930. One might speculate that in the northeastern states earlier educational momentum more than compensated for their low enrolments fifty years ago (reflecting immigration). But it could be argued equally cogently that the momentum of economic development created the stimulus for educational advance independently of early educational change. When one scans the nation today, some anomalies do stand out. In a few states high enrolments were attained and maintained despite poverty and without noticeably alleviating poverty—most notably the Dakotas. Populations which place strong emphasis upon education are providing and using it, even if their high school graduates depart for employment in more promising locales.

In an earlier study it was concluded that enrolments (of sixteen- and seventeen-year-olds in 1950) are "loosely correlated with the state median expenditures per classroom unit."[37] This association is even weaker in 1960 and not far from zero.[38] To be sure, the states in 1960 are more closely bunched so that there is less variance in enrolment to be "explained" by expenditures, but there is still a considerable range in enrolment. Idaho and West Virginia spent the same per classroom in 1960 but their enrolments are fifteen points apart. At nearly the same enrolment level, Louisiana spends roughly twice as much as Mississippi, and New York four times as much per pupil. Today, even more than earlier, what calls for explanation is not any positive correlation between enrolments and expenditure but rather their lack of statistical association.[39]

Using the share of personal income devoted to public schools in place of expenditure per classroom as an index does not produce any clearer pattern. Ohio gets 10 per cent more enrolled than Rhode Island with virtually no larger relative expenditure, and Nebraska gets 15 points more than North Carolina. Even those Southern states spending relatively more than most of the Northern states do not succeed in enrolling a larger percentage of youth than the many Southern states spending less.

37. (With M. J. Bowman), "Can Money Alone Improve the Schools?" *School Executive*, LXXIV (March, 1955), 82-84. A later section in the present chapter deals with the relationship of expenditures to school quality.

38. Perhaps in the South expenditures go disproportionately to secondary schools.

39. F. W. Harrison and E. P. McLoone, *Profiles in School Support*, Office of Education, Miscellany No. 47. (Costs of higher education are not included.) Admittedly the South has a dual school system to support, but the public in many Northern states also support a parochial system. Southern officials could have induced a higher level of attendance and expenditure in Negro schools if they chose, so there is no point in deleting Negro data before comparing regions or states.

Though enrolments rose over the war decade, 1950 rates were highly correlated with those in 1940, and precisely the same statement could be made for the 1950-1960 decade. But the rates have recently been converging as the lead states approximate what seems to be an effective ceiling of 90 per cent enrolment and comparatively large gains are scored by the most lagging states.[40] The correlation between enrolment rates in 1940 and 1950 was higher than for expenditures (in relation to income) in the same years. Over the period from 1950 to 1960, however, relative expenditures displayed slightly more correlation than did enrolments—but they are not systematically related to state income levels.

In the earlier study we plotted arithmetic differences in 1940 and 1950 enrolment rates against the ratio of 1950 to 1940 expenditures per classroom unit; the association was moderately positive, especially within the South. For the recent decade there is little correlation for the South or for the nation, though on the scale for enrolment gains the Southern states lie mainly above the Northern ones. Among the states spending 1.6 times as much in 1960 as in 1950, for example, gains in enrolment ranged from zero to 12 points and among states doubling expenditures gains ranged from 5 to 14 points. Mississippi gained just one point more in enrolment than did Louisiana through raising expenditures by a ratio of 2.6 in contrast to Louisiana's 1.6. Extreme diversity of educational performance persists within the South, a diversity that no one yet has succeeded in explaining.

A decade ago Bloom conducted an achievement survey of a sample of white pupils in every state, relating the test scores to educational and other factors presumed to underlie educational performance.[41] He found that achievement of high school seniors was moderately correlated with scores on Selective Service tests, using states as units. On the other hand, his scores were slightly negatively associated with school expenditures relative to income. There was a moderate positive relationship between scores and relative persistence of pupils from the ninth to the twelfth grade: though there was a slightly positive relationship among Southern states this correlation reflects mainly North-South contrasts, the non-South states displaying no relationship. The correlation between scores and enrolment rates for sixteen- and seventeen-year-olds was marked, especially within the Southern states. The ratio of number of high school graduates, and especially of college entrants, to the eighteen-year-old cohort was correlated with

40. The failure of high rates for leading states to rise in recent years may in part reflect heavy in-migration of families with low educational aspirations.

41. B. S. Bloom, "The Normative Study of the Tests of General Education Development," *School Review*, LXIV (March, 1956), 110-124, and scattergrams made from the original data.

scores on the tests: in each case the association is clearer among Southern than among Northern states.

These findings point to the importance of assessing the quality of schools, but that task has so far eluded the skills of educational researchers. One could ask about the assimilation of "new math" and other innovations by different school systems, and Bloom used a related measure (the proportion of science and mathematics teachers belonging to subject-matter associations); the correlation is quite low though there is some association for the Southern states taken alone. Both per capita expenditures for librarians and the level of magazine reading by states showed moderately high correlations with achievement scores (again, mainly within the South), but it is difficult to draw firm inferences about causation from that type of correlation. Here we enter the fruitful but baffling territory of identifying the contribution of schools to pupils' learning after one allows for the quality of homes and communities surrounding the schools. In this maze may be concealed many of the explanations of the low relationship between state expenditures, enrolments, and pupil achievement.[42]

Educational imparities between the races in Southern states

Where subpopulations are sharply separated in status and by barriers to association, and particularly where one group is able to determine the life-chances of the other, levels of schooling within each group and imparities between them can be linked in complex patterns. We are now familiar with the fact that in the South, as in many countries of the world, limitations upon the schooling of the subordinate group are paralleled by educational disadvantages for the lower ranges of the superordinate group. On the other hand, since the South has always shared much of the national ethos, sizable proportions of the Negroes have enjoyed better educational opportunities than many whites. Only part of this "anomaly" reflects differences in educational norms between urban and rural communities. In addition, those whites and Negroes who have moved to the North are better schooled than their fellows who remained in the South.[43]

I have shown previously that one can illuminate many features of a society's status structure by analyzing the inequality patterns for distributions of years of school completed.[44] Nam has recently repeated parts of my 1950 analysis with 1960 data, and he finds no striking changes over the

42. It is impossible to obtain expenditures by any cogent functional classification for states.
43. Bowman, in McKie, ed., *op. cit.*, p. 78.
44. Discussed in my article cited in n. 11.

decade.[45] In the North and among Southern whites the least-schooled individuals now possess a somewhat larger share of the schooling than in 1950. Among Negroes in the South, on the other hand, the best-schooled individuals today possess a slightly larger proportion of the aggregate schooling of Negroes than in 1950: in all probability this represents gains among urban Negroes.

The status correlates of schooling within the South, likewise, seem to be altering only slowly. Using 1940 data I showed that the grade in school achieved by white youth at age seventeen was strongly affected by size of community in the South but not in the North. Economic level of parental home was a dominant factor over the nation, but this factor was related to pupils' achievement differently in the South. Children from well-off homes had as much schooling in the South as in the North, but those from poorer homes were at a distinct disadvantage in the South as compared to the parallel handicap in the North. There are populous categories of whites at the bottom of the Southern status scale who suffer large disadvantages in schooling.[46]

It is necessary always to come back to a scrutiny of the racial imparities in educational opportunity. What we may call "indexes of racial differentiation" in schooling range widely among the Southern states, even for a particular generation, level of schooling, or place of residence.[47] Racial imparities in schooling are larger among old than young in 1960 and larger in the South than in the North (Table 3). For advanced levels of schooling there is more racial imparity in farm than in urban populations of the South, but at lower levels of schooling imparity between races is less marked in rural than in urban places. Imparities by place of residence are greater in the South than in the North within both races. They are larger for Negroes than for whites in the South at the upper level of schooling but smaller at the lower level: that is, urban Negroes more than urban whites find educational opportunities relatively superior to those offered to rural residents.[48]

I turn now to the racial-differentiation indexes for individual Southern states, comparing men born in the late 1880's and in the early 1920's. For men completing no more than four years of school, racial differentia-

45. See Folger and Nam, *op. cit.*

46. See my article "Social Class Differentials in the Schooling of Youth within the Regions and Community-Size Groups of the United States," *Social Forces*, XXV (May, 1947), 434-440; the results parallel those for 1960 mentioned earlier in this chapter.

47. The index is white − Negro/white + Negro percentages completing given amounts of schooling (for those with 0-4 years it is Negro − white); the range can be zero to unity. The data were not re-computed for states in 1960 but only for regions.

48. This is an aspect of the wave process discussed earlier.

tion or imparity changed little in any state. In the Southern states taken as a group, on the other hand, racial differentiation did diminish appreciably: by more than 25 points at the 8+ level of schooling in cities and on farms, and at the 12+ level of schooling by 19 points in cities and 12 points on farms. At the lowest level of schooling (0-4 years), racial imparity was less marked on farms than in cities; again the common fate of the rural lower stratum of both races comes to view. For completion of 8+ years of school the residence differences were slightly greater than for those completing 12+ years. The interstate differences in these differentiation indexes were larger for the younger men; the status structure of schooling has been loosening in recent years and some states have pulled ahead of others in the move toward racial equality of educational opportunity, but this effect was least noticeable in the farm population. For the younger men residing in cities, the disadvantages of Negroes at the 8+ and 12+ levels of schooling have been diminishing.

Charts 2 and 3 portray this index for selected demographic components of the population in ten Southern states. There is an impressive consistency of pattern for each state. Where racial differentiation in schooling was high for the older generation, it remained comparatively high for younger men. States displaying markedly high racial differentiation at one level of school tend to do so also at other levels, and this consistency is more apparent in the younger generation. Finally, those states tolerating high differentiation between the races on farms were least likely to display low differentiation within cities.

These patterns are a record of previously institutionalized connections between race relations and educational practices. The evidence is clear that states with a broadly similar race composition and economic base can work out distinct patterns for educational differentiation between races or between farm and urban residents—even without desegregation or abandonment of the "traditional way of life."

Educational finance and the quality of education

If one judges by the proportion of teachers with less than a bachelor's degree or "less than standard certificates," Southern school systems do not show up uniformly inferior. Even if one is skeptical about the quality of teachers' preparation, it will not be profitable to seek the problems of Southern education in that direction. Average salaries are low in the South, though a half dozen Southern states have instituted larger raises than the typical state over the past decade. Yet Southern localities, and rural areas in particular, are at a disadvantage on two counts in competing for able teachers: lower salaries and a less stimulating intellectual environment. The shadow of past low-quality education is extended through generations of locally acculturated teachers, as it is in some rural parts of the North.

It is often pointed out that the South does not lag in the proportion of high school graduates entering college, but not so often is it also said that the South is below the North in the proportion of the age cohort finishing high school and in the proportion entering college.[49] As already mentioned, Southern high school pupils score lower on achievement tests except in the urban schools with high-status parents. Yet it would be superficial to attribute this lower achievement exclusively to deficiencies in the schools; it is a widespread cultural impoverishment that is responsible, and this deficiency can be remedied only slowly.[50]

Expenditure data can be used along with enrolments and other measures of educational participation to reveal variant patterns of public interest in education. Contrary to a widespread impression, when judged by the percentage of personal income spent on public schools, Southern states are not distinctively high but range over the whole national span. They are no more separate from other states for the proportion of personal incomes gathered by state and local taxes. They are marked out, however, for the large proportion of school funds obtained from non-local sources.[51]

Expenditure per classroom unit ranges widely among but also within states.[52] Though it tends to be higher in states with larger per capita incomes, the variation within states may be more important in assessing school policy.[53] The index of variation (Q_3-Q_1/M) ranges from .10 to .65

49. Urban Southern populations may exceed Northern for the percentage of adults with high school graduation, reflecting favorable net in-migration and age composition. It is worth noticing that as late as 1890 only 5 per cent of the age cohort finished secondary school in the nation.

50. Educational Testing Service, *Background Factors Relating to College Plans and Enrollment among Public High School Students*, 1957. Of the sample of Southern schools, 32 per cent had at least 40 per cent of their graduates entering college while only 21 per cent of central-state schools had so large a proportion (Table B-3). On the other hand, 35 per cent of the central-state and only 10 per cent of Southern schools had at least three-fifths of the fathers of students with a secondary education (Table B-7).

51. The equivocal outcome of shifting school finance to state funds is discussed in the last section. With the preoccupation of Southern states in recruiting industry, often at large waste of public funds, and the power of state officials to control local schools, this arrangement may seriously handicap schools.

52. See the reference cited in n. 39; these data allow us to make several new approaches to analysis of school finance.

53. Personal income per school-age child varies by a factor of nearly 4:1 (1.29 to 4.4 thousand dollars) among states. But since expenditure for sub-college stu-

among states, and it is not discernibly correlated with the median level of support among states. The ratio of median/2nd percentile measures the tendency of states to allow a few districts to tail off toward extremely low expenditures. Ranging from about 1.2 to 2.6, this index also shows no association with median expenditures. Among the lowest income states, however, there is a slight positive correlation, for as incomes go down median school expenditures approach a floor that constrains the ratio. Using a parallel measure for upward dispersion among districts within states (98th percentile/M), again no overall correlation emerges.[54] The states with high upward dispersion are Southern (except North Dakota); those with large downward dispersion are non-Southern (except Missouri). Kentucky is outstanding as a state with a low median expenditure dragging major parts of the state's population while a few centers are both wealthy and culturally active. There are marked differences among the Southern states in the patterning of expenditures and of inequalities in expenditure among districts.

Utilizing the data in the *Profiles* volume one can estimate the proportion of personal income the people of any state would have to disburse beyond their present level in order to raise the lagging districts to, say, the national median without reductions in any of the presently favored districts.[55] On the accompanying Chart 4 the present expenditures as a percentage of personal income are shown on the left scale: South Dakota is highest at about 4.5 per cent. The other axis marks off the traditional percentage of income needed to raise the per-classroom expenditure in each state to the national median. For Mississippi that would be about 3.0 per cent additional, and with the increment Mississippi would spend just over 6 per cent, as would South Dakota. As the radiating lines show, that would be to approximately double present school investments in ratio to income. For South Dakota it would represent a rise of about a third, but Louisiana, on the other hand, would need to raise its expenditure level by less than 10 per cent. The increments in proportions of personal income required range among Southern states from about .25 to 3 percentage points; the Southern states and the poorer states elsewhere would have to

dents in attendance is about 5 per cent of that sum, perhaps expanding school expenditures would not be an insurmountable burden, given the political mechanisms for reaching a decision to do so.

54. However, among both low- and high-income states (especially the former), those with higher median expenditures have smaller percentages of classroom units conspicuously above the median expenditure.

55. The discussion here uses only one of several possible criteria of new expenditure levels mentioned in the source. About 0.5 per cent would have to be added for public higher education, varying somewhat by state.

add the largest increments and multiply present expenditures by the largest ratios.

Of the sixteen states that would be in the top third on the new ratios of expenditures to personal income, twelve are among the lowest third for per capita personal income and eight are Southern (including Oklahoma and West Virginia). None of the lowest third of states by level of income and only one Southern state (Florida) would find themselves in the lowest third with respect to proportion of income spent on schools. Whether these increases would be deemed bearable must be a matter of opinion. While only four Southern states would end up spending at a higher ratio to income than North and South Dakota are already doing, all except four (Louisiana, Kentucky, Virginia, and Florida) would spend more relative to income than any of the remaining non-Southern states now disburse. But some Southern states are now spending more relative to income than other Southern states would spend when raising all districts to the national median expenditure per classroom. Within the South the present range in percentage of personal income going to public elementary and secondary schools is from 2.4 to 3.6; under the hypothetical new program it would be 3.0 to 6.2. The heaviest increments would not be in those states with the largest Negro populations.

The incompatible demands on Southern universities

The education of the populace in some societies can be discussed with little reference to higher education because the underpinnings of elementary and secondary education are firm and norms of attendance are widely diffused. In the American South popular education took root very recently and for over a century higher education has been under attack in an effort to eliminate new viewpoints about popular—and not only Negro—education. Cartter points out that until about 1830 "collegiate education was both fostered and respected," that there was little distinctively Southern about universities in the region, and that half the Southern graduates had attended Northern colleges. From that date until after World War I, "higher education rather passively reflected the withdrawal of the South from the main currents of American intellectual thought."[56] During that long period the colleges "mirrored the South's concern with its past rather than helped it to face its future."

No doubt such generalizations do injustice to individual colleges. One

56. A. M. Cartter, "Role of Higher Education in the Changing South," chap. xiii in McKinney and Thompson, eds., *op. cit.*, pp. 279-283.

must particularly acknowledge that Southern universities escaped the more virulent afflictions of McCarthyism; the assumption that professors are gentlemen—whether or not they be scholars—went further to preserve poise among laymen than in the North. Southern universities less often have been subjected to the indignities of teachers' oaths.[57] During the revival of higher education in the South in recent decades, one of the shining accomplishments has been the revisionist school of Southern history, created by Southerners teaching in Southern universities: their writings were subversive in substance even if they seldom found a local audience.

In the most recent years we can observe—in colleges as in other sectors of Southern education—marked contrasts among the states; desegregation of colleges was begun suavely in South Carolina and in a few other states while professors at the University of Mississippi experienced, along with their families, an unparalleled calumny. The highly publicized students at Berkeley believed they were struggling for freedom to become fuller participants in national life; they were not upholding a university administration cowed by demagogues to persecute fellow students. While much of the marching and soul searching over Viet Nam in Northern universities may be injudicious, the absence of that overt concern would be a danger signal. The absence or belated appearance of similar demonstrations for educational and civic rights among Southern students is surely not a sign of intellectual health—especially since these problems are more within the scope of regional or national control than are events in southeast Asia. In this context the cult of the Confederate flag must be seen as childishness or atavism.

"By mid-century the intellectual non-conformist had no place in the Southern college or university"—but this quotation referred to 1850.[58] Nicholls sums up Southern withdrawal from national life as "a general intolerance of intellectual progress and the intellectual process, approbation of violence as an ultimate weapon against non-conformist and dissenter, and the stagnation of the South's institutions of higher learning."[59] While Southern scholars have published objective analyses of Southern problems, their work has seldom affected public debate.

Some would find the difficulty in the leisurely and elitist values of Southern students, tracing these characteristics back to the romanticism

57. See citation to Nicholls in n. 7, p. 139.

58. A. M. Cartter, "Qualitative Aspects of Southern University Education," chap. iii in McKie, ed., *op. cit.*, p. 41.

59. Nicholls, *op. cit.*, p. 133; his account is updated by W. P. Fidler, "Academic Freedom in the South Today," *Bulletin of the American Association of University Professors*, LI (Winter, 1965), 413-421.

of slavery days. But obviously, and especially in view of the more selective high-school attendance, there is no lack of native ability among Southern college students. To be sure, their demonstrated academic proficiency is below that in Northern colleges.[60] Student bodies with small proportions of superior students are nearly twice as frequent among Southern institutions. The North can tolerate its many hundreds of inferior colleges because it can fill many superior ones. The absence of social pressure for diligent work in high school underlies the scarcity of first-rank universities or colleges in the South, for the college years are too late to inculcate zeal for intellectual work. The same unexhilarating mental climate explains the scarcity of doctorates awarded by Southern universities and, together with ties to a familistic culture, it explains the reluctance of Southern winners of national graduate fellowships to venture into Northern universities.[61]

The inculcation of innovative behavior requires institutional embodiment: centers of advanced study and research. A few Southern states have spent more on higher education (in ratio to income or per head of population) than the national average, "but they received few concrete benefits from such costly expenditures as long as they insisted on keeping their traditions intact."[62] And just as the occupational mix in the Southern economy is weighted against the high-skill categories, so its industries tend not to be the ones requiring large expenditures for research and development. In many states, not only in the South, this problem is one of scale in creating nuclei of effective research. One or two superior professors each in a few departments of a few universities cannot generate innovative ferment. The problem, just recently being tackled in a few localities, is to move in whole departments of superior quality, for only in this way will scholarship acquire the critical mass to affect public policy. Phrase this as a problem in public opinion, as conflict among elites, as shortage of opinion leaders, or how you will, there is little vitalizing dialogue with public leaders. Yet most of the latter, one must assume, were once the students of Southern professors.

60. College Entrance Examination Board, *Manual of Freshman Class Profiles*, 1962 ed. There were 171 Northern but only 54 Southern schools reporting. I have taken the *numbers* scoring 650-699 and 450-499 as crude indexes of two levels of academic proficiency. For each region I computed the ratio of the number of entrants with the high to the number with the low score. Of the Northern schools 19 per cent and of the Southern 7 per cent had five times or more of the high- as of the low-scoring freshmen: 36 and 17 per cent respectively had as many high- as low-scoring entrants. Half the Southern but only a quarter of the Northern schools had only one high scorer for each five low scorers.

61. Cartter, in McKie, ed., *op. cit.*, pp. 45, 61-62; Cartter also shows (p. 294 in McKinney and Thompson, eds., *op. cit.*) that fewer graduates of Southern colleges go on to earn the doctorate.

62. L. Reissman, "Urbanization in the South," *ibid.*, p. 98.

In this context the popularity of the states' rights argument in a preponderantly defensive form must be laid in large part to deficiencies in Southern higher education. There has been more concern to limit the educational opportunities of Negroes and poorer whites at the educational cost of the middle and superior strata of whites than to improve the educational system of the South even if Negroes inadvertently benefited in large measure.[63] Compare the transformation in Northern thinking about labor unions and immigrants; even if these have been conversions to new fallacies, as some would say, they have manifested vigorous accommodation to challenges and willingness to face the implications of public debate.

To an unusual degree Southern universities have been prisoners of regional nationalism, of two kinds. The first is essentially exclusive, inward-looking, economically restrictionist, and politically aggressive. Those values of the larger society that would have brought indigenous economic advance have been rejected, with pretension to values that would bring financial subventions. The widening of opportunities for the populace has been resisted. The second nationalism is mainly nostalgic, striving to preserve a local tradition; in our world this aspiration can retain little vitality against the mass media so long as it is mainly a restriction on opportunities and a ritualist intoning of vestigial beliefs. A third kind of regionalism has yet to win a major place: the creative regional loyalty that searches for identity in a changing world and that could foster a breakthrough into a more open society.[64]

Some years ago a forensically brilliant plea for gradualness in desegregation was published.[65] The relevance of this document in a discussion of Southern higher education is that university faculties did not seize upon that book as the basis for a campaign to bring reasonableness into the debate. Paul's "brief" expressed the hope that the Supreme Court would permit states to act appropriately in order

> to prevent enforced mixed attendance from resulting in such conditions as: *a*) Racial antipathies seriously impairing the proper functioning of the schools, *b*) Serious impairment of the academic standards of the schools, and *c*) Threats to the health or psychological security of individual students who might be affected by a change in schools.[66]

63. L. D. Rubin, Jr., "Notes on a Rear Guard Action," in F. E. Vandiver, ed., *The Idea of the South* (Chicago: University of Chicago Press, 1964), pp. 37-39.

64. See the citation in n. 2.

65. J. C. N. Paul, *The School Segregation Decision* (Chapel Hill: University of North Carolina Press, 1954); I do not attribute the views discussed to the author personally, assuming he was writing as counsel to his governor.

66. *Ibid.*, pp. 87, 81, 111, 79.

His argument could only encourage what he deplored: "delays, dodges, and litigious confusion." He asked attention to "relevant considerations demonstrating the likelihood of strife," despite the innumerable previous examples within the South of the capacity of officials and leaders to bring public acceptance of major changes. He urged allowance for "differences in academic backgrounds between Negro and White students," and the need to consider whether pupils of one race would be able to "keep up" with those of the other race—thus ignoring a half-century of intelligence testing. He urged separate classes for some or all Negro students if they lagged academically and were unable "to participate in the white class"—the last phrase assuming the whole matter in dispute.

Many law professors have upheld the legitimacy of the Court's decisions, but the foregoing arguments are in the province rather of social scientists and educators. Yet only sporadically have Southern social scientists or schoolmen challenged those arguments. Obviously a fair proportion of white pupils cannot keep up with able Negro children; the latter should not have to sit with the less able pupils of either race if one takes the "keep up with" theme seriously. Psychological insecurity accompanies all social change and in this nation violence will arise whenever signaled by officials; these are hardly arguments against any proposal. The dereliction lies in the failure of Southern universities to put their prestige behind dissemination of the facts on desegregation as they forthrightly did with regard to combating the boll weevil, overproduction of cotton, or the search for new industry.

Converting a rising tolerance into new political structures

Southerners, along with citizens of other regions, are becoming more liberal in their views about the capacities and rights of Negroes.[67] Rising levels of schooling no doubt contributed to this re-orientation, for within some congressional districts there is evidence that candidates favoring desegregation do not always lose.[68] Overall, however, the rigidity of Southern policies on race has been disproportionate to the known pattern of attitudes among Southerners individually. Permissive positions on questions touched by race have found little political ground. Not that Northerners have been dramatically more tolerant. Yet Northern accommoda-

67. P. B. Sheatsley, "White Attitudes toward the Negro," *Daedalus* (Winter, 1966), 217-238.

68. N. Lustig, "The Relationships between Demographic Characteristics and Pro-Integration Vote," *Social Forces*, XL (March, 1962), 205-208.

tion to minority demands and acquiescence in extension of the suffrage have been more flexible.

The "delay, dodges, and litigious confusion" of Southern public life with respect to schools have kept regional educational differences wide but also have exacerbated the politics of education. "The individualism of the dominant class was extreme and socially irresponsible."[69] Most conspicuous has been the readiness of Southern leaders—which brings us again to universities—to support unequal education among the separated races long after the time when it was clear to them that separate education was doomed. Thereby many of the arguments cited by Paul for delaying segregation were given new life. A few simple illustrations of inequality in provision of schools during the 1950's illuminate the ways of Southern school politics.[70] But the data reveal at the same time how dissimilar are the Southern states in educational provision for the two races and for rural pupils.

For example, a larger proportion of white than of Negro pupils in both rural and metropolitan areas in each Southern state (except in Kentucky rural areas) were receiving federally aided lunches: differences ranged from around 20 percentage points in some states to 70 points in metropolitan Mississippi. Race differences were larger in rural areas. Transport of rural pupils by bus reveals a contrast to the foregoing pattern in some ways rather contrary to expectation. Though only in Virginia (at the end of the period) were Negro pupils more often transported, by the end of the period in no state was the difference as much as 20 points, and in all but Florida the increase in the proportion riding buses was greater for the Negro pupils.

The pattern for per-pupil expenditures is less neat. Over the short period covered, increases in expenditures were greater for rural than for urban pupils (though more so among the whites), and they were larger for Negro than for white pupils. The state levels of expenditure became less disparate over the period. To choose extremes, the range among states in ratio of expenditure on metropolitan white to that for rural Negro pupils was 3½ times as large in the first as in the last year, mainly because of a sharp leveling-up of provision for rural Negro pupils in Mississippi. In several states less was spent on urban Negro than on rural white pupils. The ratio of metropolitan to rural expenditures per pupil was slightly larger among Negroes. Almost uniformly the ratio of white to Negro expenditures was larger in rural than in metropolitan systems.

69. Nicholls, *op. cit.*, pp. 184, 105.
70. Southern Education Reporting Service, *Southern Schools: Progress and Problems*, 1959, pp. 121, 154, 165.

Even if we lacked other direct expressions of intent, white resistance to parity of education even without desegregation has been manifest. When one tries to interpret changes, the elusive question is the importance of Negro insistence as against white resistance.[71] A recent South-wide investigation of Negro registration for voting has made this pattern clearer, if not more understandable.[72]

The salient factor proved to be the percentage of Negroes in the county population, even that percentage for 1900; the negative correlations with this factor held after controlling many associated ones. The county proportion of Negroes in white-collar jobs favored registration, while education and income of Negroes were important where their percentage in the population was not large.

The most paradoxical finding was that Negro registration was negatively correlated with the level of white education; there distinctly was not the carry-over from education into public affairs that we have become accustomed to anticipate. "The usual effect of an increase in average schooling for whites in the South as a whole appears to be to give the white people more of the skills that are needed to express effectively their anti-Negro sentiment."[73] Though this negative correlation was not large, it persisted after controlling for other factors. Neither the agricultural nor the industrial features of counties nor the presence of large cities had much effect.

Equally disconcerting was the low correlation between proportions of whites and Negroes registered. White registration was not stimulated by a large proportion of Negro residents; more whites were registered in the less urban counties and in those with the lowest level of white schooling.

Withal, the multiple R^2 for the combined social and economic factors was only .28, but this was improved to .49 by allowing for political features of counties: use of tests for registration, presence of "racial" political organizations within either race, the presence of past or present violence in race relations. Most of the diversity among Southern counties in rates of Negro registration remains to be identified after this elaborate exploration.

The authors point out that those factors displaying rising trends over time (e.g., income levels or white-collar employment) are positively correlated with Negro registration, while those that are negatively correlated are declining with time. However, in view of the paradoxical relationships

71. T. F. Pettigrew, "Continuing Barriers to Desegregated Education in the South," *Sociology of Education*, XXXVIII (Winter, 1965), 99-111.

72. D. R. Matthews and J. W. Prothro, "Social and Economic Factors and Negro Voter Registration in the South," *American Political Science Review*, LXXVII (March, June, 1963), 24-44, 355-367. Included were all Southern counties with at least 1 per cent of Negroes in the population; registration data were for 1958.

73. *Ibid.*, p. 38.

between white schooling and registration by individuals of either race, one hesitates to draw confident trend inferences from this cross-section analysis. Given the historic ambivalence of elite white groups in the South toward the role of Negroes in politics, it is doubtful that optimistic predictions based only on intra-Southern influences would be warranted. The authors of the foregoing study find that "competitive politics" does favor Negro political rights if there is a candidate with permissive views on Negro rights. But factors that are influential in political situations elsewhere in the nation, such as education, have less clear-cut impact upon the responses of political leaders in the South. Not even an intense longing for economic prosperity can be depended upon to initiate educational advance or sustain a school system suited to the development of Southern human resources.

The above-mentioned investigation found fewer Negroes registered than the regression equation predicted in five states (Mississippi, South Carolina, Alabama, Virginia, Arkansas); the percentages registered varied from 3 to 28. Five states had at least the predicted registrants (Georgia, Louisiana, North Carolina, Florida, Tennessee); percentages varied from 30 to 39 and to a high of 72 in Tennessee (suspected of uncleared rolls). Earlier in this chapter I used indexes of racial differentiation in schooling and these can now be related to the foregoing grouping of the states by rate of Negro registration. There were no differences on the average in my indexes between the two five-state sets for farm or urban populations at any of the three levels of schooling. There is, however, some pattern in the scattergrams. Thus Mississippi has high indexes of racial differentiation in schooling with low registration of Negroes, while Tennessee displays the opposite combination. Though registration is high in Florida, school differentiation is also marked; in several of the graphs Georgia and Louisiana resemble Florida. A repeated pattern contains a band of states running from high differentiation with low voting in Mississippi down through South Carolina, Alabama, Virginia, North Carolina, to Tennessee with high registration and low differentiation between the races in schooling.

Agenda for research

Innumerable topics warranting further investigation have been implied or suggested in the foregoing pages. On some topics sample borings into educational data for the South have been reported. In other instances the opportunities lie principally in relating new investigations of educational topics to ongoing work by specialists in labor markets or the electoral process, for example. The following pages outline a variety of studies that would together give us a much better understanding of the place of education in Southern society.

1. Historic continuities in the cultural geography of education. Depending upon one's preference for one or another type of data, one will nod in satisfaction or raise his eyebrows in astonishment at the cited conclusion that present high-school students' test scores state by state are predicted better by army induction tests in 1917 than by present levels of school expenditures. In education as in other features of societal life, moreover, there are broad subregional stabilities from before the Civil War to the present day. Certain areas appear consistently to have moved ahead, while other localities have persistently been laggards. Exploration of these historic continuities is not antiquarianism but essential for understanding present-day educational developments as well as for design of policy. Closely related is the task of tracing out the educational histories of the major social types in Southern life: varieties of "the Negro," "poor whites," landed groups, new business groups, etc.[74]

2. Correlates of local differences in educational achievement. Mass surveys of pupil achievement (as the Bloom study or Project Talent) can enable us to distinguish and eventually to measure the quality of schools apart from the underlying community and family differences that facilitate or constrain what schools may accomplish. Only when those sets of factors can be distinguished can we assess the effects of new educational policies or explain why relative rises in expenditures bring so little improvement in pupils' qualifications. We can hope to explain why both community differences and social-status differentials in educational attainment are distinctively large in the South. With such data in hand we are prepared to take up serious inquiries about the importance of quality of teachers or the division of expenditures among categories of educational operations. Just as areas have persistently been leaders or laggards, so educational indexes of areas are correlated with occupational structure and political complexion. The analysis of process in educational advance links historical studies with contemporary area variations.[75] It is in such a context that one can seek to identify both the facilitating and the stultifying influences in different places that so strongly affect children's educational aspirations

74. Stable contrasts of educational level can be traced for French departments from late seventeenth to mid-nineteenth centuries; see C. Arnold Anderson and M. J. Bowman, eds., *Education and Economic Development* (Chicago: Aldine Publishing Company, 1965), pp. 333-339.
75. See the long quotation on p. 167.

and achievements. Of particular importance in this connection is identification of type-situations with respect to racial imparities: where Negroes receive comparatively good but whites comparatively poor instruction, where both are equally disadvantaged, and so on. Though there are broad continuities in educational level among localities as among regions over the decades, changes nevertheless occur—as the decline in New England over the past half-century. Cross-section studies using contemporary data throw light on these shifts of historic differentials, but the latter also link up with non-educational events to provide the social structure within which specifically pedagogic operations go on.

3. *Interrelationships among the levels of school.* The "educational pyramid" has become a favorite object of attention among educational planners. Under such rubrics as "survival rates," "articulation," and "selection," the same ideas have served for educational diagnosis in this country for many decades. Analyses have moved from rather simple numerical tabulations to subtle studies of student attitudes. The ante-bellum Southern eminence for college attendance has never been re-established, though one faint trace remains: comparatively large proportions of secondary graduates entering college accompanied by low ratios at both levels in relation to the age cohort. Today the numbers are of less interest than analysis of the factors associated with selectivity of secondary and college attendance: "native" ability, academic proficiency, social background, and aspirations for advanced education.[76] Especially within colleges, there is need for investigations of academic climates, school "productivity," and "student press." Only through exploration of those factors will one come to understand the deficiencies in Southern higher education.

4. *The occupational matrix.* Within the economy occupation is the link between education and income. (In the South particularly, one needs to add race to the matrix.) As the census has embraced progressively more complete data tabulated in more useful ways, it has become possible to identify the main features in which the matrix varies among subpopulations of the nation. An almost endless series of inquiries can be carried out with the computer tapes of those data, but such inquiries have barely begun for the South. Of special importance is the identification of the occupational locus of racial imparities in employment and their foundations in education particularly, and that matrix needs to be set up also

76. Comparatively few of the citations in N. Sanford, *The American College*, refer to the South. It would be profitable to replicate the Wisconsin studies of William Sewell and his collaborators (tracing college attendance back to family, school, and community factors) in a Southern state.

for representative areas and linked to other inquiries (see #2 above). Southern research men will have to move aggressively into full partnership in the twin specialties of economics and sociology of education. This matrix has no claim to monopolize attention; its merit is the ease with which, having those data in hand, one can confidently move to more subtle studies without becoming lost in speculation.

5. Confidence in acquisition of roles. The especially favorable economic position of the better-educated Southerners, and the even more distinctively unfavorable position of the less-educated Southerner of either race, stem equally from what we may call varying "confidence" in acquiring and using skills. These are subtle effects of status, parallel to the familiar effects of race on which so much has been written. As has been mentioned, the South has disproportionate representation in the less skilled occupations and in the least-paid sub-occupations. Whether schooling "pays off" depends largely upon whether the milieu encourages effective use of training. Much of the economic complexion of the South rests in differential aspirations and "confidence," qualities not identified in the conventional indexes of schooling. Measurement of actual job qualifications, as distinguished from the formal ones, for similar occupations in different regions will illuminate many of the puzzles about lagging Southern economic development. This line of inquiry leads also to studies of the specific qualifications and roles of migrants into the South and to the occupational fate of out-migrants working in the North. It is these kinds of attitudes one has in mind when he says that the capacity to use borrowed capital productively depends upon the capacity to generate capital locally—here meaning mainly human capital.

6. Assessment of alternative means for improvement of Southern education. Only superficial handling of data has allowed the faith in expenditures as an educational remedy to become so well rooted. Under this broad heading fall investigations ranging from detailed correlation of expenditures with education indexes, through studies of educational legislation, to identification of the factors in quality of education. Since many Southern states have been willing to raise expenditures more rapidly than states elsewhere and since there are such large intra-southern differences in levels of schooling provided, these kinds of studies can be prosecuted with comparative ease. Analysis of districts lying at different points along the distributions reported in the *Profiles* volume would provide firmer conclusions about the merits of different procedures for improvement of schools. In turn such data can provide the base from which to launch studies of public opinion: willingness to sacrifice for education, readiness for major transformations in school systems, or linkages to subcultures as regards racial imparities and economic readjustments in agriculture.

7. *Spill-over effects of education in the South.* Unless serious faults in the analysis can be identified, the study of factors influencing Negro registration for voting should be taken as the first step in a major research program on Southern education. Initially it would be desirable to substitute some education indexes as dependent variables and rerun the analysis. Then, juxtaposing the two studies, one would be ready for penetrating inquiries as to why the generous stock of educated men in the South has so little (apparent) effect upon public policy in education or other aspects of Southern public life. Related studies come quickly to mind. We need to compare the spheres of activity in community life of educated individuals in the South and in other parts of the country. Interviews of political and civic leaders can be related to their education, especially in college. And there is the broad topic of the outside activities of university faculties compared to the extramural contributions of similar men in other regions. It has been a platitude that formal education is distinctively cumulative in effects, yet apparently the social structure of the South has blocked this outcome. The degree to which the conclusion is warranted and the mechanisms by which the stultification has occurred (if it has) deserve scrutiny.

8. *The politics of education.* In the nation generally we are just beginning serious investigation of this broad area. The special circumstances of the South—mainly but not solely the race situation—give special importance to studies of policy-making for schools. On the higher level there are inquiries to be made about intimidation, however subtle, of university faculties. We do not yet fully understand the varying local responses to the movement for school desegregation, nor the political devices by which the varying responses have been implemented. There is the continuing relative Southern lack of interest in accepting or matching funds for compensatory schooling, for Headstart and similar programs, and for new curricula. Each of these issues is resolved by political processes, and we need to find out how those processes have worked in different places. In this connection, one doubts the wisdom of the strong Southern predilection for centralized funds of schools. Given the racial and status tensions about education, centralization may have retarded accommodation to new developments and inhibited would-be pace-setter communities from moving confidently ahead to new educa-

tional programs. This last topic leads back into the historic and sub-regional projects mentioned above (#1 and #2).

Table 1. Dropout rates for 19-year-olds, by race, residence, and state.

	Urban		*Farm*		*Negro-White*		*Farm-Urban*	
State	*White*	*Negro*	*White*	*Negro*	*Urban*	*Farm*	*White*	*Negro*
Virginia	29.8	42.9	44.7	59.3	13.1	14.6	14.9	16.4
North Carolina	24.7	37.2	38.3	53.5	12.5	15.2	13.6	16.3
South Carolina	29.3	49.0	42.9	58.5	19.7	15.6	13.6	7.5
Georgia	27.3	44.9	35.4	61.0	17.6	25.6	8.1	16.1
Alabama	26.1	40.4	38.7	50.3	14.3	11.6	12.6	9.9
Mississippi	17.4	44.7	32.0	50.1	27.3	18.1	14.6	5.4
Minnesota	13.5		23.0				9.5	
Iowa	15.0		16.3				1.3	
Missouri	24.4		30.1				5.7	
North Dakota	10.3		32.0				21.7	
South Dakota	13.4		27.3				13.9	
Nebraska	14.3		12.9				−1.4	
Kansas	20.1		14.9				−5.2	

Source: see n. 33.

Table 2. Distribution of gains in enrolment of 16-17-year-olds by periods between 1910 and 1960 by state per capita income and enrolment rate in 1960.

	1960 income per capita and enrolment rate					
	Top third		*Middle third*		*Lowest third*	
1910-1930 gain under 10%						
1930-1950 gain under 10%	—		*Texas*	3*	*Kentucky*	4
					So. Car.	4
					Arkansas	3
					Miss.	2
					Idaho	1
1930-1950 gain 10-19%	Colorado	2	Missouri	3	W. Virginia	4
			Vermont	2	No. Car.	4
			Kansas	2	Tenn.	4
					Virginia	3
					Georgia	3
					Alabama	3
					Oklahoma	2
					No. Dakota	1
					So. Dakota	1
1930-1950 gain 20%+	—		Minnesota	1	—	
1910-1930 gain 10-19%						
1930-1950 gain under 10%	*Wyoming*	1	—		—	
1930-1950 gain 10-19%	Michigan	2	N. Hampshire	3	*Louisiana*	3
	Oregon	1	Florida	3	Maine	2
			Arizona	3		
			N. Mexico	2		
			Iowa	1		
			Montana	1		
			Nebraska	1		
1930-1950 gain 20%+	Delaware	3	R. Island	4	—	
	Maryland	3				
	Penn.	2				
	Conn.	2				
	N. Jersey	2				
1910-1930 gain 20%+						
1930-1950 gain under 10%	Calif.	2	Utah	1	—	
	Nevada	1				
	Wash.	1				
1930-1950 gain 10-19%	Mass.	2	—		—	
	Ohio	2				
	Indiana	2				
1930-1950 gain 20%+	New York	2	Wisconsin	1	—	
	Illinois	2				

Italicized states are those gaining over 10% between 1950 and 1960; none gained as many as 20 points in that decade.

* Enrolment rate classes for 1960: 1, 85%+; 2, 80-84%; 3, 75-79%; 4, under 75%.

Table 3. Indexes of differentiation in schooling by race and by residence for level of school, age, and region.

	By race			
	Age 25-29 in 1960		*Age 45-54 in 1960*	
	Urban	*Farm*	*Urban*	*Farm*
Completing 0-4 years of school				
North	.37	.70*	.71	.82*
South	.57	.47	.64	.53
Completing 12+ years of school				
North	.18	.34	.36	.33
South	.32	.60	.54	.70

	By residence			
	Age 25-29 in 1960		*Age 45-54 in 1960*	
	White	*Non-white*	*White*	*Non-white*
Completing 0-4 years of school				
North	.32	.72*	.05	.30*
South	.59	.51	.37	.22
Completing 12+ years of school				
North	.06	.24	.21	.16
South	.24	.57	.43	.63

* See text comments on schooling of Indians.

Chart I. Percentage of 16-17 year-olds enrolled in school.

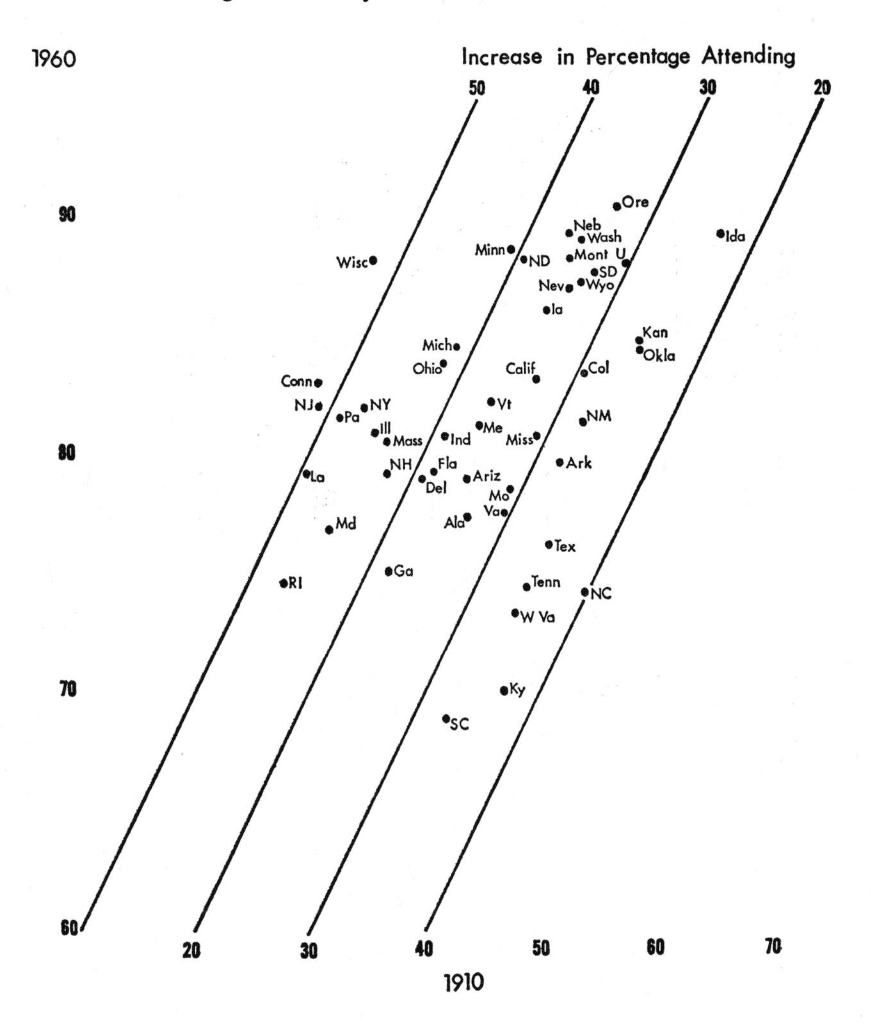

Chart II. Old and young indexes of racial differentiation.

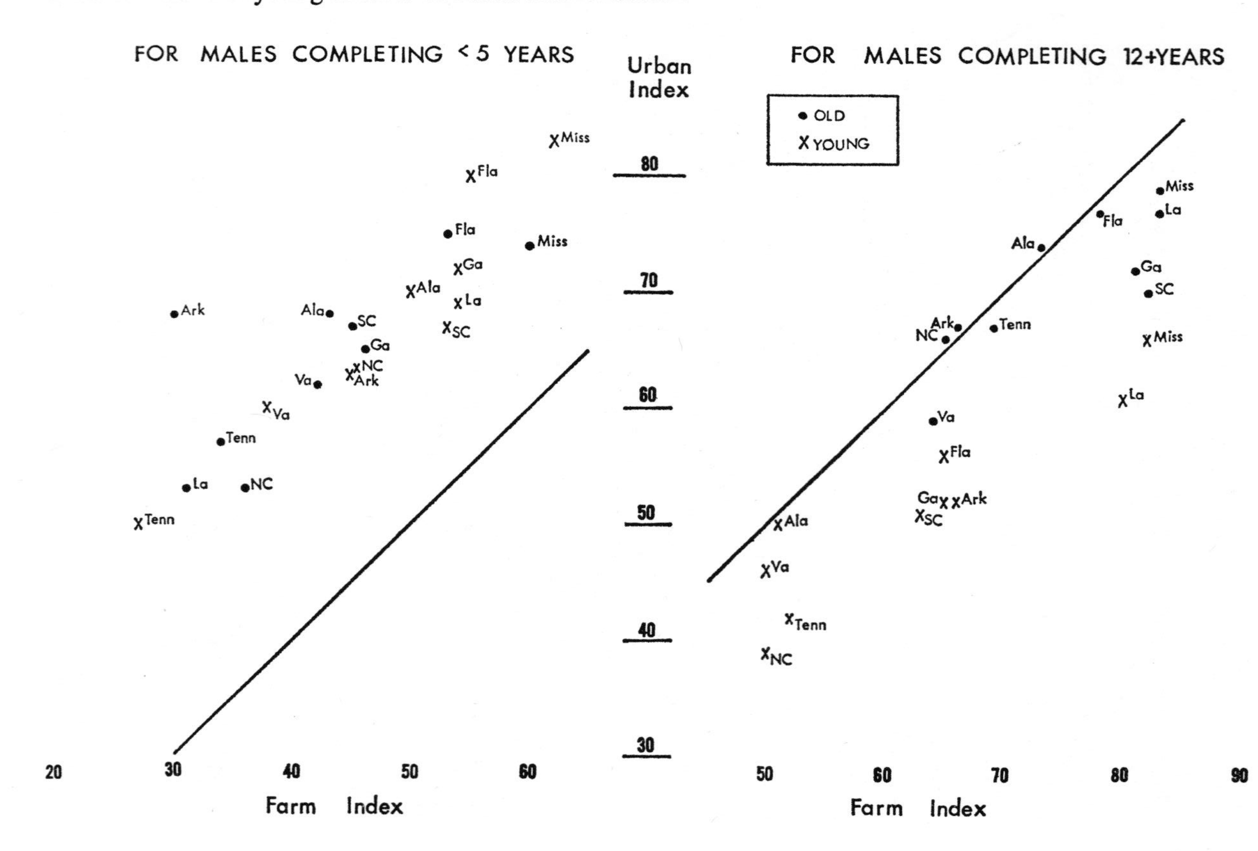

Chart III. Urban and farm indexes of racial differentiation.

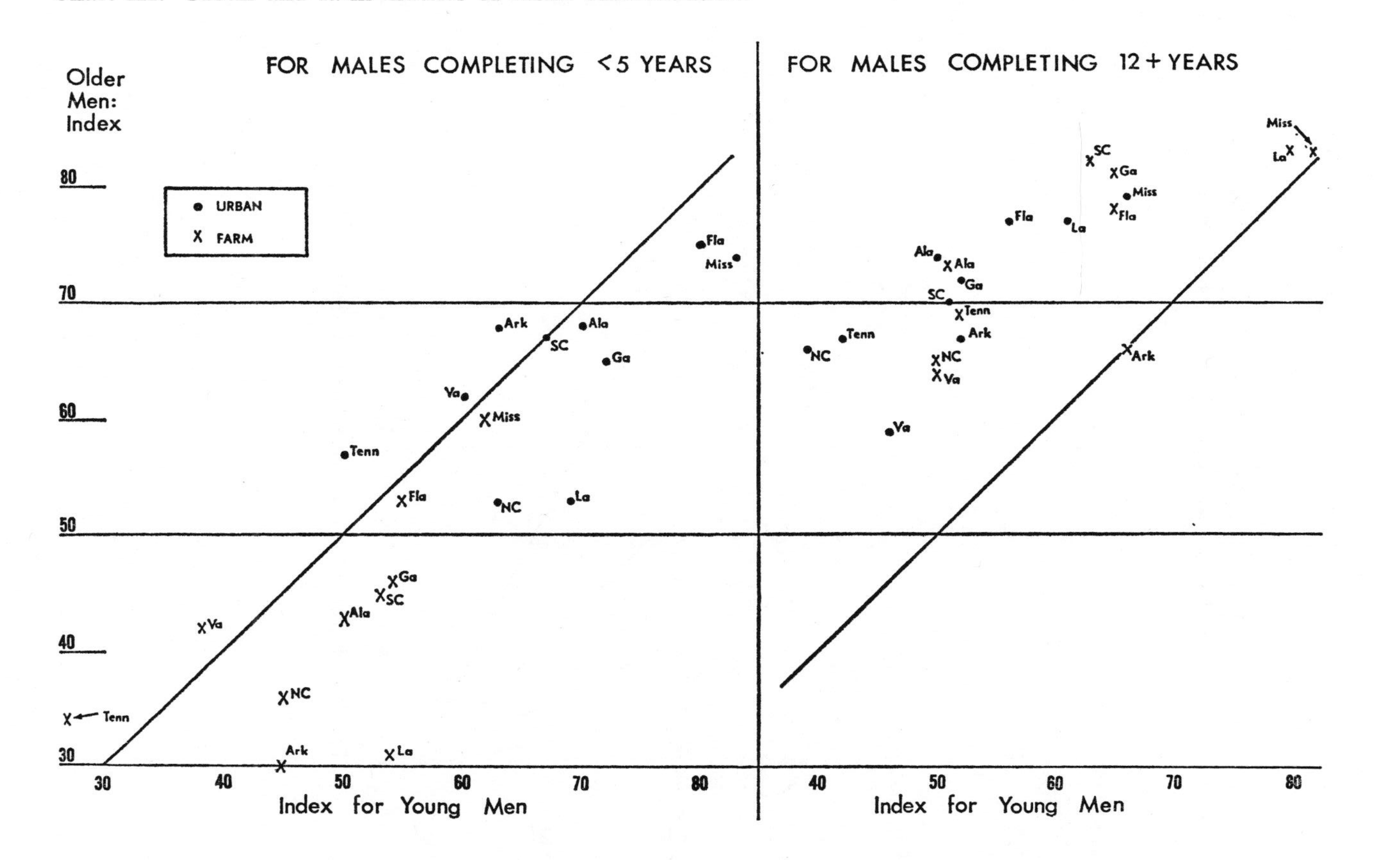

Chart IV. 1960 educational expenditures and increments needed to raise classrooms to national median, as percentage of state personal income.

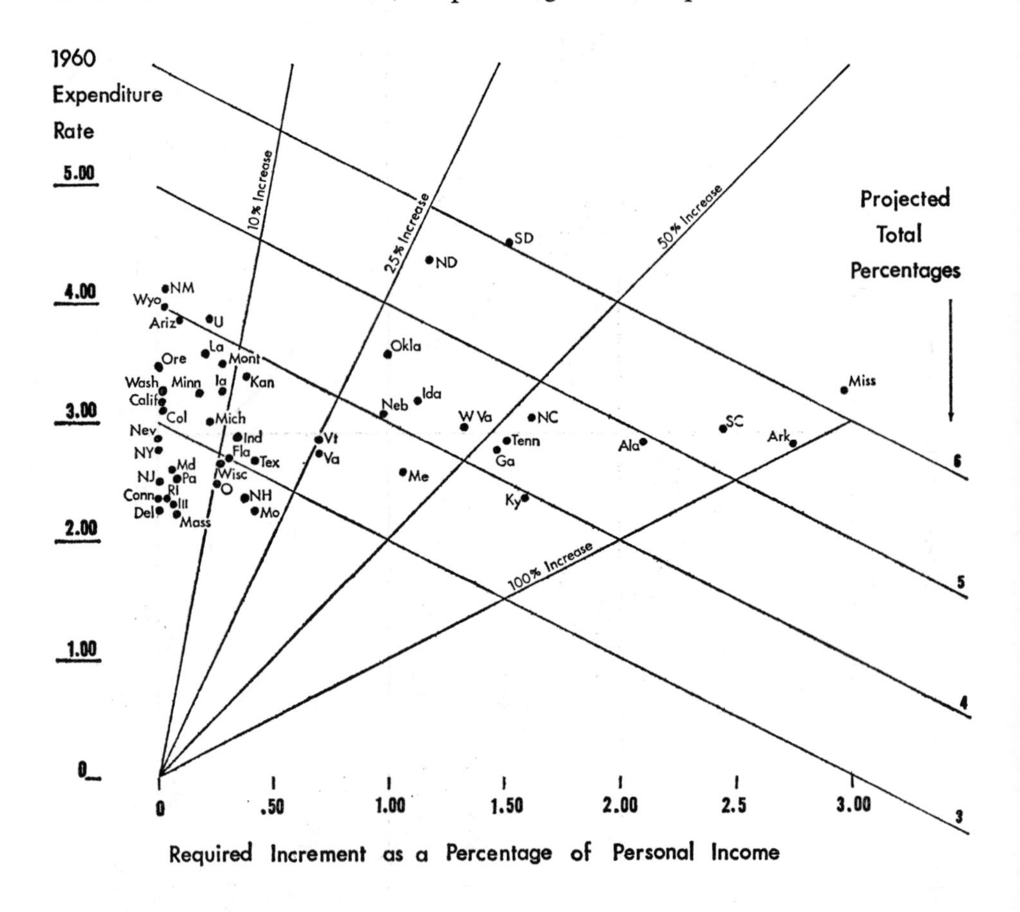

An agenda for research in religion / Samuel S. Hill, Jr.

It has been observed that the American South is the most studied region in the world. Although a great deal of comparative research would be required to support (or deny) that observation, beyond any question a ponderous amount of scholarly attention has been paid to the South. This is true of historical, political, economic, sociological, and literary inquiry—indeed inquiry into virtually the gamut of the social behavior and spiritual expressions of the Southern people.

Only one dimension of regional life has been notably neglected, the religious. It is true that histories of the South have incorporated chapters or portions of chapters describing religious developments and currents. Moreover, ecclesiastical historians have surveyed the careers of their respective denominations in full-length volumes. But exhaustive, comprehensive explorations into Southern religious history have been wanting.

Similarly, sociologists have not been unaware of the religious factor in regional life, as illustrated by Pope's *Millhands and Preachers*, chapters in such books as Dollard's *Caste and Class in a Southern Town*, Pettigrew and Campbell's on-the-spot investigations in Little Rock during the 1957 school desegregation process as reported in *Christians in Racial Crisis*, and Father Fichter's research among Catholics in the New Orleans area. In addition, many cross-sectional treatments of Southern life, from W. T. Couch's *Culture in the South* of 1934 to McKinney and Thompson's 1965 symposium, have acknowledged the religious aspect with useful chapters. At the same time, Sellers' *The Southerner as American* and Sindler's *Change in the Contemporary South*, among others, have fastened onto numerous elements of the regional experience without touching the religious element, except incidentally.

Signs of change in this respect are increasing. The year 1964 saw the publication of Kenneth K. Bailey's *Southern White Protestantism in the Twentieth Century*, a general treatment of the major movements and concerns of the popular denominations during this century. The spring meeting of the American Society of Church History in April, 1966, devoted its entire program to "Religion in the South." A good deal of excitement will greet the publication of a "Gastonia Revisited" volume now in progress at the hands of Earle, Knudsen, and Shriver. Several other studies on the topic are forthcoming. And the present symposium has solicited from among fewer than a dozen papers one dealing with religion.

One is bound to ask why so conspicuous a part of Southern life has gone relatively uninvestigated. No doubt some will respond to this query by raising questions about the query itself. But, proceeding, one cannot resist the urge to speculate on the reasons for which the religious element in Southern life has received such sparing treatment. For one thing, Edwin McNeill Poteat, writing in the Couch symposium, typified the Southern religious spirit when he suggested that religion is a profoundly personal matter: "The combination . . . of the private and sacred qualities of religion presents a formidable barrier to an essay upon it." A high degree of reverence for religious truth, authority, and experience has permeated Southern society, including men of the caliber of Poteat—whose genuine sophistication, by the way, did enable him at the same time to parallel this reverence with an assessment of the Southern religious picture requiring rare powers of discernment. But the overwhelming majority of Southerners, characteristically pietists, have adopted a hands-off policy, regarding religious faith as something pre-eminently to be lived and spread, not scrutinized.

As for the religious bodies themselves, they have had small incentive to subject their belief- and value-systems to critical analysis, for several reasons. First, they have conceived of themselves as having worlds to conquer, that is, souls to save, and a mission to be shared. Consumed by these goals, they have not been inclined to study themselves except with a view to stepping up efficiency in the accomplishment of their acknowledged tasks. Moreover, short on sophistication, in the leadership sector really as well as among the masses, they have lacked perspective on themselves. Busy doing a job, unremittingly engaged in generating conversion in the present for the sake of a future destiny, they have had no occasion to ask where their institutions came from, or whether the process of acculturation has affected their understanding, or whether social change obligates them to revise, reformulate, and redirect their positions. The religious institutions have been almost entirely devoid of any sense of history. Fabulously successful in churching the populace and impregnating the culture with their world-view and morality, they have not been provoked to sit in judgment on their own uncritically espoused norms. For example, the surprise of Southern Baptists at anyone's suggestion that they might not be classical Baptists but largely an indigenous American phenomenon would be exceeded only by a total unconcern with the whole topic, owing both to their "historylessness" and to their ensconcement as a culture-faith in a "sacred" society (in Howard Becker's sense). Similarly, Methodists in the South would take little notice, we suspect, of any accusation that they have departed significantly from many of the concerns and positions of John Wesley. Convinced of their authenticity, the popular Southern religious bodies have carried on business as usual, perpetuating their accumulated tradition without subjecting it to the Protestant principle of self-criticism and self-renewal in the light of transcendent norms.

Scholars have scarcely been any more interested in studying the religious dimensions of Southern life. Intellectual historians have not been attracted to Southern Protestantism's ideology, no doubt because of the absence of depth, complexity, and richness within it. The operative ideology of the Southern church has been, it has to be said, surpassingly simple and dull. Social scientists have shied away from inquiry into the religious factor, for the intelligible reason that it was long an assumption of their trade to regard religion as a function of social class, economic conditions, personality need, or some other *primary* phenomenon, and therefore undeserving of independent, or even serious, investigation. Strains of positivism have persisted, leading to the evaluation of traditional religion as, in Gerhard Lenski's words, "institutionalized ignorance and superstition." Scholars in the humanities have not failed to note the prevalence of religious idiom and imagery in regional life, but perhaps here, too, richness has been so generally wanting that few have deemed the religious element of sufficient import to dwell on it.

Finally, we cite two other possible causes for the common disregard of Southern religion on the part of regional analysts. First, their attention has been directed for the most part toward the South itself—quite legitimately so—and not to the Southern region under comparison and contrast with other cultures. But Southern religion, as a belief system at least, ignites the interest of the scholar only when it is set alongside other manifestations of Christianity. Cross-cultural investigation throws the Southern patterns into colorful and significant light, whereas the Southern religious ideology by itself has limited appeal and value for the researcher. Second, the genre of literature on the Southern region devoted to the subject of economic progress—a major genre in recent decades—has had no need (apparent, at any rate) for investigation of the religious dimension in Southern life. Two hypotheses may be advanced by way of accounting for this omission: one, the prevalence of a supposition that religion is not a correlate to secular progress; the other, an inchoate conviction that the Southern religious syndrome may be dysfunctional to the economic renascence to which regional leaders aspire.

Before spelling out some aspects of the Southern religious configuration which invite research, a word is in order concerning the orientation of the author of this paper. Trained in systematic and historical theology primarily, I claim no special competence as a professional social scientist.

Most of the topics to follow emerge from my chief interest in the points where historical theology, geography, and sociological theory converge. (I have not endeavored to treat Jewish and Roman Catholic patterns, though they deserve serious considerations.) It will become as clear to my readers as it is to me that a professional historian or sociologist or religious ethicist would produce a notably different list of items.

1. *Theoretical considerations*

At the outset, it must be made clear that Southern religious patterns do in fact differ from the religious picture in every other subculture of Christendom. Although middle-to-low Protestantism, the variety of Christianity which predominates in Dixie, is prominent in the American Middle West, for example, it does not have exclusive hold there. Indeed, at no other time and place in the history of Christianity, have low-church Protestant groups achieved majority status and the chief position of responsibility. (Scotland offers no real parallel inasmuch as a classical Calvinism, not associable with the subjectivist orientation of middle-to-low denominational families, is the normative influence there.) In the South the Baptists enjoy a heavy statistical preponderance, itself a remarkable fact when one considers both the Baptist theological intent—the creation of pure (regenerate) communities of faith, and historical Baptism's standard situation as a minority group on the perimeter of society's religious, as well as secular, affairs. Their near-ubiquitous companions in strength are the Methodists, who, though somewhat less accustomed to minority or perimeter status, have become in their Southern career a significantly altered communion from that formed by John Wesley, especially in respect of their heavy subjectivist propensities. Two basic points emerge here: first, the domination of the South by two denominations which have not stood as a major and continuing formative influence on religious life in other subcultures within Christendom, and second, the casting of Southern religious life into a conspicuously subjectivist—in this case, evangelical, even revivalist—mold.

These circumstances add up to the singularity of the Southern religious syndrome, a fact which though still awaiting documentation is taken for granted by all analysts of American religion. To cite an instance, N. J. Demerath III introduces *Social Class in American Protestantism* with the admission: "I should note that no Southern parishes are represented." (The character of his study makes it clear that intelligent observation, not indolence, is the basis of this notation.) Similarly, Will Herberg speaks publicly of the "semi-colonial South," with the patent implication that whereas most sectors of American religious life have witnessed recurrent waves of intellectual revolution and social change, the South's version of Christianity is relatively unchanged from the colonial period. Historians of American religion such as Sidney Mead and Winthrop Hudson generally ignore developments in Dixie without comment or make limited reference to the more dramatic of them. My recent work, *Southern Churches in Crisis* (New York, 1967), assumes the divergence of the South's ways from those of any other portion of Christendom, but its methodological base is impressionistic.

Perhaps only Wilbur Zelinsky has offered unimpeachable evidence of Southern religion's uniqueness—in an article, "An Approach to the Religious Geography of the United States: Patterns of Church Membership in 1952," wherein he argues that the South is one of the nation's seven distinct "religious regions." Zelinsky's work concentrates on delineating denominational strength in various locales. So far as it goes, his is an admirable study, but it does not pretend to investigate quite conceivable differences between, say, Baptists or Methodists in the South and their colleagues in other national subcultures. For example, it is far from impossible that Methodism in the South might turn out on inspection to be a different expression of Christianity from Methodism in some other American region, in terms of theological particularity or its conception of responsibility to society (as formulated, say, in the "Christ and culture" typology).

Initially, then, a great deal of work is needed to explicate the widely held theoretical assumption that the South is a "religious region" in more fundamental senses than Zelinsky's usage conveys.

Mention of the "Christ and culture" typological program (constructed by H. Richard Niebuhr in a book by that name) brings to mind the theoretical issue of which it is an elaboration—the church-sect distinction, the classic taxonomical device for the study of religious phenomena. Refined along many lines since it was devised by Weber and Troeltsch, the church-sect typology is still useful for describing religious institutions' conception of their fundamental responsibilities. Apropos of the South, it has unusual efficacy in providing a grip on the seeming incompatibility between the basic impulses of the popular churches to assume a narrow range of responsibility and on the other hand, the breadth of contribution the society would seem to have a right to expect from such massive groups. That is, the Baptist and Methodist bodies, especially, have evolved from meager, inauspicious origins in the eighteenth-century South, with concomitantly limited and simple duties, to their present standing as immense, wealthy, and highly organized institutions, with accordingly expanded capacities. As I have contended in my recent book, both made their appearance in the South as sectarian groups. They harbored no notions of accomplishing anything beyond the conversion of all the unchurched, the sanctification of all the justified, and, later on, the rectification of public morality. Only gradually did their congregations come to include the elite—economic, political, or intellectual—in the larger population, and even then they held no grandiose ambitions of creating a Christian civilization abounding in academic, aesthetic, or social-political achievements. In terms of Milton Yinger's refinement of the church-sect dichotomy, they were concerned with a ministry to individuals, not to the society at large.

One of Christian history's more ironic happenings is the conferral of church-type responsibility upon these simple sectarian families—owing to their enormous success as converters of most citizens (regardless of class) and molder of the culture's value-system. In a nutshell, the new situation was, by the 1920's anyway, the domination of a Protestant Christian civilization by Protestant groups unequipped either by ideology or experience to assume their role.[1] Following upon my own study of this confusion between role-intention and role-expectation, there is need now for inquiry into the true nature and extent of the putative confusion. Perhaps still another elaboration of the classic church-sect distinction will suggest itself to the investigators, or possibly an altogether novel analytic instrument. In the latter category, the Southern religious situation might even suggest a theoretical device correlating the churches' task-commitment and the orientation of their theology (objective or subjective).

Having proposed that theoretical research be done, first, into the divergence of Southern religious patterns from those of the American mainstream, and then into the pertinence of church-sect typology for organizing regional religious phenomena, I must observe that whatever theoretical tools are employed in the analysis of *white* Southern religion, none of them has the same—or perhaps any—pertinence to the popular faith-expressions of the region's Negro people. To illustrate: the application of church-sect typological considerations to Negro bodies is practically fruitless, since neither their intellectual responses nor their theology nor the general social conditions have prompted them to reflect on their responsibility to the culture at large. It is true that the same issue, dif-

1. An interesting concrete instance might be (the hypothesis needs testing) the alleged determination of the Mennonites residing in the northern Valley of Virginia to exercise decisive control over public morality there, a posture seemingly out of keeping with their less aggressive attitude in most places outside the sect-controlled South, that is, their typical willingness to "live and let live."

ferently framed, indicates that perhaps the Southern Negro churches epitomize the sect-type religious institution. Nevertheless, this supposition collapses before the recognition that there are *two* Southern cultures, Negro and white. In relation to one of these, "black religion" is not hostile or tolerant or indifferent (Troeltsch's characterization of sects). But it is effectively excluded from any sort of relation to the other, the white culture, not by any determination of its own. In a word, for Negro religious beliefs, values, and attitudes to be researched accurately, the unique nature and social role of the Negro subculture must be borne in mind. It is instructive to remember that the germane social science theory has been formulated in the light of *white* Christianity's career in Europe and America.

2. *Cross-cultural studies*

If Southern religion deviates from classical and contemporary Christianity, as we are contending, the confrontation of the Southern religious syndrome with alien ecclesiastical cultures and collectivities is certain to prove illuminating. To the extent of my knowledge this is an unmined territory, and it surely promises a rich treasure to the laborer. The proclivity for confining Southern studies to developments within the region itself must be overcome in the religious realm (at least) so that, first, the impact of the interaction between Southern segments and other segments within *national* churches can be measured, and, second, Southern socio-religious colonies in the North can be described.

Concerning the latter, few empirical projects in contemporary American religion bid fair to be more rewarding than investigations of Southern Baptist congregations in the North. Since the close of World War II, scores of such churches have been planted in the North by the Convention's Home Mission Board or have emerged from the accidental collocation of Southerners who moved north in search of better economic opportunities. New congregations have sprouted from West 57th Street in Manhattan to Pittsburgh, to Detroit, and thence to Denver and Los Angeles. By the admission of everyone who has addressed himself to the issue, including Board officials whose vested interests might be expected to produce comments to the contrary were they anywhere near admissible, these churches attract transplanted Southerners almost exclusively. Numbers of inquiries need to be made, first of all, to confirm the impression that the membership is solidly Southern, and further, to discover such things as who *precisely* these people are and what their attitudes are vis-à-vis both the institutional religious headquarters "down home" and the Yankee culture surrounding them.

Perhaps insufficient time has elapsed to permit any large yield of information on whether or not the second generation of displaced Southerners will hold onto the faith of their parents. Whenever that time does arrive, it will be fascinating to gather data on the attitudinal and affiliational changes which may accompany the maturation of the sons and daughters of adults born and bred in Dixie. Perhaps Hansen's three-generation hypothesis ought to be applied to their behavior. One may speculate that the second generation, when it comes to maturity, will dissociate itself from the ecclesiastical enclaves of Southern culture, perhaps more because of felt "ethical deprivation" (Glock) than from ethnic alienation. Should this prove to be the case, "Hansen's Law" would be not so much discredited as irrelevant, since this *variety* of ethnic alienation is rather easily overcome—compared to the estrangement experienced by Eastern European immigrants to this country seventy-five years ago. As a corollary, interested analysts must keep their eyes open to see if these culture-congregations change character with the passing of the years, and if so, whether the change is significantly influenced by the greater or lesser tendency of migrating Southerners to identify with these "ethnic" congregations. It may be that the membership will be unable to reproduce itself by natural means, owing to the defection of the second generation (for whatever reasons), and it will consequently be dependent upon "fresh arrivals from the old country." Still another consideration is whether these churches will be able to make any dent on the non-Southern population around them. Should they do so, it may be presumed that the congregation will eventually sever ties with the Nashville-based denomination (Bryan Wilson's scheme is pertinent here). All this is conjecture. What really matters is the phenomenon, the Southern-constituted and -oriented congregation in the North, and its responses to continual social change.

Already ripe for the plucking are other aspects of this Southern-Northern ecclesiastical phenomenon. The degree of religious involvement manifested by the "immigrant" in his new setting, as compared with his earlier religious habits under the Southern sun, must be examined. One wonders to what extent the yearning for small-group identification, especially with a group whose rhetoric is familiar, motivates active affiliation. That is, it is entirely possible that the removal northward arouses religious instincts which had been latent or torpid previously. Careful field research may disclose interesting variations on the classic issue of the social functionality of religious participation.

Turning to geographical considerations, there is real need to test for possible differences between displaced Southern Baptists in, say, New Jersey and eastern Pennsylvania on the one hand and Ohio and Michigan on the other. For one thing, what sections of the South do the members come from? If those who live in the Middle Atlantic states come predominantly from the cis-Appalachian South, does this produce a differently toned congregational life—and is there, for example, a relatively small percentage of these people who affiliate with *Southern* Baptist churches in their new communities? On the other hand, what is the point of origin of the constituents of the churches in the Middle West? Are they principally from trans-Appalachian areas, and if so is there any correlation between the tone of their newly founded churches and the rather more conservative brand of Baptist churches which predominate in the transmontane South (itself an item for research, as we shall suggest later)? In other words, we are raising the question whether there is not a demonstrable differentiation between various subtypes of Southern Baptist churches in the North (corresponding to variations within the South itself, perhaps).

In line with our assumption that Baptist churches in the South manifest certain church-type traits, alongside their fundamental sectarian impulses, we have now to ask how Southern Baptist churches in the North should be classified on the church-sect spectrum. Almost certainly they are regarded by the in-groups of Northern society as sectarian, and they may well see themselves in the same light—for aggressive as well as defensive reasons. But how do they compare with admittedly sectarian bodies? Are the Southern Baptists in Fargo, North Dakota, importantly different from the Pentecostalists of that city, with reference to income, educational standing, vocational identity, and the like? Does the fact of their domination of and acceptance by the culture of the South affect their attitudes toward their mission in the North at such points as, say, their dealings with other denominational bodies, the confidence with which they advance their cause, and the degree of their ideological dogmatism? In other words, what effect do the altered ecological conditions of these people have on their self-consciousness, self-conception, and degree of involvement in parish life?

The situation of Methodists from the South who have out-migrated to Northern industrial centers, though markedly different, likewise invites research. Owing to Methodism's structure, these persons have not instinctively thought to found congregations constituted almost wholly of displaced Tennesseans or Georgians or Virginians. In that important respect there is no analogy between the Baptist and Methodist experience. But that fact does not necessarily imply that the differences between the yearnings, needs, and outlooks of the two groups are great. Deserving of careful inquiry is the entire matter of what difference, if any, is made in the lives of the new arrivals by the character of the churches to which they have belonged in their Southern home communities. From the ecclesiastical standpoint, certain preliminary conjectures can be made. Methodists have not planted enclaves of Southern culture because: (1) their greater subjectivism has not inclined them to do battle in behalf of a highly particularistic theology; (2) their polity makes them less disposed to divisive action, leading them rather to assimilate or infiltrate existing churches in preference to splintering; (3) the Methodist Church is one and elastic, allowing for considerable diversity within an acknowledged unity; (4) an ecumenical spirit is at least as prevalent as a strident and self-conscious denominationalist spirit. On the more personal level, a number of questions need to be raised: What percentage of the adopted Buckeyes, Hoosiers, and the like are conserved as Methodist? Is there a significant defection to the sects (which may resemble certain aspects of some varieties of Methodism in the South)? Is there a high degree of *conscious* infiltration of "liberal" Northern Methodist churches with a view to making them "more Southern" (the words used would be "more vital," "more consecrated," "more evangelistic")? Are there many cases in which Southern Baptist successes nearby are pointed to as models?

Cross-cultural studies of these sorts are rewarding in their own right. More than this, however, they would shed light on developments which may be expected in the South itself as rapid social change assaults (and probably erodes) the religious establishment. It is not too much to predict that there will be a second-generation phenomenon within the region's indigenous population, and that a clash will ensue between the traditional church patterns and new (for the South) forms. Present trends in Ohio, New Jersey, and Michigan may afford some advance insight into emerging conditions in Dixie itself.

3. *Historical studies*

The prescription of the terms of this symposium, that the papers are to focus attention on the present, and not on the past as such, clearly is not meant to obviate the historical dimension of a proposed research agenda. Two lines of inquiry will suffice to show that historical and contemporary considerations are correlative for the study of religion in the South.

Any casual observer of the present-day South is likely to react incredulously to the report of the low spiritual condition of the colonial and early republican South. Yet the fact remains that religious institutions fared exceedingly poorly before the eruption of the frontier revivals after 1755 and during 1800-1810. The established Anglican Church was generally ineffective, and the other denominations represented in the region, Presbyterian, Roman Catholic, Lutheran, Baptist, and Quaker, enjoyed only occasional and isolated strength before 1755. By all odds the one body in the best position to claim the populace was the Church of England, that is, until the Scotch-Irish pincer appeared, the Ulster Scots in the Lower Cape Fear territory and the Scotch-Irish in the Valley of Virginia from the 1720's to the 1740's. At that juncture it appeared that the South was the Presbyterians' for the taking. Soon, however, Baptists lighted revival fires, trailed a decade later by the Methodists. German immigration brought a steady stream of Lutherans into certain portions of the upper South. To sum up, by the dawn of the nineteenth century, several Protestant families had entrenched themselves, both the older "sure winners" and the late-comers. Religious pluralism was a fact—admittedly only extraneously or incipiently in some places and for some local societies. And it was *religious* pluralism, not general ideological pluralism, for unreligious and liberal stances lost their hold. The case of Deism, which flourished here and there for some forty years after the Revolution and then disappeared after 1830, stands as the most illustrious example of this point.

It is, of course, impossible to fix turning-point dates precisely, but about 1830 a religious consolidation occurred. The traditional denominations endured both in name and in fact, but a particular version of Christianity won wide acceptance and became the common universe of discourse multilaterally. "Evangelical Protestantism," more an attitude than an institution or particular creed, came to power and was destined to inform popular religious views for many decades, even taking its toll of hallowed Lutheran, Episcopal, and Presbyterian positions.

In other words, the period about 1830 stands as the era of *convergence* in the religious (not to mention, general) life of the South. A curious, and not always equal, balance of revivalist concerns and fundamentalist ideology occupied a normative place in the society from that time forward. What concerns us here is the inverse parallel that gives evidence of becoming a mark of the 1960's. If 1830 was marked by convergence, perhaps 1960 will be remembered as inaugurating the period of *divergence.* On every hand there are signs that the old Evangelicalism is losing its grip under the impetus of assaults from the right and the left. On the right there is a heightening commitment to traditional Christianity (reformulated), and on the left, the incursions of secularism grow steadily more conspicuous.

Just how effective the breakup of the old sacred society already has become is exhibited by two series of reports produced and published by the *Charlotte Observer* in 1964 and again in January of 1966. Sample questions having to do with the place of religion in the lives of the general population yielded answers which reflect the new pattern of divergence. Whereas a generation ago ministers were accorded high respect, almost reverence, when they spoke on a religious or moral issue, today there is smaller penchant for accepting their pronouncements uncritically. The same openness also applies to the literality with which the Bible should be interpreted, the necessity of regular church involvement, the part played by good works in one's salvation, descriptions of judgment and hell, the propriety of tithing, and so on. On one matter after another, the *Observer*'s findings indicate a sure exchange of subservience to the older soteriological and ecclesiastical religion for the posture of free inquiry and the right of private interpretation. To date, not many people are making much fuss, nor are most disposed to challenge the validity of the Christian world-view. But the hold of Evangelical Protestantism has been relaxed, especially in the sense that in many instances the Southerner's duty to respond to the exhortation, "be justified and sanctified, or else . . .," no longer organizes his entire life. This will undoubtedly mean—in time, as today's youth arrive at maturity—that growing numbers will be religiously unaffiliated or quite casual about religious practices. The chances are that it will mean that another segment, those who continue to take their faith seriously, will gravitate to the classical churches which retain the essence of traditional Christianity while at the same time reformulating it. In violation of popular Southern opinion, this type of mobility reflects a conservative, not a liberal, urge.

To sum up, the contrast between the two watersheds, 1830 and 1960, affords insight into the effect of social change on the South. One suspects that there is some kind of inverse correlation between social patterns under religious convergence (relative uniformity and closedness) and those which will emerge under divergence (genuine pluralism and openness). In any event, careful assessment of the present religious situation should be instructive for the region's social planners.

A second inviting historical consideration is whether, and if so to what extent, the so-called "Methodist Age" of American religious history, covering the century following the Great Awakening of the 1740's, was in fact institutionalized by the Southern churches and endures as their prevalent characteristic to the present. Coined by the Presbyterian church historian Robert Ellis Thompson in a publication of 1895 and used extensively by several contemporary scholars, the term refers to a particular way of thinking about Christianity, a "distinct expression of Christianity," as C. C. Goen puts it. Its central features are: an intensive religious experience involving repentance, commitment to the Saviour, and inward assurance of "new birth"; the view that churches are composed of the regenerate only, resulting in a rather sharp distinction between the church and the "world"; and a conception of the Christian ethic which progressively narrowed this ethic until it came to be expressed solely in terms of individual piety (Goen).

In mainstream America, the Methodist Age faded during the middle third of the nineteenth century as new intellectual systems were introduced and when the corporate social problems resulting from urbanization and industrialization rendered suspect any exclusive concern for private morality. But what stood as a transitional phase in the larger American Protestant experience seems to have crystallized in the South. A careful analysis of the Methodist Age in the light of popular Southern beliefs and values today would be immensely instructive. If the findings were positive, further confirmation for the insulation of the Southern culture and for the South's reflection of the national culture as it looked fifty to a hundred years ago would have been adduced.

4. *Interdenominational studies*

After a recent intensive survey in four northern California counties, Glock and Stark concluded that a "new denominationalism" has appeared on the American scene in the form of five theological camps. In response to basic questions of doctrine, church members of most denominations followed no particular party line. Congregationalists, Methodists, and Episcopalians commonly took a "liberal" position, Disciples and Presbyterians a "moderate" position, and so on. For the purpose of this essay it is significant that Methodists placed in the liberal camp, and that the Southern Baptists were "fundamentalist." We hypothesize that research among Southerners would turn up important modifications of the Bay Area pattern—and we suspect that some variation would prevail between the various subsections of the South.

Glock and Stark directed to their sample of church members questions about: (1) their belief in God—"Do you know God really exists?" "Do you both have some doubts and believe in God?" and so on down to a totally negative query; (2) their belief in the divinity of Jesus, from an altogether affirmative faith down to one which denies any semblance of divinity; (3) selected additional beliefs about Jesus; (4) the miracles of Jesus; and (5) life beyond death—all in terms of a wide spectrum of possible answers. Similar research needs to be done among Southern churchmen, taking into account denominational affiliation, geographical location, and subtle shades of difference between quite generally orthodox answers.

Among the things to be on the lookout for in such research is the crossing of denominational lines, thanks to variables like rural-urban setting, membership in "people's churches" or "First" churches, and the socio-economic status of the respondents. A relatively high degree of theological particularity will almost certainly be discovered, but the reasons for such variations as appear will be illuminating.

A testing of the supposition that there are four fairly distinct geographico-theological subsections of the South—the "Old South" (the upper Atlantic states), the Deep South, the "Frontier South" (from Kentucky and Tennessee west and northwest to Missouri), and the Southwest—would be useful. Any annual meeting of the Southern Baptist Convention amply exhibits diversity, seemingly geographically conditioned. Moreover, it is intriguing to observe the way in which one portion of the South which is theologically fundamentalist is liberal on ethical issues such as race relations while the opposite pattern reveals in another portion. Interview questions exploring the geographical issue ought to deal with doctrinal stance, moral positions, attitude toward the ecumenical movement, and the like. Uniformity of posture is most unlikely to be found in any subsection.

Scrutiny of denominational relations and patterns should also consider what influence, if any, the popular evangelical theology has had upon those denominations of Protestantism which traditionally stand to the right of Evangelicalism. By all historical standards, the Episcopal and Lutheran churches, and really the Presbyterian as well, ought to loom as Christian institutions which are recognizably distinct from the popular religion of the Southern masses. Yet one hears and sees much evidence suggesting that the lines between the "high" and "low" churches are blurred in the sense that "high" churches actually operate as "low." To cite an instance, many Episcopal priests talk quite openly about the difficulty they encounter in trying to persuade their parishioners that they are Episcopalians, not Methodists or Baptists, and that an awareness of their tradition's distinctiveness, while no cause for hauteur or self-righteousness, is a distinction worth making for the sake of the gospel.

It may be even more difficult for the patches of Lutheran churches in such places as upstate South Carolina, the southern Valley of Virginia, and North Carolina's western Piedmont, to retain their denominational identity. We speculate that the generally upper-class status of the Episcopalians goes some distance toward preserving denominational awareness, in contrast to the Lutheran social situation where the members are the common population of the area, coming from the bourgeoisie and the proletariat. Not infrequently, Lutheran churches will sponsor Sunday evening or week-night services in which gospel hymns are sung, and one gets the feeling that institutional investments and the ethnic factor may be the principal restraints on their turning evangelical.

Popular Southern patterns fit somewhat more naturally in the case of the Presbyterians, owing to the Calvinist tradition's central position on the Protestant spectrum, where it is poised between objectivist Christianity as manifest in Episcopal and Lutheran life, and the subjectivist orientation of the Baptists and Methodists. Nevertheless, despite their rather greater objectivism, Southern Presbyterians often appear to be virtually indistinguishable from or at least remarkably close to the popular bodies. One of their foremost church historians wrote recently of the way in which sizable segments in that denomination tend to "reduce presbyterianism to congregationalism, thus reflecting the omnipresent influence of the Southern Baptists." It is time to explore just how great an influence the massive evangelical bodies have wielded on the more traditional denominations which are part of the Southern religious landscape.

Inter-denominational research should put to rigorous examination the matter of denominational mobility, so often alluded to in discussions of Southern religion but concerning which so little is actually known. It is incontestably true that Baptists and Methodists experience leakage in the direction of the "higher" churches and at least in the case of the Baptists, also toward "lower" independent or sectarian congregations. In need of documentation are such items as the extent of the mobility, the precise denominational sources and destinations of the transference, and the conscious reasons for which people change churches. Further, the class location of the mobile churchmen should be analyzed, with full attention to "status discrepancy." Are the Methodists who become Episcopalians socially prominent individuals who seem to be desirous of improving their peer rating? Are the Presbyterianized Baptists intellectuals who "jump" for theological reasons? Just what are the prevalent incentives for denominational change? And in a related vein, which are the "status churches" in various Southern communities? Is the Episcopal church always at the top? Do Baptist or Methodist churches ever command the highest social ranking? As for those individuals who are downwardly mobile, does status discrepancy figure as a prominent element? Is there any basis to the allegation that the clerical ranks of the "higher" churches are supplied to a conspicuous extent by apostate low churchmen?

Finally, is any differentiation to be made between Southern churchmen's attitudes toward other denominations as representations of Christianity, on the one hand, and their feelings toward persons in those other denominations, on the other? In certain quarters, strident in-group self-consciousness prevails, making for a closed spirit and challenging the legitimacy of other institutionalized expressions of the faith. Yet there seems to be no correlation between dogmatism on this score and interpersonal relations in the Southern society. One suspects that denominational exclusivism has relatively little bearing on the practical lives of the denominational absolutists. Are certain denominations, or certain geographical sectors of denominations, more exclusivistic in their attitudes? And for whom would one cast a political vote under a variety of circumstances: would a Baptist vote for an Episcopalian governor? a Methodist for a Roman Catholic senator? a Presbyterian for a Jewish president? In other words, how deep do denominational loyalties and claims run?

5. *The Southern clergy*

For a long time, the voice of the Southern minister has been regarded as the voice of God. Pretty consistently, the local minister has enjoyed a position of respect and prestige. Almost without having to qualify for it in his own right, the "preacher" has stepped into a role of community leadership. There are signs now that his previously automatic peerage is being severely challenged, or at any rate that it is not taken for granted. It appears that he is less and less drawn into the top-level councils of town and city power structures. Increasingly he is overlooked—not ignored or attacked—and expected to *earn* through his own initiative whatever position of respect he may occupy in the community.

This decline of status for the ministerial role, reflecting as it does a dramatic change, is certain to have telling effects upon Southern life. Research ought to be directed toward a number of aspects of the decline. The real standing of the clergy ought to be assessed. To what extent and among what groups is there a continuing disposition to accord to the clergy high estate on the grounds that they are the authentic messengers of a real God? Alternatively, is there any considerable segment which defers to ministers but without any profound conviction concerning the ontology of their role, that is, simply from habit or out of uncritical acquiescence to regional tradition? Interview questions here must be carefully designed, because clearly there are shades of opinion on the clerical role.

The impact of this decline on the incumbents themselves is a critical item. Although it would be difficult to prove the point, one suspects that the promise of high-status rewards has figured in the decision of many Southern clergymen to follow that vocation. At any rate, ministers have been aware of and gratified by the standing their role-occupancy has conferred upon them, and no doubt some men have undergone a change of personality in reaction to the blandishments of their position. What effects will relative loss of status produce? Will this new circumstance result in serious emotional disorders on the part of clergymen? Will the ministerial vocation attract fewer individuals? And the people in the congregations, to whom will they look as authority figures once the clergy have been nudged from their former magisterium? Who will be the intellectual and leadership elite in the post-New South? Investigation now is likely to indicate incipient deviations from past patterns, and to provide useful material for imagining the future.

Where are the seminarians coming from? Informal studies from time to time have intimated that ministers belong for the most part to the lower socio-economic classes, that many are first generation college-trained persons, and that rural areas and small towns have been the major demographic sources of supply. Light would be shed on the larger cultural scene if inquiry of this sort were pursued.

Finally, the influence of seminary training on the actual role-performance of the South's parish ministers calls for scrutiny. In certain of the major denominations, regional seminaries belong to the mainstream of world Christianity—which, it hardly needs remarking, is distantly removed from the consensus of popular Southern Evangelicalism. One wonders what really happens to the young product of a representative Southern congregation and community when he breathes the air of progressive theological scholarship for three years. Does he respond by reverting to his traditional posture after a period of flirtation with the new? Does he drink so deeply of the new wine that, heady, he forsakes his calling for secular enterprises—or, alternatively, espouses the new position with such vigor as to place an unbridgeable chasm between himself and the constituency? Again, does he leave the seminary smitten with the acquired perspective and a courageous exponent of it, only to wither under criticism and threatened ostracism at the hands of his colleagues? Or does he never really join the issues being raised, so that his three years of theological education register no appreciable modification of his thought and of his conception of the task he is about to take up? Shifting the terms of the discussion somewhat, what patterns emerge among ordinands who enrol in the conservative (principally Baptist) seminaries of the region? Are there significant differences in the two cases, and if so, of what factors are they functions?

6. *Miscellaneous items*

On any showing, the racial issue is the ranking social problem of the contemporary South. Its tentacles have of course stretched into the religious dimensions of regional life in all sorts of ways, and these demand investigation. Most prominently, the distinction, if any, between the attitudes of Southern white churchmen and non-churchmen toward the racial issue ought to be established. Or, since so high a percentage of Southern whites in the middle and upper classes are church members, it would be more realistic to frame the inquiry in terms of degree of church involvement, and perhaps also in terms of denominational affiliation and class location. Quite possibly, religious affiliation is not an independent variable in the Southern whites' assessment of the Negro's identity. In that case, the fact ought to be disclosed. Then inquiry should be made into the social responsibility the whites believe churchmanship imposes upon them.

Another ethical issue, the one on which the popular churches are the most articulate, is the matter of social drinking. Since the Civil War particularly, preachers have instructed their laymen to regard this as the number one evil of the Christian life. Their strictures have been widely accepted, resulting in Blue Laws, prohibition crusades, and a general absence of the cocktail hour and the wine glass from festive evenings. Nevertheless, many a church-going farmer has fermented his own wine for occasional use, and numbers of believing businessmen have partaken of a highball in the company of associates. Moreover in recent years a growing percentage of (educated?) Southerners have included the drinking of beer, and distilled spirits as well, in their ordinary social life. Of central significance is the fact that these drinkers continue to hear forthright directives against the use of alcohol from the church pulpits and still feel obliged to imbibe under somewhat secretive circumstances. They are able to live a "double life" without really seeing any moral gravity in their behavior, on the one hand, or taking steps to silence the ministers on the other. How do Southern churchmen really feel about social drinking? What are their actual practices? What responses do they make to the official stand of the church on this issue? And what part do the usual variables, denominational affiliation, social class, vocation, etc., play in their comportment?

A full agenda on Southern religion would be of course endless. But now, as a last item, we mention the urban-rural dichotomy in Southern life and its bearing upon religious patterns. Partly because Southern cities have not been typically urban, social life in these heavily populated communities has differed less from rural ways than might be postulated on theoretical grounds. The similarity of approach, tone, and belief in city and country churches impresses itself upon any careful observer of the two types. In many instances it would appear that urban congregations are merely rural colonies transplanted to cities, where under the impetus of new social and economic conditions people and institutions "spruce up," but without making basic changes. It is time, now that rapid social change has been in full swing for a dozen or more years, to compare and contrast these types of churches, the truly rural, the "country churches moved to town," and the truly urban, to discover where the differences lie, what becomes of the devout of various age and social groups when they become city-dwellers, how long it takes for the impact of urbanization to alter existing patterns, and to what extent the churches of the cities serve as outposts of the agrarian culture identified with the older South. Studious elaboration of this item may be singularly transparent to the role which the religious dimension occupies in Southern life.

The Contributors

C. ARNOLD ANDERSON is co-editor of *Education and Economic Development* (1965) and of *Education, Economy and Society* (1961), and author of "The American South—a Region in Transition" (published in Svensk geografisk arsbok, 1955). Born in Platte, South Dakota, in 1907, he completed his undergraduate studies and his Ph.D. degree at the University of Minnesota, and is now Professor of Education and Sociology and Director of the Comparative Education Center of the University of Chicago. Dr. Anderson is one of the editors of the *American Journal of Sociology*, a member of the World Bank Mission to Kenya, and was a research professor in Sweden on a Fulbright grant from 1955 to 1956.

GORDON W. BLACKWELL was born in Timmonsville, South Carolina, in 1911. He was graduated *summa cum laude* from Furman University, received his M.A. degree from the University of North Carolina, and his Ph.D. degree from Harvard University. A former Kenan Professor at the University of North Carolina, he later served as Chancellor of the Woman's College of the University of North Carolina and as President of Florida State University. He is now President of Furman University. Dr. Blackwell is the author of *Toward Community Understanding* (1943), *New Farms for Old* (1946), *Church and Community of the South* (1949), and *Game Theory and Defense against Community Disaster* (1954).

JOHN TYLER CALDWELL was born in Yazoo City, Mississippi, in 1911. Educated at Mississippi State College, he received M.A. degrees from both Duke University and Columbia University, and his Ph.D. degree from Princeton University. His principal field of study has been political science. Presently Chancellor of North Carolina State University at Raleigh, he has been a consultant to the Ford Foundation, President of the Association of State Universities and Land-Grant Colleges, and a member of the Select Committee on the Government Research Advisory Panel.

MARSHALL R. COLBERG is a native of Chicago, Illinois. He received his A.B. and M.A. degrees from the University of Chicago and his Ph.D. degree from the University of Michigan in economics. Dr. Colberg is the author of *Human Capital in Southern Development* (1965), and is co-author of *Business Economic Principles and Cases* (1963), *Prices, Income and Public Policy* (1959), and *Factors in the Location of Florida Industry* (1962). In May of 1966, Dr. Colberg received a grant from the Social Security Administration for a study of lifetime earning patterns of Americans by race. He is presently Professor and Chairman of the Department of Economics at Florida State University at Tallahassee, Florida.

ROBERT J. HARRIS is Professor of Political Science and Dean of the Faculty of Arts and Sciences at the University of Virginia. Born in Wilson County, Tennessee, in 1907, Dr. Harris is a Phi Beta Kappa graduate, *magna cum laude*, of Vanderbilt University; he received his M.A. degree from the University of Illinois, and his Ph.D. degree from Princeton University. He is the author of *Judicial Power of the United States* (1940), *The Quest for Equality: The Constitution, Congress, and the Supreme Court* (1960), a co-author of *Continuing Crisis in American Politics* (1963), and a collaborator on *The Constitution of the United States: Analysis and Interpretation* (1953).

SAMUEL S. HILL, JR., was born in Richmond, Virginia, in 1927. He graduated *magna cum laude* from Georgetown College, received his M.A. degree from Vanderbilt University, his B.D. degree from Southern Baptist Theological Seminary, and his Ph.D. degree from Duke University. Dr. Hill studied at Cambridge University, England, on a Rotary International Fellowship. He is the author of numerous articles investigating religion and race relations in the South, including *Baptists—North and South* (1964) with Robert G. Torbet, and *Southern Churches in Crisis* (1967). Associate Professor of Religion and Chairman of the Department of Religion at the University of North Carolina at Chapel Hill, Dr. Hill received the Tanner Award in 1964 for "excellence in undergraduate teaching" and the Alumni Achievement Award from Georgetown College in 1966.

EDWIN C. KIRKLAND was born in Charleston, South Carolina, in 1902. He was a Phi Beta Kappa graduate of Wofford College, received his M.A. degree from Vanderbilt University, and his Ph.D. degree from Northwestern University. He is the author of many articles in *The Tennessee Folklore Society Bulletin*, *Southern Folklore Quarterly*, *Journal of American Folklore*, and *Asian Folklore Studies*, and has compiled a monograph, *A Bibliography of South Asian Folklore* (1966). He is a member of the Council of the American Folklore Society and managing editor of the *Southern Folklore Quarterly*. Dr. Kirkland is presently Professor of English at the University of Florida.

AVERY LEISERSON, Chairman of the Political Science Department at Vanderbilt University from 1952 to 1965, took his A.B. degree at the University of Illinois and his Ph.D. degree at the University of Chicago. He has taught at Princeton University and the Universities of Chicago, Michigan, and Washington. His government employment includes the National Labor Relations Board, the United States Bureau of the Budget, public member of the Chicago Regional Wage Stabilization Board, and the Secretary of Labor's Advisory Council on Welfare and Pension Plans. Dr. Leiserson is a Fellow of the American Association for the Advancement of Science and current President of the Southern Political Science Association. His publications include *Administrative Regulation* (1942) and *Politics and Parties* (1958). He was editor of the *Journal of Politics* from 1961 to 1964, and of the symposium volume *The American South in the 1960's* (1965). The politics of science, political theory, and comparative political systems are his current fields of research.

RAVEN I. McDAVID, JR., has been Professor of English at the University of Chicago since 1958. He is editor of the *Linguistic Atlas of the Middle and South Atlantic States, 1941* ——, which is being compiled for publication, and is Vice-President of the American Dialect Society. The best known of his many scholarly publications is his abridgment of H. L. Mencken's *The American Language* (1963). Born in Greenville, South Carolina, in 1911, he studied as an undergraduate at Furman University and received his M.A. and Ph.D. degrees from Duke University. In addition to the University of Chicago, he has been a faculty member at The Citadel, Michigan State University, Southwestern Louisiana Institute, and Western Reserve University. He has also held visiting appointments in a number of colleges and universities. During the summer of 1965, he was a Senior Fulbright Lecturer at the University of Mainz, West Germany.

J. KENNETH MORLAND was born in Huntsville, Alabama, in 1916. A Phi Beta Kappa graduate of Birmingham-Southern College, he received his B.D. degree from Yale Divinity School and his Ph.D. from the University of North Carolina. He is the author of *Southern Schools: Token Desegregation and Beyond* (1963), *School Desegregation: Help Needed?* (1962), and numerous articles in scholarly journals concerning racial awareness and education. Dr. Morland is Professor of Sociology and Chairman of the Department of Sociology and Anthropology at Randolph-Macon Woman's College, and is serving as Visiting Professor at the Chinese University of Hong Kong for 1966-67 as a Fulbright Scholar.

DAVID M. POTTER was Walgreen Lecturer at the University of Chicago and Commonwealth Lecturer at University College, London, and is presently William Robertson Coe Professor of American History at Stanford

University. Born in Augusta, Georgia, in 1910, Dr. Potter studied at Emory University, received the M.A. degree from Oxford University, and the M.A. and Ph.D. degrees from Yale University. His publications include *Lincoln and His Party in the Secession Crisis* (1942), *Trail to California: The Overland Diary of Vincent Geiger and Wakeman Bryarly* (1945). He has co-authored *Nationalism and Sectionalism in America* (1949), *A Union Officer in the Reconstruction* (1948), and *People of Plenty: Economic Abundance and the American Character* (1954).

BENJAMIN U. RATCHFORD, Professor of Economics at Duke University between 1928 and 1960, has served as Chairman of the Inter-University Committee for Economic Research on the South, as Deputy Chief of the Program Review section of the Economic Cooperative Administration in Paris, and was appointed by the United States Government to serve as Economic Advisor for the Level of Industry to the Office of Military Government for Germany in Berlin. He is presently Vice-President and Senior Advisor of the Federal Reserve Bank of Richmond, Virginia. Dr. Ratchford was born in Gastonia, North Carolina, in 1902, was educated at Davidson College, and received his Ph.D. degree from Duke University. His publications include *American State Debts* (1941); he has co-authored *The Future Level of German Industry* (1946), *Berlin Reparations Assignment* (1947), *The Impact of Federal Policies on the South* (1949), and *Economic Resources and Policies of the South* (1951), with Calvin B. Hoover.

LOUIS D. RUBIN, JR., was born in Charleston, South Carolina, in 1923. A Phi Beta Kappa graduate of the University of Richmond, he received his M.A. and Ph.D. degrees from Johns Hopkins University. He is the author of a novel, *The Golden Weather* (1961), as well as critical studies of Thomas Wolfe, Ellen Glasgow, and James Branch Cabell; he has written a study of modern Southern literature entitled *The Faraway Country* (1963). Dr. Rubin is serving as general editor of a new series of scholarly works, *Southern Literary Studies,* published by the Louisiana State University Press. Recently at Hollins College, where he was Professor and Chairman of the Department of English, Dr. Rubin now is a member of the English Department at the University of North Carolina at Chapel Hill.

WILLARD THORP is credited with the development of the Special Program in American Civilization at Princeton University where he is Holmes Professor of Belles Lettres. Born in Sidney, New York, in 1899, Dr. Thorp was a Phi Beta Kappa graduate of Hamilton College, and received his

Ph.D. degree from Princeton University. Dr. Thorp is editor of *A Southern Reader* (1955), and a co-editor of *An Oxford Anthology of English Poetry* (1947) and *Literary History of the United States* (1948).

GEORGE B. TINDALL is Professor of History at the University of North Carolina at Chapel Hill, where he earned his M.A. and Ph.D. degrees. Dr. Tindall was born in Greenville, South Carolina, in 1921, and completed his undergraduate degree at Furman University. He was a Guggenheim Fellow in 1957-58 and was at the Institute for Advanced Studies at Princeton from 1963 to 1964. His publications include his book, *South Carolina Negroes, 1877-1900* (1952), and he is currently preparing a manuscript for a history of the South from 1913-1946, the final volume in a ten-volume *History of the South.*

RUPERT B. VANCE is Kenan Professor of Sociology and Research Professor in the Institute for Research in Social Science at the University of North Carolina at Chapel Hill. In 1963 he received the Thomas Jefferson Award, which is presented annually to the faculty member "whose work and life is in the best tradition and spirit of Thomas Jefferson." Born in Plumerville, Arkansas, in 1899, Professor Vance was educated at Henderson-Brown College, received the M.A. degree from Vanderbilt University, and the Ph.D. degree from the University of North Carolina at Chapel Hill. He is the author of *Human Factors in Cotton Culture* (1929), *Human Geography of the South* (1932), and *All These People: The Nation's Human Resources in the South* (1945). Professor Vance is a former President of the Southern Sociological Society, the American Sociological Society, and the Population Association of America.

Index